POLAND BETWEEN EAST

AND WEST

POLAND
BETWEEN EAST AND WEST

SOVIET AND GERMAN DIPLOMACY

TOWARD POLAND, 1919–1933

BY JOSEF KORBEL

PRINCETON, NEW JERSEY

PRINCETON UNIVERSITY PRESS

1963

TO R. RUSSELL PORTER

PREFACE

■ RELATIONS between Russia and Germany have profoundly influenced the modern history of Europe. In a
more narrow sense, their policies toward Poland, "the land
between," have frequently determined the fate of East Europe
and have had, therefore, a decisive impact upon European
peace.

World War I brought about revolutionary changes in Central and East Europe: the Czarist Empire changed into a communist state, Imperial Germany into a democratic Republic,
the Austro-Hungarian Empire collapsed, and out of this same
period of upheaval an independent, vigorous Poland emerged.
But the historical pattern of clashes and convulsions, of plotting and maneuvering, soon reappeared, and the familiar
shadow of unrest and apprehension once again hovered over
the Continent.

Although the policies of the Soviet Union and the Weimar
Republic toward Poland have been the subject of a number
of other studies, such studies have been made within a broader
European context. However, the opening of the files of the
German Foreign Office and the private papers of some leading
German personalities invited a new and deeper look into this
exciting and revealing period of recent history. They also
helped to throw new light on certain motivations of Soviet
foreign policy.

This is, then, a study of Soviet and German diplomacy toward Poland. Polish foreign policy, per se, is here analyzed
only to the extent to which it reflected Moscow's and Berlin's
diplomatic moves toward Warsaw.

The preparation of this work required several years, and
many institutions and persons deserve my deep gratitude for
precious assistance. The John Simon Guggenheim Memorial
Foundation appointed me as its Fellow. The National Ar-

chives, Washington, D.C., the Russian Research Center, Widener and Houghton Library, Harvard University, Hoover Institution on War, Revolution, and Peace, and the University of Denver made their sources available; the assistance of their archivists and librarians was of inestimable value. Carl L. Lokke, the National Archives, Paul R. Sweet, the Department of State, Hans Gatzke, E. Raymond Platig, Marshall Shulman, Zigmund Gasiorowski, Easton Rothwell, Witold Sworakowski, Mrs. Arline Paul, and Mrs. Harriet Lawton were most helpful at the early stage of the research. Professors Hans Kohn, Marek Korowicz, and Edward Rozek read the manuscript. Miss Mary Jaeger, Mrs. Lavonne Delahunty, Miss Ruth Davis, and Mrs. Laurel C. Voight extended their most cooperative secretarial help. Exceptionally careful editorial assistance was contributed by Mrs. William Hanle, of the Princeton University Press. To all of them I am greatly indebted.

Special thanks go to my friend and colleague, Professor R. Russell Porter, who gave me again the rare service of his literary talents by editing the manuscript, for which, however, I am solely responsible.

Due acknowledgment is given to the sources used in the book. In particular, my thanks go to das Militärgeschichtliche Forschungsamt, Freiburg/Breisgau, Federal Republic of Germany, for the permission to quote from *General von Seeckt's Personal Papers*, and to Harcourt, Brace & World, Inc., for their consent to excerpt materials from Gerald Freund's *The Unholy Alliance*.

Denver, Colorado   J O S E F   K O R B E L
June, 1963

CONTENTS

A HISTORY OF HATRED   3

PART I: 1919–1920:
Years of Military Campaigns

1. SETTING THE SCENE — 1   9

2. RUSSIA VERSUS POLAND   16
     Travesty of Self-Determination
     Pilsudski
     Pilsudski-Lenin Secret Contacts
     Soviet Political Offensive
     Polish Political Offensive
     Diplomatic Maneuvering
     The War
     Aftermath of the War

3. GERMANY VERSUS POLAND   68
     Groener's Plan
     Seeckt's Plan
     Maltzan's Alternatives
     Germany and the Soviet-Polish War

PART II: 1921–1925:
Years of Diplomatic Campaigns

4. SETTING THE SCENE — 2   97

5. CURRENTS AND CROSSCURRENTS   103
     Semblance of Consolidation
     Reality of Hostility

Similarity on the Western Border
"The Polish Card"
The Genoa-Rapallo Tangle
Unity in Diversity
Rantzau
Chicherin
Rantzau's First Experience

6. THE RUHR CRISIS   129

The Soviet Game
Stresemann
A Lost Opportunity

7. SHIFTS IN POWER   152

A Prelude
The Polish Bait
A Frontal Attack
The Tug of War
A Critical Conversation

PART III: 1926–1933:
Years of Precarious Balance

8. SETTING THE SCENE — 3   183

9. GERMANY ON THE MOVE   188

Mending of Soviet-German Fences
"East Locarno"
Germany Intervenes
Poland's Economic Isolation
Struggle in the League of Nations
Re-enter Pilsudski
Soviet-Polish Moves and the German Reaction
German-Polish Moves and the Soviet Reaction

CONTENTS

A War Scare
Germany Threatens—Russia Retreats

10. BETTING ON THE "LITHUANIAN
    HORSE"   223

11. INDEPENDENT POLICIES   240

    Improvement in Polish-German Relations
    Improvement in Polish-Soviet Relations
    Deterioration in German-Soviet Relations
    Change of Guard
    Renewed Polish-German Tensions

12. AN EQUILIBRIUM   266

    The Polish-Soviet Pact of Nonaggression
    The Polish-German Pact of Nonaggression

POSTSCRIPT: THE FULL CIRCLE   287

BIBLIOGRAPHY   290

INDEX   311

LIST OF ABBREVIATIONS

AA   Auswärtiges Amt. Files of the German Foreign Office, on microfilms deposited with the National Archives, Washington, D.C. Numbers refer to reel, serial number, and frame, in that sequence.

Ciechanowski Deposit. Files of the Polish Embassy in Washington, D.C., deposited with the Hoover Institution on War, Revolution and Peace at Stanford University, Stanford, California.

D.B.F.P.   Documents on British Foreign Policy, 1919–1939.

D.G.F.P.   Documents on German Foreign Policy, 1918–1945.

Foreign Relations Papers.   Papers Relating to the Foreign Relations of the United States.

Groener Papers.   General Wilhelm Groener's Papers. Personal files of General Wilhelm von Groener, on microfilms deposited with Houghton Library, Harvard University, Cambridge, Massachusetts.

Seeckt Papers.   General von Seeckt's Papers. Personal files of General H. von Seeckt, on microfilms deposited with Houghton Library, Harvard University, Cambridge, Massachusetts.

POLAND BETWEEN EAST

AND WEST

A HISTORY OF HATRED

NATIONALISM seems to survive all human progress. At
times, it has directed its creative forces toward lofty ideals
of peace, toward stability and construction. More often, however, it has generated unbridled passions of hatred and destruction. Nowhere is this truth more evident than in the triangular
relationship between Russia, Germany, and Poland. This is a
dark story of scorn and fear, of contempt and hostility. What
was to one country a period of national glory was to another a
period of national humiliation. The fortune of one seemed
inevitably to be purchased through the misfortune of another.

When, in the tenth century, Poland laid the foundations of
a consolidated state, Russia was still a primitive country, re-
mote and largely unexplored. When, six centuries later, Poland
came to bask in the glory of her power, which stretched from
the Baltic to the Black Sea, she did so at the price of Russia's
humiliation before Polish invasions and occupations. In Central Europe, in that same period, West and East Prussia also
owed allegiance to the Polish crown, though only a few centuries before the Teutonic knights had inflicted grievous hurt
upon the Polish people. For centuries the seesaw battle of as-
cendancy continued. Wars knew no end, territories changed
hands and again changed hands. And through the centuries the
roots of mutual hatred sank deep into this fertile soil.

By the dawn of the eighteenth century the tables were turning once again. At different levels and with different designs,
both Russia and Prussia were becoming modern states while
Poland's strength was being lessened by internal dissension. As
might be expected, her neighbors converged on the once proud
Poland and began, with Austria's eager participation, to carve
away her national territory. By the close of the century, in
1795, the year of her Third Partition, Poland disappeared from

3

the map of Europe. To Prussia and Russia now went the glory; the price—the humiliation of Poland.

For more than one hundred years Russia and Germany shared the common crime of Poland's partition. In 1914, however, the embers of Polish nationalism, fanned by the events of war, suddenly burst into flame. The common ties, which had for so long suppressed the voice of Polish freedom, suddenly were broken by an armed conflict between the Central powers and Czarist Russia. Expedients of war therefore necessitated some revisions in the thinking of both Berlin and Petrograd about the fate of Poland. As a result, promises of national self-determination came to the Polish people from both her enemies. However, it was soon apparent that these promises were merely an instrument to further expansion and meant only to dull their patriotic spirit.

The end of the war brought a period of political and social revolutions. Once again the wheel had turned. New banners of nationalism now rose where others had fallen. The Austro-Hungarian Empire was buried in its own ruins; the German Empire had disappeared, and after a critical period of revolutionary activities was replaced by the democratic Weimar Republic; and Czarist Russia was shattered by the revolution. Out of such upheavals independent Poland was reborn, made up of territories that had long been considered by her neighbors as their natural property. Her western boundary was partially determined by the Versailles Treaty, the fate of some important regions still to be decided by a plebiscite. Nor did the Versailles Conference, in the absence of Russia, determine the Polish-Soviet boundary; it was left open to mutual challenge and to decision by arms.

Neither Poland nor her neighbors were satisfied with such a situation. She dreamed of a re-establishment of the powerful and vast country which once was the Kingdom of Poland. Her neighbors remained unreconciled, not only to the boundaries of the Polish Republic but even to its mere existence.

A bizarre situation, offering many possible contradictions, developed in European politics. Poland, never lacking in audacity, was more than ready to defend her national interests in a determined defiance of heavy odds. Germany, fighting for the salvation of democracy on her own soil against both communist and monarchist dangers, sought Bolshevik cooperation against Poland. And Russia, though setting high hopes on a revolutionary situation in Germany, paradoxically, sought close contacts with the conservative elements of the German democratic government. Although their motives were mutually exclusive, Germany and Russia shared at least one common interest: to destroy Poland's independence, or at least to reduce her to political impotence. What followed was a stubborn and deceitful diplomatic struggle which affected the whole of Europe and contributed to the final climax of another world conflagration.

It is the first phase of this struggle, from 1919 to 1933, which forms the object of this study; the other phase, from 1934 to 1939, equally if not more exciting and enlightening, still remains to be written.

PART I. 1919–1920

YEARS OF MILITARY CAMPAIGNS

CHAPTER 1

SETTING THE SCENE—1

◢ THE "ten days that shook the world," to borrow from John Reed, were prolonged to a hundred and then a thousand days. The October Revolution occurred in 1917, but for the next three years Soviet leaders fought for its preservation. The rest of the world continued to suffer from the partial paralysis of shock and expected and hoped for an internal collapse of the communist regime. The Allied armies, posed on the Russian soil in the north and south and in the far east, first watched and then indirectly assisted the counterrevolutionary forces in their ill-conceived struggle against the Red army. But when their main hope, Admiral Kolchak, was captured in February 1920, it was time for them (except the Japanese) to withdraw. When another counterrevolutionary attempt led by General Denikin from southern Russia had collapsed in December 1919, and when a third though feeble effort by General Wrangel had come to naught, the Western world could no longer realistically hope that the communist edifice would crumble. The brutal methods of war communism which affected every phase of Russian life prevented any further major disruptions from within.

Now the Soviet leaders concentrated their energies on the consolidation of their power, on the recognition of the Soviet State by the outside world, and on the acquisition of credits and trade for their ravaged country.

At the beginning of 1920 the Allied Council lifted the barriers of the blockade against Russia and opened the doors to trade negotiations. However, this prospect of trade came to nothing because individual Western countries insisted on

9

negotiating settlements of Russian prewar and wartime debts and indemnification for seized property, and the Soviet government resolutely refused all such attempts. For the same reasons, there was no inclination in the West to extend to Soviet Russia her eagerly sought diplomatic recognition. Thus, in the first years of the 1920's she remained in quarantine, left to suffer the terrible sickness of her economic misery and political convulsions, a result in part of her long history of feudalism, in part of the chaos of the revolution.

There were, however, additional reasons for the West's negative attitude toward the new situation in Russia. As eager as the Soviet government was for normalization of its contacts with the rest of the world, it was at the same time passionately imbued with a revolutionary mission. Lenin, who commanded supreme authority in the Communist Party of Soviet Russia and who was not only a brilliant thinker but an equally outstanding political strategist, did not see any inconsistency in Soviet official endeavors for recognition on the one hand and, on the other, revolutionary subversion of the very governments from which he sought the stamp of legitimacy. The Third International, which he established in March 1919, started as an unrepresentative body of haphazardly collected communist individuals but soon developed into a powerful instrument of Soviet foreign policy. Commanding absolute obedience from the leaders of the newly founded communist parties the world over (and especially in Europe), Moscow appealed incessantly to proletarian masses for the revolutionary seizure of power in their own countries.

Though Great Britain was for a time the chief enemy of Soviet Russia—for it remained even after an exhausting war the world's banker and largest imperium—there was little chance of subverting the quiet-minded population of the Isles. It was in the vast colonies and in China that Soviet communists worked toward cutting the arteries of British economic and political life. France, suffering from her war-inflicted wounds, was troubled by strong currents of social discontent. But the firm direction of its conservative leaders kept developments under control and led her to display an irreconcilable attitude toward the Soviet regime.

It was Germany which seemed to justify Lenin's high hopes for revolution. Disgruntled, economically exhausted, aching from the moral malaise which inevitably follows defeat in war, she appeared to offer to the determined, communist-inspired Spartacist movement potential grounds for action. Three times —through 1919, in the spring of 1921, and again in October 1923—a communist revolution seemed about to succeed.

Poland, for obvious reasons of geography, played a key role in Soviet designs. As the Moscow leaders said on frequent occasions, she was to serve either as a bridge or a barrier to the spread of communism; if the latter, she must be smashed; if the former, she must become a Soviet Poland.

To the Marxist analyst in Moscow, the situation in Poland was one of contradictions, both promising and foreboding. The country had no administrative cohesion. Composed of three separate territories, which had lived for so long under three different political systems, postwar Poland was a mosaic of heterogeneity. Three currencies circulated in the nation. Numerous political parties were burdened with the tradition of orienting policy in three different directions: toward Berlin, toward Vienna, and toward Petrograd. The two most important parties, the Polish Socialist Party and the National Democratic Party, bequeathed to their new country their ferocious rivalry. The first was socially progressive and irreconcilably anti-Russian; the latter consisted of small *bourgeoisie* and landowners and was reactionary in its social outlook. Its main wrath was directed, however, not against Russia but against Germany. Political freedom existed, but it merely seemed to encourage the constant bickering of political parties in their relentless struggle for power.

The economic and social scene was gloomy. Famine and

disease were common; landowners and industrialists enjoyed luxuries of life while the peasantry was destitute. High illiteracy bred ignorance and irresponsible passions. These were conditions that bode well for Soviet plans, and the Communist Party of Poland, active in major towns, was to serve as the forerunner of the country's eventual sovietization. However, there existed one single foreboding which the Soviet Union could not ignore. This was the patriotism of Polish leaders and the strong national feelings of the Polish masses—an anti-Russian nationalism that affected the whole nation, encouraged as it was by the dominant European power, France, who wished to build between Russia and Germany a strong, vigorous Poland.

Within a few months after the cessation of hostilities, the Polish government succeeded in fielding some 600,000 soldiers, composed of wartime legionaries, rifle regiments, the French-trained army commanded by General Haller, and new conscripts. However, even this impressive figure was diluted by weaknesses in the country and by the necessity of fighting at one time or another four of Poland's six neighbors: Russia, Germany, Lithuania, and Czechoslovakia. Only with Latvia and Rumania was Poland able to establish friendly relations.

Postwar Poland was indeed a paper tiger, but it was her good fortune that Russia was also a paper tiger. Though her government succeeded in whipping together a remarkably disciplined army whose leaders were filled with revolutionary vigor, the country could do little more than lick the wounds caused by war and revolution. Peasants slaughtered cattle and hid grain; the urban populace, suffering from hunger, took to the countryside. Organized resistance was suppressed, but the spirit of opposition spread through vast regions. The revolution was not yet firmly established and in its leaders' opinion continued to be threatened by outside intervention.

It was with these circumstances in mind that Lenin looked across the plains of Poland to Germany, another outlaw, whose

Bolshevik revolution would not only help to maintain the Soviet regime but also signal a communist victory all over Europe.

Germany seemed to fit perfectly the pattern of the communist theory on revolution. The ruling circles of prewar and wartime years, the military, the *Junkers,* big industry, high bureaucracy, had lost the symbol of their power: the monarchy. The Allies had cut the German arteries of trade by a total blockade and had withheld assistance from a dying German conservatism. The workers, on the other hand, schooled in street battles and led by Spartacists, seethed with revolutionary fervor and received encouragement, if not by way of arms, then by plentiful revolutionary appeals from Bolshevik Moscow. In between was the vast gray area of neutral masses—the amorphous masses as communist terminology calls them—disoriented, confused, waiting passively and opportunistically for the victor in this class-motivated struggle. All the German people, whatever their social interests, felt deeply the pains of humiliation from a dictated peace in a war which they thought they had not lost and for which they were convinced they were never responsible.

Toward the end of 1918 and in 1919 all signs pointed to a favorable revolutionary action. But most of these appearances were superficial and soon proved the fallacy of Bolshevik theoreticians. Germany was not ready for revolution.

After a short period of rule by a Council of People's Commissars, the Socialist movement split; the moderate Social Democrats, aware of their responsibility, remained the central force in the government and the radical Independent Socialists went into the opposition. The victory of the Social Democrats in the elections in January 1919 and the weakening of the Independents signified that German workers, long conditioned to follow an established authority, were not imbued with a revolutionary spirit after all. The communist attempts to seize power in the same January in Berlin, Hamburg, and a few

13

other German cities were quelled by the swift action of the government. So was the communist-inspired but short-lived Bavarian Soviet Republic in April 1919 and the "Red Army" upheaval in the Ruhr the following April.

The strange combination of forces which defeated these communist thrusts for power destroyed the myth that anticommunist elements in Germany were sure to be hopelessly lost in the scramble for power. To save the German Republic from communization, the ruling Social Democrats allied themselves with monarchists. The military, presumably rendered powerless by the clauses of the Versailles Treaty, were promised a respectable place in German life; the *Junkers* retained their vast properties in Prussia; big industry was at a later date invited to share in power; and the aristocratic bureaucrats retained key positions in government administration. In return, the antirepublican, conservative military, aided by the Free Corps, converged on the Spartacists, on the Bavarian Soviets, and on the Ruhr "Reds," and liquidated them without major effort. The Weimar Republic was saved, but the tragedy of this socialist-reactionary misalliance lingered over the work of all subsequent governments. The Weimar Constitution was democratic but it remained an artificial structure without a democratic interior. In such a situation, the seeds of violent extremism found fertile soil. Communists staged strikes and disorders. On the Right, the Free Corps desperadoes (after their own ephemeral seizure of power, the Kapp Putsch, in March 1920 and an enforced dissolution) went underground, from whence they perpetrated a series of political murders.

Germany was obviously ill. The people could not accept her defeat and the legend that her glorious army, unbeaten on the battlefield, was "stabbed in the back" by the rotten, demoralized rearland, quickly found comforting accommodation in the mind of the population. Naturally, then, the harsh stipulations of the Versailles Treaty, whether they referred to the war guilt, or deprived Germany of colonies and territories in Europe, or dictated severe limitations on the German army and armament, or imposed on her the heavy burden of reparations —all were viewed as grave injustices and humiliation.

In the short period of five years after the war, Germany had nine governments and they were all harassed by the extreme Left and Right which hampered their efforts to find some direction in either their domestic or external policy. Perhaps there was only one cardinal issue on which the whole nation and all political parties were agreed: Poland. This country, a good part of which had been attached to Germany before the war and exposed to Bismarckian *Kulturträger* activities—a country despised and scorned by the "superior" German race—had now emerged victorious and had seized great chunks of territory, once the cradle of Prussian power. East Prussia was separated physically from the rest of Germany; Danzig was proclaimed a free city but made economically dependent on Poland. The struggle for Upper Silesia, rich in minerals, was yet to culminate in another disappointment for the German people. The tradition of hatred and contempt for the Polish nation was now reinforced by a spirit of vengeance.

CHAPTER 2

RUSSIA VERSUS POLAND

TRAVESTY OF SELF-DETERMINATION

✍ IN THE arsenal of Soviet strategy against the Polish nation, the principle of self-determination became one of the chief weapons. Even before the Russian communists seized power, the future of Poland had occupied their minds. Lenin and Rosa Luxemburg, the erudite leader of the German radical Left, had exchanged sharp polemics on the subject. Rosa Luxemburg had rejected the idea of an independent Poland while Lenin had defended it, though in a strictly Marxist sense. When the Seventh All-Russian Conference of the Russian Social Democratic Labor Party met in April 1917—at the time when the fate of the Polish nation was discussed by all the belligerent powers—it passed a resolution on the National Question which stated that "the right of all nations forming part of Russia freely to secede and form independent states must be recognized." But it quickly qualified this commitment by adding that "it is only the recognition by the proletariat of the right of nations to secede that can ensure complete solidarity among workers of the various nations. . . . The right of nations freely to secede must not be confused with the expediency of secession of a given nation at a given moment." [1]

Stalin accompanied the resolution with a clear explanation that the prerogative of decision about secession belonged to "the party of the proletariat" which was "at liberty to agitate for or against secession, according to the interest of the proletariat, of the proletarian revolution." The bourgeois right of

[1] *The Essentials of Lenin* (2 vols.; London: Lawrence and Wishart, 1947), II, p. 53.

16

Polish self-determination was to him, as he stated at a later date, "only a semblance of independence," only "an illusion." [2] Indeed, in the crucial months that followed the October Revolution the Russian Bolsheviks felt at liberty to agitate for an independent proletarian Poland, to attack the illusion of her independence, or to sacrifice the idea altogether to their own power interests.

Their appeal for peace November 8, 1917, condemned annexations of foreign territories, including those perpetrated by Czarist Russia, and asked for the opportunity of any nation to express their wish freely in the press, in popular assemblies, or through political parties and rebellions.[3] They hoped that this and similar appeals would lead to a disintegration of the front and hasten the process of social and national revolutions.

At the Brest-Litovsk armistice negotiations, the Soviet negotiators defended vehemently the right of the Polish people to self-determination. In Petrograd, meetings were held and resolutions were passed asking for Polish freedom. Trotsky even threatened a resumption of hostilities if the Poles should not be allowed to determine their destiny. The All-Russian Central Executive Committee stood "for the effective self-determination of Poland. . . ." [4]

As the wrangling and agitation about the Polish question continued at Brest-Litovsk, the Austro-Hungarian Foreign Minister, Count Czernin (as though he himself represented a government of liberalism and justice), confided melancholically to his diary, "These people [the Soviet delegates] are not honest, and in falsity surpass all that cunning diplomacy has been accused of, for to oppress decent citizens in this fashion and then talk at the same time of the universal blessing of

---

[2] Joseph Stalin, *Marxism and the National and Colonial Question* (New York: International Publishers [n.d.]), pp. 64, 79.

[3] *Mezhdunarodnaia politika noveishego vremeni v dogovorakh, notakh i deklaratsiiakh,* eds. I. V. Kliuchnikov and A. V. Sabanin (3 vols.; Moscow: 1925–1928), II, pp. 88–90.

[4] *Soviet Documents on Foreign Policy.* Selected and edited by Jane Degras (3 vols.; London: Oxford University Press, 1951), I, p. 25.

freedom—it is a sheer lying." [5] In retrospect, Czernin's observation is remarkable only for the fact that he belonged to a group of the first statesmen who ever negotiated with Soviet representatives.

This was a period which lent itself to agitating for secession: Poland was in ferment and the Slavic nations of the Austro-Hungarian Empire were clamoring for independence. However, as the threat of a renewed German advance into Russia cast its shadow over the existence of the Soviet regime, this particular agitation was hastily superseded by a policy of Soviet power interests. Lenin, expressing the conviction of a forthcoming socialist revolution in Europe, stated in his "Twenty-one Theses of Peace"—in clearly Marxist terms—that a Marxist put the interests of socialism above the right such nations as Poland had to self-determination.[6]

On March 3, 1918, the comedy of Brest-Litovsk was brought to a tragic end. The peace was signed; its stipulations, ignoring completely the professed principle of self-determination, were the result of the power relationship between the two antagonists. German imperialism triumphed and Soviet helplessness was exposed. One-third of the vast Czarist Russian territory in Europe was lost to the Central Powers, including the Russian part of Poland.

It was, however, the military development on the western front which determined the future of Poland. The "black days" of August sealed the fate of Imperial Germany and three months later, November 11, the Armistice was signed. Allied victory not only assured Poland of independence and unification, but it did for Russia what she would have been unable to do for herself: it nullified the Brest-Litovsk Treaty. Thus, the end of the war opened wide not only the question of the

[5] Ottakar Czernin, *In the World War* (New York: Harper and Bros., 1920), p. 246.
[6] James Bunyan and H. H. Fisher, *The Bolshevik Revolution 1917–1918; Documents and Materials* (Stanford: Stanford University Press, 1934), p. 505.

Soviet-Polish boundary, but also a host of vexatious problems of Soviet-Polish relations.

The new Poland was not, of course, created in the Soviet image of self-determination. Though its first government was led by the Polish Socialist Party, it did not represent the proletariat in the communist sense and its national aspirations were at odds with the Marxist interpretation of the right of independence, which was only "an illusion." It was, in the Soviet view, a Poland of squires and *bourgeoisie,* a product of Western imperialism and capitalism. It was an anti-Russian and anticommunist Poland, and no one personified this spirit of Polish policy more convincingly than did the Head of State, Joseph Pilsudski.

PILSUDSKI

Under Pilsudski's leadership, the national affairs of Poland carried the unmistakable imprint of his colorful personality. Pilsudski was a hero of his nation's period of suffering as well as its period of glory. He was a Shakespearian figure in Poland's turbulent history, both admirable and repulsive, loved and hated.

He was born in Lithuania, which was then a part of Czarist Russia (though centuries before united with Poland), and reared in the tradition of a hatred of everything Russian, particularly Czarist. As a young man, he was arrested and exiled for five years to Siberia for participation in terroristic activities. The torture which he suffered from the Czarist jailors only deepened his hatred and nurtured his patriotic dedication; he became more reassured in his plans, less radical in their execution, a basically taciturn man, preoccupied with his own thoughts and little concerned with his environment. In 1892 he joined the Polish Socialist Party, still in its infancy, and edited its secret newspaper. At the outbreak of the Japanese-Russian war he sped to Tokyo, seeking from the Japanese government political help for the Polish nation only to find

19

Roman Dmowski, the leader of National Democrats, already there and offering markedly different advice. The two men developed a hatred of each other that persisted until death.

Pilsudski was supposedly a socialist, though he himself confessed never to have read Marx; but he was sincerely concerned with the plight of the Polish worker who, in his opinion, suffered even more than the other members of the Polish society. Dmowski represented the Polish middle class, conservative, chauvinistic, anti-Semitic. Though working, too, toward Polish independence, he believed that this national goal could be achieved only through cooperation with Russia, against Germany and the Austro-Hungarian Empire. In this respect, also, Pilsudski differed fundamentally with Dmowski.

By 1905 Pilsudski had moved from Russia into the Austrian part of Poland. He organized in Cracow a kind of military institute, lecturing on revolutionary tactics and training a group of dedicated followers in revolutionary activities. As the Austrian-Russian tensions grew, he was allowed to establish a League of Riflemen; when the war broke out, he led three Polish infantry companies into action against the Czarist army. Repelled, and forced to withdraw, he opened negotiations with the German high command to organize a Polish Legion which would fight alongside the German army if the German government would solemnly promise to give Poland independence after the war. When Germany hesitated, Pilsudski refused all cooperation and was promptly arrested and interned for the rest of the war.

In November 1918 Pilsudski returned triumphantly to Warsaw, now the capital of a free and independent Poland. Through a curious twist of history, the man who was ready to gamble that his nation would find its freedom through a German victory over Russia found himself, through Germany's defeat at the hands of the Entente, its first Head of State. In the days that followed, with his country facing innumerable political, administrative, and economic problems, qualities of his greatness and of his weaknesses quickly emerged. Basically of a soldier's mind, utterly unselfish, he would have liked to see the whole nation attack these problems in the simple fashion of soldierly devotion and sacrifice. He knew no political philosophy, in spite of his hazy socialist inclinations, other than a romantic belief in the greatness of his country. Party politics, which he saw as a despicable product of democracy, were repugnant to him. He had a profound distrust of democracy, but it must be remembered that Poland, split by irresponsible party struggles, was obviously not ready for democracy. Disgusted, he retired in 1923, but even then his towering figure, in a de-Gaullian manner, cast its influential shadow on the unruly political scene. In 1926 he struck back and through a *putsch* established himself in power and resolutely set about shaping Poland's political practices according to his dictatorial inclinations. Rejecting his socialist past completely (though it was still accepted by part of the working class), he swung to the Right to be finally completely surrounded by a group of reactionary colonels who had followed him blindly since the days of the Polish Legion. He listened to their views, he ordered them to execute his policies; but all major decisions were his own. These he reached after days and nights of thinking, a solitary figure who frequently talked to himself. Eventually, as his body was weakened by malignancy, his mind became increasingly bitter and, disillusioned with his own nation, he often heaped vituperative criticism on his fellow countrymen.

Pilsudski's hatred of Russia, indeed, of anything Russian, was in part the product of irrational sentiments, and partly nourished by his knowledge of history. Toward Germany he directed an equally deep mistrust, justified by the lessons of the past; but this was somewhat mollified by his respect for the German sense of order and discipline, and particularly for German achievements on the battlefields of World War I. France was his first love, though it was an idol which eventually disappointed him. In his youth he worshiped Napoleon, but as he grew older, he became critical of France's internal political heterogeneity and distrustful of her foreign policy. He resented the paternal attitude of the French government toward Poland and did not conceal his contempt for the French Military Mission in Warsaw, viewing its mere presence as an insult to his national and military pride.

Marshal Pilsudski was a great man, but his intellect lacked the sophistication to grasp the complex political and social forces of his time and to see beyond his own lifetime. Thus, wishing to give his nation the greatness it deserved, he bequeathed to it instead those weaknesses which only a few years after his death proved to be his nation's undoing.[7]

PILSUDSKI-LENIN SECRET CONTACTS

The terms of the Compiègne Armistice ordered the German army in the east, under the command of General Max Hoffmann, to remain in its positions and to withdraw only when "the Allies shall consider this desirable." The Allies obviously wished to establish some political order before German withdrawal and attempted thereby to prevent the Red army from occupying the evacuated territory. However, General Hoffmann did start the withdrawal and, as he himself testified, thus facilitated the movement of Soviet troops into this vacuum. Alarmed, the Polish army, hastily organized from various elements, in February 1919 launched a counteraction. It penetrated into Belorussia and forced the Red army out of Lithuania. In July it succeeded in breaking down the opposition of Ukrainian nationalists in Eastern Galicia.

At the same time, the Soviet regime was seriously threatened by the counterrevolutionary forces of Admiral Kolchak, General Yudenich, and General Denikin. Indeed, the possibility of a combined attack by the forces of Denikin and Pilsudski

[7] The brief sketch of Pilsudski's life is based on Robert Machray, *The Poland of Pilsudski* (New York: E. P. Dutton and Co., 1937) and W. F. Reddaway, *Marshal Pilsudski* (London: George Routledge & Sons, 1939); and on personal reminiscences of some of Pilsudski's contemporaries.

seemed to the Soviet Union to constitute a grave threat. The fact was that although these two leaders were negotiating about common action, they failed to reach any agreement concerning the future relations of Poland and Russia. Their aims were basically contradictory: Pilsudski wanted to establish a powerful Poland and to detach the Ukraine and Belorussia from Russia; Denikin wished to restore an old, indivisible Russian empire.[8] Nevertheless, whether the danger was real or fictional, Soviet Russia planned to paralyze it by a countermove.

In July 1919 a prominent Polish communist leader, Julian Marchlewski, appeared suddenly in Warsaw. As a man who was well known in the political and intellectual circles of Warsaw, he did not find it difficult to establish contact with a confidant of Pilsudski, a certain Wencikowski. Marchlewski suggested to him—personally, supposedly not acting on anybody's instructions—the possibility of peace negotiations in which Russia, as he stated, would be ready to make far-reaching concessions to Poland. He received a noncommittal though not quite unpromising answer that no official negotiations were possible at that time.[9]

And, indeed, the time for Soviet-Polish peace negotiations was not propitious. Even then the Polish government was trying to convince the Supreme Council of the wisdom of permitting the Polish army to march into the interior of Russia, with the Entente's financial assistance. Paris and London, however, vacillated. Disappointed, Pilsudski decided to explore the Soviet offer.[10]

Not quite coincidentally, an opportunity soon presented itself which provided for a more concrete exploration of Marchlewski's suggestions. In the autumn of 1919, at the small

[8] The Pilsudski-Denikin negotiations are extensively described in Titus Komarnicki, *Rebirth of the Polish Republic* (London: William Heinemann, 1957), pp. 418–24, 467–69. Also in A. J. Denikin, *Kto spas' sovetskuiu vlast' ot gibeli* (Paris: Izdanie Dobrovol'tsev', 1937).

[9] I. Markhlevskii, *Voina i mir mezhdu burzhuaznoi Pol'shei i proletarskoi Rossiei* (Moscow: Gosudarstvennoe izdatel'stvo, 1921), p. 12.

[10] Komarnicki, *op. cit.*, pp. 469–76.

Polish town of Mikaszewicze, a delegation of the Russian Red Cross was taking part in the negotiations with Poland on the organization of the exchange of prisoners of war and hostages. It was led by none other than Marchlewski.[11] He was met by a Captain Boerner who confided to him a secret message from Pilsudski saying that the Polish army would be given orders not to cross the existing fighting line but that, in return, the communists must stop any agitation in the Polish army. In case of the acceptance of Pilsudski's proposal a Polish delegate would be sent to Moscow to negotiate with Lenin, but the contacts must be kept in absolute secrecy.[12]

Pilsudski's delegate, Boerner, was further to inform Marchlewski on his own behalf that "Poland [was] not Europe's policeman and [did] not wish to be" and was acting exclusively in her own interests. Poland was not interested in helping Denikin; she could strike on her own front but had not done so. "Shouldn't this point open the Bolsheviks' eyes?" ended Pilsudski's message.[13]

Soviet eyes were wide open. As they were engaged in a critical battle with Denikin, Pilsudski's offer not to strike on his front was of inestimable value to them. Marchlewski returned with Pilsudski's proposal to Moscow. The Politburo held a meeting November 14, during which it decided "to instruct comrades Trotsky and Chicherin to elaborate in details an armistice with the Poles viewing the conditions handed over to comrade Marchlewski as acceptable in general. . . ." [14]

---

[11] On November 2 and 9 two conventions were signed between the Russian Red Cross Society and the Polish Red Cross Society. The first dealt with the return of Polish hostages and prisoners of war, the second with the exchange of civilian prisoners. *Livre Rouge.* Recueil des documents diplomatiques relatifs aux relations entre la Russie et la Pologne, 1918–1920. Edition d'état (Moscow: 1920), pp. 76–81.

[12] General Tadeusz Kutrzeba, *Wyprawa Kijowska, 1920 roku* (Warsaw: Naklad Gebethnera i Wolfa, 1937), pp. 26–7. The account is based on the diary of Boerner.

[13] *Ibid.*, p. 27.

[14] *Trotsky Archives.* Houghton Library, Harvard University.

Marchlewski met Boerner on November 23 to communicate Lenin's answer to him. However, it was an entirely new proposal which clearly implied the Soviet government's wish to improve, through a negotiated settlement, its military and political position.[15] Three days later, Boerner was received by Marshal Pilsudski, who instructed him, in a highly commanding fashion, to reject the Soviet proposal. On the whole, Pilsudski saw in it a maneuver to draw him into negotiations which would compromise Poland in the eyes of France, who continued to be Soviet Russia's archenemy and who saw in Poland her chief ally. Nevertheless, Pilsudski insisted "that he did not wish to allow the Russian reactionaries to triumph in Russia. Therefore, he [would] do all he [could], despite the risk of being misunderstood by the Soviet government." Pilsudski further expressed surprise that the Soviet government did not use this opportunity to come to an agreement, the more so because "the Chief of State . . . a long time ago proved by deeds [not fighting the Red army when it was preoccupied with Denikin] what his intentions were." If Lenin understood, Pilsudski was willing to send to him his plenipotentiary. He did not wish to fight with the Soviets, but if they wish to wage war with Poland, "he will pick up the glove." [16]

Early in December 1919 Boerner communicated Pilsudski's answer to Marchlewski who promised to pass it on to Moscow through a special courier. The two men met no more and the strange dealings between Pilsudski and Lenin were kept secret for two years. The blanket of mystery was first slightly removed by Karl Radek. In 1921 he wrote that "Mr. Pilsudski and the Polish social patriots betrayed the despicable Denikin and the Entente. They were afraid of the Czarist generals more than of Soviet Russia. . . . In the moment of the decisive struggle

---

[15] The Soviet proposal is in Boerner's diary as published in Kutrzeba, *op. cit.*, pp. 27-8.

[16] *Ibid.*, pp. 29-31. See also Louis Fischer, *The Soviets in World Affairs* (2nd ed., 2 vols.; Princeton: Princeton University Press, 1951), I, pp. 239-41.

with the Russian counterrevolution Soviet Russia signed a secret treaty with Pilsudski. . . ." [17]

The purpose of the statement seemed obvious at that time—to discredit the Polish government in the eyes of the Western European countries in general, and the French government in particular. But Radek's assertions were not accepted at face value; nor did the writings of Marchlewski two years later, in which he described his meetings with representatives of Pilsudski, command much confidence. The story was, therefore, largely ignored.[18]

After Pilsudski's death, General Kutrzeba, at one time the chief of strategic planning in the Polish general staff, published in 1937 the documents concerning the Marchlewski-Boerner meetings. He stated bluntly that to Pilsudski it was the lesser of two evils to facilitate Soviet Russia's defeat of Denikin. A war against the Soviets with Denikin as an ally would have been a war about Russia; while a war by Poland against the Soviets, without Denikin, would be a war about Poland. Based on this reasoning, "Pilsudski entirely consciously helped the Soviets in their war with Denikin. . . ." [19]

By the end of December Denikin was defeated. The two rivals, Moscow and Warsaw, had eliminated their common enemy, the first through military action, the latter through military inaction. Now they were in a position to revert to their previous and major goals.

SOVIET POLITICAL OFFENSIVE

Soviet Russia was on the defensive in 1919 on the Polish front. Her weapons against Poland were mainly of a political nature and she was busily engaged in public diplomacy. Diplo-

---

[17] Karl Radek, *Die Auswärtige Politik Sowjet-Russlands* (Hamburg: Verlag der Kommunistischen Internationale, 1921), pp. 16, 56. Also, K. Radek and R. Stefanovich, *Perevorot v Pol'she i Pilsudski* (Moscow: Gosudarstvennoe izdatel'stvo, 1926).

[18] Marchlewski, *op. cit.*, pp. 12–15.

[19] Kutrzeba, *op. cit.*, p. 25.

matic notes, addressed to Warsaw by open radio, were a mixture of requests for peace negotiations and revolutionary appeals. They were directed both to the government and to the Polish proletariat.

While the Polish Ministry of Foreign Affairs at first ignored these communications, the Communist Party of Poland, founded in the last days of 1918, responded to Moscow's exhortations with great revolutionary zeal. It published proclamations, distributed leaflets which appealed for insurrection, organized Workers' Soviets in a few Polish cities and even succeeded in arming some of them.[20] The Party, rejecting for a few months after the war even the thought of an independent Polish state, declared in its platform at the First Congress, "The Polish proletariat rejects all such political slogans as autonomy, self-determination. . . ."[21]

Indeed, in the expectation of direct assistance from the Red army, one of the Party's numerous proclamations to the Polish people declared that aid to the approaching Polish revolution on the part of the Russian proletariat "would not be considered an invasion."[22] There are indications that if such an invasion was not planned by Soviet leaders the thought of it was at least utilized for political purposes. At about the same time that Marchlewski embarked upon his secret mission of peace with Pilsudski, the German Ministry for Foreign Affairs received, on July 15, 1919, certain information from a person reportedly close to the Communist Prime Minister of Hungary, Bela Kun, "who [was] thoroughly acquainted with Lenin's plans." Lenin,

---

[20] The *Wislowski Collection*, Box VII, Hoover Institution, contains relevant materials. See also E. Brand and Waletsky, *Le communisme en Pologne* (Paris: Librairie de l'Humanité, 1922), pp. 24ff. On the foundation of the Communist Workers' Party of Poland see the highly documented M. K. Dziewanowski, *The Communist Party of Poland* (Cambridge: Harvard University Press, 1959), pp. 76ff.

[21] Jan Regula, *Historja Komunistycznej Partji Polski* (2nd ed., Warsaw: Drukprasa, 1934), p. 34 (on microfilm, Russian Research Center, Harvard University).

[22] Brand and Waletsky, *op. cit.*, p. 29.

according to this source of information, which is not identified in the German Foreign Office files, "wanted peace in Europe to encourage general demobilization. When, however, Europe is then in a state of defenselessness and has a feeling of security, he [Lenin] will march with his army against Germany. . . . Lenin hopes to be able to open the advance this autumn and then to push to the Rhine. He counts, of course, upon the support of the Bolshevik elements in Poland and Germany. . . ." [23] It is difficult to believe that the perceptive Lenin would have overlooked the strength of the French army, which did not entertain any thought of demobilizing and, one may safely surmise, would have resisted a Red army invasion of Central Europe.

Nevertheless, reports about a Soviet military move against Poland persisted. A few months later, on February 7, 1920, a German diplomat in Berlin received a mysterious visitor who insisted that his name not be mentioned in any written report. He is identified only as a political personality from the Soviet Ukraine. The visitor first gave his host a glowing report about the Red army, which had in the field two and a half million men (as well as the reserves), of an iron discipline, sufficiently equipped. Having impressed the German diplomat with the imposing military strength of Soviet Russia, the visitor continued, "The army will go into action very soon, not only in Russia but also abroad, and the next objective is Poland. Strong Russian forces are seemingly concentrated in the area of Kiev. However, this is in fact only a fake maneuver. The main operation will be conducted over Minsk. . . . One of the main goals is Warsaw and one can expect that from Warsaw, shortly thereafter, Toruń [near the old German-Russian border] will be reached." The visitor "had no doubts about the absolute suc-

[23] *St. Antony's Collection*, The National Archives, Washington, D.C., reel no. 103; July 15, 1919; the report is signed by Dr. Victor Naumann. Baron A. von Maltzan, a central figure of the German policy toward Russia after World War I, after having read the report, wrote in the margin, "To my knowledge Lenin is much too prudent a man to have such plans."

cess of the operation because the Poles in no way can match the Russians in numbers, equipment, or leadership of the army. Besides, an agitation has been in process in Poland for a month to render the country hostile to the present government. This agitation works extremely well. . . ." At the end of the visit, which was reported to Maltzan, the Ukrainian declared categorically that "the fate of Poland [was] altogether sealed."

Then the visitor came to the chief purpose of his visit. "The fateful hour for Germany has struck," he said, and pointed to the great future which was in store for Germany if she decided to go with Russia. This would bring an end to Versailles and the old East German boundary would be re-established. The visitor urged the German government to send someone to Moscow and the Ukraine immediately to establish contacts when the Russian army passed through Poland. "The Ukrainian assured me again that we must surely count on the Russian attack and equally surely assume that it will succeed . . . ," a statement which Maltzan accompanied in the margin with a one-syllable *ja*. As to the date of the Russian attack—it was to take place during the first half of March.[24]

It seems that the Ukrainian emissary sought out the German diplomat to prepare the way for another and even more important and informative visit. Two days later, on February 9, the German received his guest again. This time he came in the company of another man "who is a close friend of Litvinov and receives regular news from Russia." The Russian covisitor repeated to the German diplomat the information about the strength of the Red army, though in a more detailed and even more impressive manner. The German official wrote, "as far as the offensive intention against Poland is concerned, the man said exactly the same as the other gentleman had. He [the Russian] added that Poland will either have a position of an

[24] *St. Antony's Collection*, reel no. 33; A.S. 261, February 7, 1920. The report dated February 9 is initialed A.S. At the end of the nine-page report, Maltzan this time commented that with some few exceptions the information was in accordance with his own.

autonomous province in the Russian Reich, or in case of bitter opposition, she would have the same position as she had under the Czarist government. [Russia] does not think, however, of claiming any part of German Poland which should belong to Germany." [25]

It may well be that the anonymous Soviet emissaries deliberately overstated their case in order to impress the German government with the Red army's offensive strength. They probably hoped to dissuade Germany from joining the Entente in an ever-feared crusade against communist Russia, and indeed to lure her into full cooperation by the offer of the glittering prize of another common division of Poland. Such an offer would always find a sympathetic consideration in Berlin. On the other hand, direct Soviet sources do not indicate that an invasion of Poland was planned. Rather, they reflect the Soviet leaders' conviction that the Poles were making preparations for decisive operations and that Soviet offensive preparedness was therefore imperative.

Outwardly, the Soviet government professed to have a sincere longing for peace. On December 22, 1919, Chicherin sent an open radio telegram to the Polish Minister of Foreign Affairs, Stanislas Patek. He assured him of Russia's ardent desire to remove any misunderstanding between the two countries, to end the bloodshed and "enter immediately into negotiations" to achieve a stable peace. He, therefore, asked the Polish government to propose the place and time for peace negotiations.[26]

When this diplomatic note was not answered, the Council of the Commissars addressed a new declaration to Poland on January 28, 1920. It warned her of the consequences of her aggres-

---

[25] *St. Antony's Collection*, reel no. 33; A.S. 272, February 11, 1920. The report is dated February 11, 1920. The Polish intelligence service was also in possession of documents pointing to Soviet preparations for war against Poland. Kutrzeba, *op. cit.*, pp. 43, 69–72.

[26] *Vneshniaia Politika SSSR. Sbornik dokumentov. 1917–1944,* 4 vols. [n.p., n.d.], I, pp. 333–34.

sive policy but reiterated previous assurances of unreserved Soviet respect for Polish independence and promised that the Red army would not cross the fighting line as of the moment. It declared solemnly that the "Soviet government did not enter into any agreements or pacts with Germany or any other country, aimed directly or indirectly against Poland, and that the character and spirit of the international policy of the Soviet authorities excluded the very possibility of any agreements . . . [which] would violate Poland's independence and her territorial integrity." [27] The sincerity of the pledge can be judged by the offer which was supposedly made only a few days later in Berlin by the two Soviet representatives.

This official governmental appeal was accompanied by a series of other public communications. On February 2 the All-Russian Central Executive Committee (VTsIK) addressed a fiery appeal directly "to the Polish people." It expressed understanding for the traditional Polish suspicion of the old imperialist Russia. However, it stated, times have changed and "the freedom of Poland is an indispensable condition for the development of Russia," which does not want to impose communism on Poland by way of the Red army's bayonets. The Russian communists' longing for peace with Poland is sincere, stated the proclamation.[28]

The Executive Committee of the Communist International (ECCI) added its voice to such appeals and published on February 17 a manifesto which accused the Western powers, France, Great Britain, and the United States, of inciting Poland to fight against Soviet Russia, "the same Poland which received its freedom and independence not from the hands of these imperialist governments, but thanks only to the revolution in Russia and Germany." [29] This last part of the proc-

---

[27] *Krasnaia Kniga. Sbornik diplomaticheskikh dokumentov o russko-pol'skikh otnosheniiakh, 1918–1920* (Moscow: N.K.I.D., 1920), pp. 84–5.

[28] Kliuchnikov and Sabanin, *op. cit.*, Vol. III, Part I, pp. 9–11.

[29] Jane Degras, *The Communist International, 1919–43*. Documents. (2 vols.; London: Oxford University Press, 1956), 1, p. 80.

lamation, in obvious contradiction to historical fact, has remained a Soviet political shibboleth to this day.

While pursuing this intensive peace offensive, the Soviet government made political and military preparations for war. Lenin sent to his closest associates a series of telegrams urging intensified efforts.[30] On March 11 he stated publicly that the Red army "will never cross the line on which it stands now—and it is considerably farther [east] from the area where the Polish populace lives. . . ." However, if Poland continues to be silent to the Soviet peace proposal and attacks Russia, she will then suffer and "will never forget it," he warned.[31]

If the war was indeed inevitable, the military leaders were planning to react to a Polish move by a counteroffensive. "In the middle of February 1920 the chief of the operational division of the staff, comrade Shaposhnikov, pointed in a detailed report to the premises of a plan of future operations against Poland." [32] Accordingly, the past experience of leaving the Soviet troops outnumbered on the western front and remaining passive was to be substituted by energetic and decisive blows. Shaposhnikov planned "the principal blow on the front at Vilna-Lida"; to achieve this goal he ordered that "all the transport must be accomplished in April, and at that time decisive operations must start." [33]

[30] February 19, to Trotsky: ". . . We shall prove to be idiots if we allow ourselves to be drawn by a silly agitation into the depth of Siberia and at that time Denikin revives and the Poles strike. This will be a crime." February 27, to Trotsky: "All indications are that Poland will present us absolutely unacceptable, even insolent conditions. All attention must be directed to the preparation and strengthening of the Western front. . . ." March 1, to Josef Unshlikht, a communist leader of Polish nationality: "Top secret. The Poles, we see, will fight. We do everything we can to strengthen our defense; we must intensify to the highest degree agitation in Polish. We'll help you if necessary with people, money, paper." March 11, 1920, to Z. Ordzhonikidze: "The Poles are making war inevitable." All of the above from *Trotsky Archives*, file A.

[31] V. I. Lenin, *Sochineniia* (35 vols.; 4th ed. Moscow: Ogiz, 1950), Vol. 30, p. 369.

[32] H. E. Kakurin and V. A. Melikov, *Voina s Belopoliakami 1920 g* (Moscow: Gosudarstvennoe voennoe izdatel'stvo, 1925), p. 67.

[33] *Ibid.*, pp. 68–70.

Another authoritative account of the role of the Red army in the political struggle within and without Russia describes in detail the Soviet leaders' anticipation of war with Poland and the country's political and military preparations. It quotes Lenin as declaring, "We resolved to have by spring [1920] a one-million man army; now, we need an army of three million men. We can have it. We shall have it." [34] From the beginning of 1920 the Soviet high command considered the Polish front, particularly the Belorussian front, as of primary importance because through it was the shortest route to Warsaw and (in case of defense) also to Moscow.[35]

By the spring of 1920 the Soviet leaders considered the outbreak of hostilities only a matter of time. Trotsky explained the delay in Polish operations as a maneuver to provoke Russia into a major military action which would allow the West to intervene in "great style." He proposed an intensive political campaign of preparation for war and a "general mobilization of the Polish communists." [36]

POLISH POLITICAL OFFENSIVE

The Polish government answered the Soviet policy in kind; it, too, spoke publicly of peace and, in fact, prepared for war. It was not a secret that Pilsudski intended to limit the Soviet power to Russia herself, to support the Ukrainian quest for independence and a self-government in Belorussia, and integrate them, together with Lithuania, into one strong, imposing federation, under Polish leadership.[37]

[34] *Grazhdanskaia Voina 1918–1921*, eds. A. S. Bubnov, S. S. Kamenev, R. P. Eideman (3 vols.; Moscow: Gosud. Izdatel'stvo, 1930), III, p. 120.

[35] *Ibid.*, pp. 308–13, 317, 319.

[36] *Trotsky Archives*, file A.

[37] An official Polish source and at least one Polish scholar made liberal deductions from the Soviet government decree of August 29, 1918, by which Soviet Russia annulled all Partition treaties signed by Czarist Russia, Prussia, and Austria. They maintained that this act of the Soviet government recognized the Polish right of restitution of the 1772 boundaries or at least was an expression of Soviet disinterest in the area. *Polish-Soviet Relations 1918–1943*. Official Documents. Issued by the Polish Embassy in

General Kutrzeba testified that "already in the spring of 1919 [he] prepared, as the head of the section for planning of the Chief Command, an operational study the task of which was to weigh the Polish army's offensive in the Ukraine. . . ." "The Kiev Expedition," as the subsequent Polish invasion of the Ukraine was called, was not something new; "as an operational idea [it] existed over one whole year." [38]

Pilsudski first ignored the Soviet messages suggesting peace negotiations. Then, on February 15, he gave an interview to *Le Matin* in which he stated somewhat cryptically, "The time for concluding peace with Russia has come. It has come not only for us, but for all States of the Entente." Implying further that the Western powers failed to understand "enormous changes [that] have taken place in Eastern Europe," he declared that Poland must take the initiative and therefore was preparing a "plan aiming to establish a legal status for Eastern Europe." [39]

What kind of legal status he had in mind can be deduced from events which followed. A few days later, toward the end of February 1920, the Committee on Foreign Affairs of the *Sejm* reacted to the Soviet peace offers and expressed in a statement the readiness of Poland to negotiate peace. However, the statement concluded, the Polish Republic had the right to insist "that the population of the territories which are situated beyond the present line of Polish administration and [which] belonged to Poland before 1772 be given the opportunity of a free expression of will about their own future allegiance." [40] As another authoritative witness stated ". . . The federalist theory was at its height. The [Soviet] proposal was not given any serious consideration." [41]

Washington by the Authority of the Government of the Republic of Poland [n.d.], p. 3. Jan Ochota, "Uniewaznienie aktow rozbiorowych przez Rosje," *Sprawy obce* (Warsaw), January 1930, No. 11, pp. 283–314.

[38] Kutrzeba, *op. cit.*, p. 49.
[39] Komarnicki, *op. cit.*, pp. 542–43.
[40] Jan Dąbski, *Pokój Ryski* (Warsaw: [n.p.], 1931), p. 17.
[41] Count Alexander Skrzyński, *Poland and Peace* (London: George Allen & Unwin, 1923), p. 40.

On March 13 the Polish government sent a note to the Entente powers in which it outlined certain conditions for peace negotiations with Soviet Russia.[42] In a circular telegram from the Polish Ministry of Foreign Affairs to its diplomatic mission these conditions were formulated as follows: (1) abrogation of the partition treaties of 1772; (2) detachment from Russia of the territories west of the 1772 boundary; (3) recognition by Russia of independence of the states of the former Russian empire which have governments *de facto;* (4) renunciation of socialist propaganda outside Soviet Russia's boundaries; (5) the fate of the countries west of the 1772 boundary to be decided without Russia's intervention entirely according to the will of the population; (6) Russia's obligation to pay reparations to Poland on the basis of the situation as it existed in 1772.[43]

Even Mr. Hugh Gibson, the American Envoy to Warsaw, who had previously championed Pilsudski's policy, considered it now his duty to comment that "the intentions of the Polish Government have manifestly undergone material change both as to substance and procedure. . . . The Polish [conditions] are much more far-reaching than Patek had led the representatives of the powers to believe and leave him open to the charge of imperialism. . . ."[44]

There is no reason to doubt that the Soviet government would never have considered engaging in peace negotiations on the basis of such expensive territorial demands; by that time Belorussia and the Ukraine, or rather the regions which were under communist rule, formed an integral part of the Soviet system. Moreover, the Entente powers would not have been prepared to support such claims; members of the Allied Council, particularly Lloyd George, repeatedly warned the Polish government that it would not support its quest for territory which extended beyond the Polish ethnic line. How-

[42] Komarnicki, *op. cit.,* p. 565.

[43] *Ciechanowski Deposit,* Hoover Institution.

[44] *Foreign Relations Papers,* III, p. 381.

ever, the Polish conditions of peace were never presented to
Soviet Russia; Pilsudski created a situation which prevented
the two belligerents even from meeting.

DIPLOMATIC MANEUVERING

On March 27, 1920, after a two months' delay, the Polish
government at last answered the Soviet diplomatic notes and
expressed willingness to open negotiations on April 10 at
Borisov, a place close to the front line in the area of the northern part of the Soviet-Polish front. Here only, the Polish note
suggested, would the fighting stop; there would be no cessation
of hostilities along the rest of the front.

For a moment Moscow hesitated as to whether it should, as
Chicherin suggested, ignore the Polish proposal altogether.[45] It
then decided to engage in a battle of words. It wished the
negotiations to be conducted at a neutral place, preferably in
Estonia but was ready to accept such places as Moscow, Petrograd, Warsaw, Paris, or London. It also desired the cessation
of hostilities along the entire front. As the Polish government
continued to insist upon its original conditions for negotiation,
the Soviet government finally turned to the Entente countries
with a request for intervention with the adamant Poles. This
last communication is dated April 8.[46]

One cannot but question sincerity of such official expressions
of the Soviet government's wish for peace. They certainly find
little support in less official statements made by the Third International representatives. Karl Radek, for instance, made a
lengthy speech on April 20 in which he belabored his favorite
subject, the views of Marx, Engels, and Lenin on the desirability of an independent Poland, and in which he spoke for
an independent Soviet Poland, closely allied with Soviet Russia
and the forthcoming proletarian Germany.[47]

[45] *Trotsky Archives,* file A.
[46] The texts of the diplomatic notes are in *Vneshniaia Politika,* I, pp.
414–19.
[47] Karl Radek, *Piat' let Kominterna* (Moscow: Krasnaia Nov', 1924), pp.
232–51.

It appears incomprehensible that the possibility of peace negotiations were to be made dependent upon an agreement about the place of the meeting. Nevertheless, each side had paramount reasons for insisting on its position; the Russians were opposed to Borisov for exactly the reasons that the Poles insisted upon it. After the defeat of Denikin, the Soviet high command, as has been stated, began moving troops to the western front to take positions for a counteroffensive thrust in the direction of Warsaw. To negotiate and cease hostilities near Borisov, where these Soviet forces were concentrated, would have paralyzed their plan. Moreover, it would have meant the danger of opening their southern flank to a Polish offensive. This is exactly why Pilsudski is known to have insisted on Borisov; "he *pretended* [author's italics] to agree with negotiations but made such conditions as Borisov—which Russia did not nor could not accept. . . ." [48] His "guiding ideas on the plans of our war with Russia in the spring of 1920 arose at the time of the break of 1919/20," [49] writes Kutrzeba, and reveals, in another source, that Pilsudski "reckoned that Poland must conquer her boundary by sword and not accept it as a present from Russia's hand." [50]

On April 23 Chicherin made a last attempt. Sensing the desperate situation, he now indicated his readiness to meet a Polish delegation at Grodno or Bialystok in the northwest sector of the front rather than at Borisov.[51] He did not know that by this time a date had been set by Pilsudski to invade the Ukraine; nor did he know that two days earlier the representa-

---

[48] Both the Polish and Soviet sources agree on this interpretation of the diplomatic game around Borisov; J. Pilsudski, *L'Année 1920*. Édition Complète avec le Texte de l'Ouvrage de M. Toukhatchevski "La Marche au delà de la Vistule" (Paris: La renaissance du Livre, 1929), pp. 267–68. *Grazhdanskaia Voina*, pp. 327ff; Marchlewski, *op. cit.*, pp. 15ff; Karl Radek, *op. cit.*, p. 59; Kutrzeba, *op. cit.*, p. 74. Waclaw Jedrzejewicz, "Rokowania borysowskie w 1920 roku," *Niepodległość*, III (1951), pp. 47–59.

[49] Kutrzeba, *op. cit.*, p. 42.

[50] *Polska Zbrojna* (Warsaw), May 7, 1937, as quoted in E. G. Val', *Kak Pilsudski pogubil Denikina* (Talinn: Izdanie avtora, 1938), p. 3.

[51] K. W. Kumaniecki, *Odbudowa Panstwowości Polskiej. Najważniejsze Dokumenty* (Warsaw: J. Czerniecki, 1924), p. 266.

tives of Poland and the Ukrainian National Republic had signed a secret political convention which was followed on April 24 by a military agreement. This convention recognized an independent Ukraine with Simon Petlura as head of the government; the military agreement envisaged, in case of common war against Soviet Russia, that the two allied armies would operate under the command of the Polish Commander-in-Chief and that the newly occupied territories would be under a provisional Polish administration.[52]

Nor did the next event leave anyone in doubt about the ultimate prospects of Soviet-Polish peace negotiations. On April 26, 1920, Marshal Pilsudski issued the following proclamation: "At my order the army of the Republic of Poland has resumed its advance and has penetrated deeply into the Ukraine. I want the population of these regions to know that the Polish army entering the territory which belongs to the Ukrainian citizens will remain in the Ukraine only as long as it will be necessary to transfer the country to the administration of a legitimate Ukrainian government. When the national government of the Ukrainian Republic will have established its authority, when the troops of the Ukrainian nation will have taken hold of its borders to protect their country against new intrusions, when the free nation itself will be in a position to decide its destiny, then the Polish soldiers will withdraw behind the frontier of the free Republic of Poland, after having brought to an end their glorious campaign for the liberty of nations. Together with Polish troops, there will return to the Ukraine, under the direction of Ataman general Simon Petlura, the legions which, in the days of the gravest tests of the Ukrainian people, found support in the Polish Republic. I am convinced that the Ukrainian nation will use all its efforts to achieve by arms and with the aid of the Polish Republic its

[52] Kliuchnikov and Sabanin, *op. cit.*, III, II, pp. 5–8. The text of the military convention is in I. Mazepa, *Ukraina v ogni i buri revoliutsii, 1917–1921* (Paris: Prometej, 1950), III, pp. 204–207.

real freedom and secure to the fertile soil of its homeland happiness and prosperity which will result from work and calm, once peace is re-established. The army of the Polish Republic guarantees to all people of the Ukraine—regardless of class, origin or religion—defense and protection." [53]

A new and fatal phase in Soviet-Polish relations had begun.

THE WAR

The Soviet-Polish war lasted less than six months. However, in the light of its political consequences, of the failure of either side to achieve its stated goal, of changing military fortunes and of the vacillating policy of the Entente, the Soviet-Polish war is surely one of the decisive events of our times.[54]

The swift advance of the Polish army into the interior of the Ukraine prompted the Polish government to take a political stand on the future of the Soviet borderland. Only three days after the attack had been launched, the Ministry of Foreign Affairs in Warsaw sent to its diplomatic representatives a circular note which defined the aim of the Polish military campaign. The note stated in the opening sentence, "It is in the interest of Poland to root out Russian imperialism and to reduce Russia to her own boundaries." It then continued with an analysis of the political situation, an analysis which was not lacking in foresight. "It is unquestionable that should Russia succeed, with one or another internal system, in achieving territorial boundaries more or less the same as they were in Europe before the war, she will do so only with German help; and at any rate such a Russia, even if she were so restored with the ill-considered assistance of the Western governments, would have to seek support for its policy in the very near future through the closest alliance with Germany." Continuing its

---

[53] *Livre Rouge.* Edition d'état. (Moscow: 1920), pp. 106–107.

[54] The chief military and political developments of the war have been the subject of many studies. They are mentioned here only in conjunction with some new or lesser-known materials as they may throw some new light on the complex and colorful scene of this military and political battle.

political analysis, the note stated, "Between the Russian imperialism . . . and Poland there is no compromise. It is, therefore, in Poland's interest that all territories, the population of which is not of Russian nationality, remain separated from Russia."

The document then analyzed the political position of the Baltic States and outlined the future of Belorussia and the Ukraine. In the case of Finland, the note asserted that her independence was for the time being assured and it pointed to recent negotiations with Finland, held in Warsaw, which had opened a prospect for a joint policy toward the common enemy in the east. Estonia's future, on the other hand, was not so clear, in view of Russian ambition to make her a bridge to the Baltic Sea. Furthermore, the document stated, Poland was eminently interested in Latvia and hoped shortly to open friendly negotiations with her. In addition, Poland would endeavor to reach an agreement with Lithuania in the absence of complete union. As to the non-Polish territories which were hers until 1772, Poland categorically requested their disannexation from Russia.

In the case of Belorussia, the document stated, "Poland does not want to cut the Belorussian nation in two. In view of the geographical situation and the lack of any considerable number of politically minded elements it is necessary to speak about independence for Belorussia." However, the analysis continued, "Belorussia will eventually be found in the sphere of influence either of Poland or Russia. The latter would be fatal to Poland." Poland recognized the Ukraine's right to independence and that this idea of independence must be encouraged in the West. This remarkable document concluded, however, with the statement that "the conviction has to be aroused that the Ukraine can be oriented only toward Poland, with the financial help of the West." [55]

No sooner had the invasion of the Ukraine begun than the

[55] *Ciechanowski Deposit.* The document, not otherwise identifiable, is dated Warsaw, April 29, 1920.

Polish government came to realize that some of its political expectations were without foundation. The Ukrainians' memory of fighting against the Poles for Eastern Galicia in 1919 was still fresh; nor were they free of their traditional hostility toward the Poles. As a result, they failed to give to the Polish units the anticipated enthusiastic welcome and active support. Although they hated the Bolshevik terror, they had little confidence in Polish promises.

In the middle of May Pilsudski made a speech at Vinitsa in the Ukraine in which he pledged to his audience the independence of their country—a pledge already qualified by expectation of an agreement with Poland. At Vinitsa he met Ataman Petlura and the two commanders "embraced each other" as "national anthems were played and the sun was setting." However, even at this solemn occasion, difficulties were already arising concerning the extent of Ukrainian independence, as was related by the former Prime Minister of the Ukrainian Republic, I. Mazepa.[56] It became quickly apparent that Pilsudski planned to treat the Ukraine as a satellite of Poland.

The triumphant advance of the Polish army was short lived. During the first days of May, it captured Kiev; on June 13 it was in full retreat. At the beginning of July, the Soviet army launched the long-planned and powerful offensive on the western front which brought the Red army to the gates of Warsaw.

These spectacular military events were accompanied by some frantic political moves. The Soviet political and military leaders based their military plans upon the expectations of class warfare and revolutionary upheavals within Poland. General

[56] Józef Pilsudski, *Erinnerungen und Dokumente* (Essen: Essener Verlagsanstalt, 1936), IV, p. 62. Waclaw Grzybowski, "Spotkania i rozmowy z Józefem Piłsudskim," *Niepodległość* (London), I, 1948, p. 91. Mazepa's description of the events at Vinitsa is in *Kultura* (Paris), No. 9/59, September 1952, pp. 104–109. (The date of the meeting differs, some sources putting it at May 16, others at May 17.) For a critical appraisal of the Polish campaign in the Ukraine, see John S. Reshetar, Jr., *The Ukrainian Revolution, 1917–1920* (Princeton: Princeton University Press, 1952), pp. 300–14.

Mikhail Tukhachevsky, who was responsible for the strategic planning of the offensive, described in a lecture held subsequently at the Moscow Military Academy, the minute political preparations made in advance of the Soviet moves.[57]

The war had been given the quality of a class struggle at a mass meeting organized in Moscow on May 5, a few days after the Polish attack in the Ukraine. Lenin, Trotsky, Kamenev, Sokolnikov, Radek, Martov, and Marchlewski climbed the rostrum and hurled flamboyant speeches against the Polish imperialists, landowners, and the *bourgeoisie*. Promising self-determination to Poland, they appealed to the Polish workers and the peasants to revolt.[58]

Words of caution, however, were uttered, too, in view of the past hatred between the Russian and Polish people. Radek, who knew Poland better than many other Soviet leaders, appears to be the first person who struck a word of public warning. Writing in *Izvestiia*, he pointed to the fact that even the small *bourgeoisie* in Poland was convinced of Russian annexationist aims, for it did not trust Russia, whether Czarist or Red. Then, he proceeded, "We must crush the white guard Poland completely. She has proved to us by deeds that she cannot exist side by side with Soviet Russia. If the white guard Poland cannot exist side by side with Soviet Russia, then a Soviet Poland will."[59]

Trotsky wrote at a later date that on May 1 he had warned, "that the war *will end* with the workers' revolution in Poland, there can be no doubt; but at the same time there is no basis for supposing that the war *will begin* with such a revolution."[60] On May 10, when the situation in the Ukraine was

[57] J. Pilsudski, *L'Année 1920*, p. 215. In a series of shorter studies written before the Soviet-Polish war, Tukhachevsky analyzed the role of the Red army, its strategy and tactics in the light of a class warfare. *Voina Klassov*. Stat'i, 1919–1920 gg (Moscow: Gosudarstvennoe izdatel'stvo, 1921).

[58] L. Trotsky *et al.*, *Sowjetrussland und Polen. Reden von Kamenev, Lenin, Trotzki . . .* (Berlin: Russische Korrespondenz, 1920).

[59] May 4, 1920.

[60] Leon Trotsky, *Stalin* (New York: Harper and Bros., 1941), p. 328.

extremely serious and he was sending out instructions to make persons in responsible positions aware of the gravity of the crisis, he instructed the commanding officers to treat the Polish people well.[61] These instructions were to be interpreted, of course, in the Marxist way, in an attempt not to antagonize the workers' and peasants' masses and to separate them from the hated landlords and the *bourgeoisie*. For that purpose intensive preparations were made in the field of political activities. In May the Communist Party of Soviet Russia founded a Polish Bureau which was attached to the Central Committee of the Ukrainian communist party. Polish communists were brought in to participate in a course which was to train them for political work, particularly among the Polish peasants.[62] Quantities of materials were translated into Polish for dissemination among the Polish people.[63]

The Communist Party of Poland was used as the avant-garde of the Red army advance. It established a Central Army Revolutionary Committee to concentrate on political work among Polish soldiers.[64] On a broader scene, it issued appeals and proclamations, all of which denounced the "capitalist" Polish war against Soviet Russia. Soviet Russia was greeted as liberator, and, to strike a nationalist tune, as the only country which had guaranteed the inviolability of the Polish boundaries.[65]

To supplement this two-pronged Soviet and Polish communist political operation, the Comintern sent a group of professional revolutionaries and agents to the front to operate secretly behind the Polish lines. Their tasks were "to shatter

[61] *Trotsky Archives*, file A; a series of telegrams to *Orgburo* in May. Also L. Trotsky, *Sovetskaia Rossiia i burzhuaznaia Pol'sha* (Praga: Izdatel'stvo gazety "Pravda," 1920), p. 10. Also his appeals, speeches, and orders in *Kak vooruzhalas' revoliutsiia*.

[62] Tadeusz Teslar, *Propaganda bolszewicka podczas wojny polsko-rosyjskiej 1920 roku* (Warsaw: Wojskowy instytut naukowo-oświatowy, 1938), pp. 41–7.

[63] *Ibid.*, pp. 296–303.

[64] *Ibid.*, p. 97.

[65] *KPP w obronie niepodległości Polski: Materiały i dokumenty* (Warsaw: Książka i Wiedza, 1953), pp. 45ff.

the morale of the Polish army by propaganda," to publish a revolutionary newspaper *Świt* (Dawn), to operate closely with the Communist Party of Poland in organizing acts of sabotage, strikes, etc.[66]

The party work was accompanied by a series of public statements originating in Moscow. On May 18 the Executive Committee of the Communist International issued a manifesto, addressed to the proletariat of all countries, asking workers to sabotage the war of "the shameless bandits of Polish imperialism." It assured the Poles that Soviet Russia was bringing them "not oppression, but national freedom." [67]

The real meaning of the communist interpretation of the term "national freedom" was illuminated a month later, on June 17, when the All-Russian Central Executive Committee addressed an appeal to the "Polish soldiers-legionaries, workers, and peasants." The calamity of the Polish army's occupation of Kiev had by then been averted and the authors of the appeal, always thinking of the war in class-conflict terms, this time spoke of a "workers' and peasants' " Poland and offered such a Poland "help against [her] internal and external enemies. . . ." The proclamation asked Poles to cease "this bloody, dishonorable, cursed struggle" and to come over, armed or unarmed, "under the true brotherly protection of the workers' and peasants' Red army, and thus to secure, surely and quickly, an independent socialist Poland." [68]

Another month passed, and the Red army was in full attack. On July 19, 1920, the Second Congress of the Communist International opened in Moscow. The sign of victory, of an irresistible march of revolution, dominated the scene. The representatives of various communist parties the world over followed the military developments with "breathless" excitement. The scene was recalled at a later day by Zinoviev; the group,

[66] W. G. Krivitsky, *In Stalin's Secret Service* (New York: Harper and Bros., 1939), pp. 29–30.
[67] Degras, *The Communist International*, pp. 91–2.
[68] Kliuchnikov and Sabanin, *op. cit.*, III, I, pp. 28–9.

facing a large map hung in the Congress Hall, was "led to understand that the very fate of the international proletarian revolution depended on every step forward of the Red army." [69]

The Congress sent a fiery greeting to that same army which, it said, was fighting "not only in the interest of Soviet Russia, but also in the interest of all laboring mankind, for the Communist International." [70] This resolution was followed by an appeal to the "proletarian men and women of all countries." Though anticipating that the fires of revolution would sweep not only Poland but Europe itself, it pointedly mentioned, in the past tense, that "Soviet Russia was ready to conclude peace even with the Polish capitalists and she not only recognized, for the sake of peace, Poland's independence, but even ceded her a large portion of the frontier region." The appeal confirmed Poland's right of self-determination, but its last words, "Long live Soviet Poland," carried again the unmistakable imprint of the Marxist interpretation of this right.[71]

At the time of the Second Congress, Karl Radek once again reviewed, in a lengthy article, the thinking of Engels, Marx, Lenin, and Rosa Luxemburg about the problem of Polish independence and underlined again the class nature of the struggle. Anticipating a communist victory in Germany, he was at the same time deeply aware of the mistrust which even a Polish communist might harbor toward either Russia or Germany, although these countries had been sovietized. He wrote, "No proletarian government (neither Soviet Russia, nor the future proletarian Germany) is interested in imposing upon the Polish nation its own government. On the contrary, such a government is interested in strengthening the position of the

[69] *Protokoly S'ezdov i Konferentsii Vsesoiuznoi Kommunisticheskoi Partii* (b). Desiatyi S'ezd RKP (b). Mart 1921 g (Moscow: Partiinoe Izdatel'stvo, 1933), p. 505.

[70] *Vtoroi Kongress Kommunisticheskogo Internatsionala*. Stenograficheskii otchet (Petrograd: Izdatel'stvo Kom. Internatsionala, 1921), p. 41.

[71] *Kommunisticheskii Internatsional v dokumentakh. Resheniia, tezisy i rozzvaniia Kongressov Kominterna i Plenumov IKKI. 1919–1932,* ed. Bela Kun (Moscow: Partinoe izdatel'stvo, 1933), pp. 159–62.

Polish working class when it achieves victory; it is, therefore, interested in the disappearance of any national mistrust among the Polish small-bourgeois masses. . . . [It] recognizes fully the independence of Soviet Poland." Poland is not a fence against Russia but "a bridge which unites Soviet Russia with proletarian Germany," concluded Radek.[72]

Wide horizons were appearing beyond the plains of Poland in these days of July and the visions of the communist leaders extended still further. Everything seemed to develop more successfully than the Soviet leaders had anticipated. On July 20 the German government proclaimed neutrality and denied France the right to send supplies to the hard-pressed Poles through German territory. That same day the Danzig workers went on strike, refusing to unload shipments of arms sent to Poland by the only passage open to her. British workers went on a sympathetic strike and Czechoslovakia sealed her boundary and refused transit of equipment.

Then on July 31, in complete miscalculation of the reaction of the Polish nation, the Soviet government set up a ready-made Provisional Revolutionary Committee composed of a group of Polish communists. Marchlewski was its chairman.[73] So blinded were the Soviet leaders by their own "class-warfare" concept, they failed completely to sense the temper of the Polish people, who, as Poles, were passionately anti-Russian and, as individualists, passionately anticommunist. Their response to the Soviets' and to the Polish Committee's appeals was altogether negative, with the exception of a few workers' organizations in some industrial centers.

In an attempt to alleviate this deep-rooted misapprehension of the Polish people, the Soviet Revolutionary War Council on August 6 issued an order to the Red army. It was to behave in such a way that "Poland sees in it a liberator, not a con-

[72] *Kommunisticheskii Internatsional.* Organ Ispolnitel'nogo Komiteta Kommunisticheskogo Internatsionala, II, No. 12, July 20, 1920, cols. 2172–2187.

[73] L. Fischer, *op. cit.,* I, pp. 268–70.

queror"; to avoid everything that might be remindful of the Czarist army; to exert no acts of banditry or violence; but, at the same time, to be merciless with Polish counterrevolutionaries and "help the Polish comrades as quickly as possible to organize their own units in the areas liberated from the lords' army. Above all," stated the Soviet order, "look up local organizations of the Communist Party of Poland, and cooperate with them on the strengthening and extending of these organizations; [however do] not make decisions about any important and rather complicated problem without seeking counsel with them." [74]

In the midst of the Soviet advance the Soviet leaders had to make a fateful decision: to stop at the Polish ethnographic line or to cross it. They had to consider the possibility of the Entente's intervention in the conflict should they follow the latter course. The Entente powers had several times in the past advised the Polish government not to cross the ethnic boundaries which, they had proposed, were to be taken as a basis for delineation of the future Soviet-Polish border. Conversely, they promised Poland assistance if the Red army should attack her and cross this line.

Soviet diplomacy therefore concentrated on preventing a possible British move in favor of Poland, its chances in London being more promising than in the other Entente capitals. On frequent occasions Lloyd George had been openly critical of Pilsudski's policy and, moreover, he was anxious to open trade relations with Soviet Russia. France, the Soviet government knew, was willing to give military assistance to Poland; indeed, she encouraged the Polish government in the war with Russia. However, her hands were tied by her recognition of General Wrangel, who had picked up the remnants of Denikin's army and was harassing the Soviet army in the south. Pilsudski distrusted him as much as he had Denikin and was suspicious of French policy toward Wrangel. Also, in her anx-

[74] Teslar, *op. cit.*, pp. 242–43.

iety to keep Germany powerless, France depended considerably on Great Britain and could not, therefore, afford to oppose openly the British attitude toward Poland. The United States showed friendly feelings toward Poland, but Soviet Russia could safely presume that her isolationist position excluded any thought of active intervention in the war. Also, the American attitude was still colored by the expectation that the Bolshevik regime would collapse from within and a new, undivided, hopefully liberal Russia would arise.[75]

The British government, then, held the key to the solution of the critical question of further military developments on the Polish front. After a desperate plea for assistance by the Polish Prime Minister, Wladyslaw Grabski, before the meeting of the Supreme Council at Spa, Lloyd George seized upon the opportunity to compel Grabski to agree to the Entente's previous proposal to negotiate a Polish-Soviet peace on the basis of the ethnic line of the Soviet-Polish boundary. Lloyd George wished to convene a conference in London, but was ready to give Poland British help should the Russians cross the line. On July 11, Lord Curzon sent a note to the Soviet government worded accordingly. The note, however, suggested negotiation not only about the Polish front but also in regard to the Crimea, where General Wrangel's forces were engaged.[76] The Soviet government faced a dilemma: to accept the British offer and honor its former pledge to respect an independent, ethnographic Poland or to exploit her military success, pursue the enemy, and establish a communist Poland—with the expectation of communizing Germany as well—but with the risk of an Allied intervention on the side of Poland.

Sergei Kamenev, the chief commander on the Soviet-Polish front, was worried about the military implications of continu-

---

[75] The Entente powers' policy toward the Soviet-Polish conflict throughout its duration is exposed in detail in Komarnicki, *op. cit.*, pp. 397–406, 587–601, 608–617, 619–35, 655–70, 685–88, 704–706.

[76] *D.B.F.P.* First Series, VIII, pp. 441–42, 502–506, 513–18, 524–30; Kliuchnikov and Sabanin, *op. cit.*, III, 1, pp. 34–5.

ing the war and submitted a report to the Revolutionary War Council, whose chairman was Trotsky. He proposed a halt in the advance.[77] Trotsky had already put on record his views. On July 13 he had sent a telegram to the members of the Politburo in which he recommended acceptance of the British mediation offer. Russia, he stated, recognized Poland as an independent nation and was ready in principle to guarantee the inviolability of the Polish boundaries as proposed by the Entente, without prejudice to the final solution of the question. But Russia refused English mediation as to the Crimea which was not an independent country.[78]

Lenin evaluated the Curzon note differently and pressed for the continuation of the war. He sent a message (the date is not known) to Sklianski, a member of the Revolutionary War Council and Deputy Commissar for War, stating that "the international situation, particularly Curzon's proposal (annexation of the Crimea . . .), demands a tremendous acceleration of the attack on Poland. Are you set? Everyone? Energetically?" [79]

On July 12 or 13 Lenin informed Stalin, who was in Kharkov in charge of military operations against Wrangel, about the Curzon note. He asked him to speed up all efforts for attack and wished to know his opinion about the Curzon note. "I personally think," wrote Lenin, "it is a complete swindle, bent on the annexation of the Crimea which suddenly comes out in the note. They want to snatch victory from our hands by swindling promises." [80]

On July 17 the Revolutionary War Council met to consider

[77] J. Pilsudski, *L'Année 1920,* p. 280.
[78] *Trotsky Archives,* file A.
[79] *Ibid.*
[80] Lenin, *Sochineniia,* Vol. 31, p. 179. In Stalin's collected works his answer to Lenin's telegram is omitted. The omission was undoubtedly prompted by the fact that the Soviet advance, undertaken against Trotsky's view, was subsequently recognized by Lenin and other communist leaders as a mistake. Nevertheless, the footnote to the text of Lenin's telegram, published in his collected works, reveals that Stalin agreed with Lenin's evaluation of the Curzon note. Vol. 31, p. 511.

Kamenev's report and made a decision which proved to be fatal. "The Revolutionary War Council of the Soviet Republic and its chairman, Trotsky, took a position which was directly opposed [to Kamenev's recommendation] but nevertheless categoric and decisive," recorded two Soviet military writers in 1925 (undoubtedly already under Stalin's instruction to throw the blame for this immense blunder on Trotsky).[81] The Council ordered the Red army to cross the ethnic line and advance into the heart of Poland.

A directive to chief commander Kamenev explains the reasoning which prompted the Revolutionary War Council's decision. "Curzon's note," states the document, "offers the best proof that the success of the Soviets on the Polish front threatens to a considerable extent the situation" created by the Versailles Treaty. The British mediation offer was only a pretext to gain time for preparation of a new attack on Soviet Russia and to reorganize the forces of Poland and Wrangel. "We cannot permit them to gain this time." The offensive must be pursued "without the slightest pause [and] without taking account of the limitations defined in the Curzon note." [82]

Some attempt was made to camouflage the military operations with a diplomatic move. The same day, July 17, Chicherin replied to Lord Curzon. He expressed the general desire of Soviet Russia to establish peaceful relations with all countries, "even with Poland." However, he stated, Poland has not made direct proposals to the Soviet government, a fact which made the cessation of hostilities difficult. Taking into consideration the interests of the Russian and the Polish toiling masses, the Soviet government considered it possible to conclude peace with Poland only through direct negotiations. It was ready to offer to the Poles a boundary which would be even more favorable to them than the Supreme Council's and Lord Curzon's proposal, and give them even more advantageous conditions of

---

[81] H. E. Kakurin and V. A. Melikov, *op. cit.*, p. 475.
[82] *Ibid.*

peace if—and here the ominous note was struck—"the Polish people proceed in their internal life along a path which will establish a solid foundation for truly fraternal relations between the working masses of Poland, Russia, and the Ukraine, Belorussia, and Lithuania and will guarantee that Poland will stop serving as an instrument of aggression and intrigue against the workers and peasants of Soviet Russia and other countries." [83]

During the early years of the Soviet government, its revolutionary leaders, still faithful to the spirit of proletarian internationalism, were ready to subordinate the territorial interests of Russia to the spread of communist ideology and rule. This explains why Chicherin alluded to the Soviet willingness to cede to Poland some regions which extended beyond the Curzon line and why, on the other hand, he stressed class relations between Poland's workers and her eastern neighbors. A communist Poland could expect a generous solution to the territorial question.

On July 22 the Poles, under military pressure from the East and diplomatic pressure from the West, radioed a message to the Soviets proposing armistice negotiations. Unimpressed by this direct message, even though it complied with Chicherin's request to Curzon, the Soviet high command issued the following day an order to take Warsaw on August 12.[84] However, to maintain the illusion of willingness to negotiate, the Soviet commander in the field agreed, after some delay, to meet the Polish delegates in the area of fighting, at Baranowicze, on July 30. By reason of various complications on both sides, however, the armistice negotiations did not open until August 17, and then at Minsk.

Meanwhile, developments on the front against General Wrangel apparently created some further hesitation in Moscow in regard to the war with Poland. As late as August 2, Lenin in-

[83] Kliuchnikov and Sabanin, *op. cit.*, III, I, pp. 35–7. The diplomatic move was accompanied by a public declaration of the Council of Commissars, July 20; *ibid.*, pp. 41–6.

[84] Pilsudski, *L'Année 1920*, p. 211.

quired of Stalin about the military situation in the south, for "in the Central Committee opinion grows that we should immediately sign a peace treaty with Poland" because of the danger from Wrangel.[85]

The Central Committee's hesitations were overcome, however, and military operations proceeded. They continued to be concealed, not only by devious contacts with the Poles but also by major diplomatic moves on the larger scene of international politics. The Soviets had not forgotten the statements of Lloyd George and the Supreme Council, which promised aid to Poland from the Entente powers should the Red army cross the ethnographic boundary. The beginning of August saw the Red army deep in Polish territory; at this time Leo Kamenev, who since spring had been negotiating trade contacts in London, began a diplomatic move calculated to take care of this threat. He submitted to Lloyd George a Soviet proposal for peace with Poland. Interestingly enough, he both failed to include and altered certain paragraphs which were in the text prepared for negotiation with the Polish delegation.[86] These paragraphs were of major significance, for if accepted, their intent would have provided a key to the complete communization of Poland. Lloyd George, misinformed about the full text of the Soviet proposal, considered it just.[87]

Elated by Kamenev's success in London, Lenin sent a telegram on August 11 to Stalin in which he explained the British attitude as a result of "lost courage because of the general strike" in England and further stated, not quite truthfully, that Lloyd George had recommended that Poland accept the Soviet conditions of peace "including everything, disarmament, hand-

---

[85] Lenin, *Sochineniia*, Vol. 31, p. 239. A footnote to Lenin's telegram, p. 513, indicates that Stalin, despite Trotsky's failure to send him promised reinforcements, expected to defeat Wrangel at the beginning of fall. The text of Stalin's answer, however, is not published in his *Sochineniia*.

[86] Komarnicki, *op. cit.*, pp. 655–56.

[87] There is in Komarnicki, *op. cit.*, pp. 670–73, an illuminating comparison between Kamenev's proposal and the conditions of peace presented to the Polish delegation at Minsk.

ing over of arms to workers, and land and the rest." [88]

That same day, Lenin instructed Karol Daniszewski, the head of the Soviet delegation at the Minsk negotiations: "You know from Chicherin about our major diplomatic success in England concerning Poland. I hope you will take full advantage of this situation and, as adroitly as possible, include Warsaw in these conditions (along the lines we have discussed) as well as the complete security of the rest." [89] It is not clear what Lenin meant by his mention of Warsaw, but one can surmise he meant that should the Polish capital not be taken by arms, the Soviet delegation was expected to take it by way of negotiations. Indeed, the peace conditions submitted at Minsk included a paragraph which placed Warsaw within a "neutral" zone.

There was a last-minute controversy about this prized goal. According to the plan, Warsaw was to be taken August 12. Two days before this date, the *Glavkom* (chief command) and Tukhachevsky exchanged barbed messages on further moves, disagreeing on their evaluation of intelligence reports concerning the concentration of Polish troops.[90] On August 12 Trotsky published a strange article. Soviet Russia, he wrote, was ready to sign an armistice but Poland was maneuvering and delaying negotiations. Why? She wanted the Red army to take Warsaw. If the army did not do this, Soviet Russia would deny herself the fruit of victory; if the army continued to pursue the defeated Polish army "we shall move farther onto Polish territory and shall be compelled to take Warsaw." This would enable the Polish government to accuse Russia of an annexationist policy and imperialist aims and she would then ask for Western intervention.[91]

It was probably Trotsky's article, reflecting again his opposition to Lenin's views on the war, which provoked the latter's

[88] Lenin, *Sochineniia,* Vol. 31, p. 241.
[89] *Trotsky Archives,* file A.
[90] Kakurin and Melikov, *op. cit.,* pp. 281–84.
[91] *Izvestiia,* August 12, 1920.

terse telegram to Sklianski, "The *Glavkom* mustn't hesitate. If the War Department or the *Glavkom* believe Warsaw can be taken, it must be taken. What are the requirements to accomplish that? Will you say? To speak about armistice when the enemy marches—idiocy." And the telegram is amplified (in Lenin's handwriting), "If it is possible from the military point of view. We'll beat Wrangel without it. But from the *political* [point of view it is] most important to kill Poland." [92]

On August 12 the Red army reached the vicinity of the Polish capital. A session of the Council of Ministers, held the next day for the purpose of preparing instructions for the armistice delegation, was interrupted by the news that the Russians were at Praga, the outskirts of Warsaw. The news proved to be false. Nevertheless, everyone expected its fall at any moment—everyone, that is, except a handful of Polish military leaders, led by their determined commander, Joseph Pilsudski.

The events of August 16, 1920, will not soon be forgotten. Marshal Pilsudski's army opened a counteroffensive which forced the Red army to retreat as rapidly as it had advanced only a few days before. Exhaustive studies of the military aspect of the Soviet advance, of the battle for Warsaw, and of the victorious Polish counteroffensive have been made by competent writers on both the Soviet and Polish sides. They are of no concern to this study. However, it must be stated that in contrast to the general opinion expressed after the war, ascribing the Polish victory to the strategic advice of General Weygand, the plan of the counteroffensive was actually the product of Pilsudski's military brain and its successful pursuit the product of the national pride, devotion, and courage of the Polish nation.[93]

---

[92] *Trotsky Archives*, file A. The telegrams are dated August 1920.

[93] None other than General Weygand himself stated as late as 1953, ". . . I came to Warsaw with the Ambassadors' [Lord d'Abernon and M. Jusserand] mission and the Polish government entrusted me with the organization of the resistance of the Polish army in cooperation with the

When the truce negotiations were opened at Minsk on August 17, neither of the two opposing sides knew of the changing fortunes of the war. The Polish delegation was at first without contact with Warsaw and when radio communication was established, it was constantly jammed. "It was torture for us," wrote the Polish chairman, "that for days we knew nothing of what was happening in Warsaw, whether the Warsaw battle was won, where at the moment the front line might be. The first days, [the news was that] the Bolsheviks had triumphed. Through a Soviet paper, *Gwiazda,* they spread the news that Warsaw had fallen, that 'the red flag waves over Warsaw.' " [94]

Moscow, if it knew about the turn of events on the battlefield, seemed not to realize the consequences. On August 19 the Politburo decided to "recognize the Wrangel front as principal" and to take appropriate measures, acting as though the war with Poland had been brought to a successful end.[95]

At Minsk, Soviet delegate Daniszewski, equally ignorant of the real situation, presented the Poles with a 15-point proposal which reflected the victorious mood of the Soviet government. Recognizing Poland's independence and willing to make certain territorial concessions to her which went further than the British proposal of July 11, Soviet Russia, however, wished to limit Poland's army to 50,000 men. In addition, there was the "Trojan Horse," the creation of a civilian militia, "to be recruited from among the workers. . . ." Arms and military equipment were to be adjusted to the needs of such an army. The surplus arms were to be distributed by a Soviet-controlled commission to the workers' militia. Poland would stop manufacturing arms and dismantle her war industry. She would not receive arms

chief of staff, General Rozwadowski. Marshal Pilsudski always pretended not to know this decision of his government, and my relations with him were difficult from the beginning. It must be admitted that the strategical plan which was put into operation . . . was prepared by the Polish General Staff and it was better than mine." K. A. Jelenski, "Wywiad z gen. Weygand," *Kultura* (Paris), No. 6/68, June 1953, p. 84.

[94] Dąbski, *op. cit.,* p. 53.

[95] *Trotsky Archives,* file A; extract from the Politburo session protocol.

from other states, nor allow foreign troops on her territory; nor would she permit existence of any organization hostile to Soviet Russia. The Polish army would withdraw 33 miles to the west, thus forming a neutral zone which would be under the control of a common commission and, significantly enough, of a special trade-union commission. Poland would legislate free distribution of land and would finally grant to Russia unconditional right of passage through her territory.[96] Acceptance of such conditions certainly would have meant, and was intended to mean, the communization of Poland, as well as her complete dependence on Moscow and isolation from her powerful ally, France.

On August 20 Moscow began to realize the magnitude of the calamity on the Polish front. Lenin sent a message to T. Smilga, the political commissar of the front, saying, ". . . It is urgent to press with all vigor [the recruitment of] Belorussian laborers and peasants, if even in beggars shoes and bathing costumes, but with immediate revolutionary rapidity, to give you reinforcements in triple and quadruple quantity. Subsequently [it is necessary] to increase ten times our agitation among Polish laborers and peasants [and tell them] that their capitalists are destroying peace and condemning them to senseless bloodshed." [97]

By this time even the negotiators at Minsk had heard about the change. "Whoever had it, pulled out a bottle of cognac or wine and drank to the health and success of the Polish army," reminisced Dąbski and remarked that the Soviet delegates' mood had changed, too—in a different direction.[98]

---

[96] Kliuchnikov and Sabanin, *op. cit.*, IV, I, pp. 47–9. It was this proposal which differed from Kamenev's note to Lloyd George. When the British government protested in an ultimative form (*D.B.F.P.*, First Series, VIII, p. 379n). Chicherin, in a reply of August 26, cynically explained that "it was on [the Soviet] side a concession to Poland to agree with an armed civilian militia, over this number [of 50,000 men] which is in fact a supplementary force." *Vneshniaia Politika*, I, pp. 491–92, 492–93.

[97] *Trotsky Archives*, file A.

[98] Dąbski, *op. cit.*, p. 54.

On August 25 Dąbski answered the Soviet proposal, submitted a week before, and triumphantly rejected it point by point.[99] Both sides continued to argue in the hope that subsequent events would be on their side. On September 2 the last meeting took place at Minsk at which time it was agreed to transfer the negotiations to Riga.

While the Polish war communiqués were announcing the further advance of the Polish army, the British and Soviet governments continued to exchange recriminatory notes about the meaning of the peace proposal which Kamenev had made to Lloyd George. In a note of September 2 calculated to reassure the Polish delegation at Minsk, Balfour stated that H.M. Government had not agreed to the imposition of military limitations on Poland. It had only "stated that such a condition of peace would not be considered either by the British government or the British people as a sufficient reason for an active intervention." Chicherin, on September 5, accused the British of shifting their position to meet the changing military situation. He even stated, with tongue in cheek undoubtedly, that the military situation had changed, indeed, but to Soviet advantage.[100]

Thus the Poles, left to themselves, met the Soviet peace negotiators in Riga on September 23. At the opening session the Soviet chief delegate, Adolf Ioffe, stated that the Soviet government was giving up its previous demand for the reduction and demobilization of the Polish army. It was ready to offer Poland a more favorable boundary than the Entente powers had been. It stood by this proposition for ten days. The negotiations were difficult; at points there was danger of their suspension. However, with both sides anxious to relieve their respective nations of the gruesome prospect of winter fighting, neither was bold enough to break them off.[101] Lenin,

[99] Kumaniecki, *Odbudowa* . . . , pp. 403–405.
[100] *Vneshniaia Politika,* I, pp. 493–95, 495–97.
[101] Kumaniecki, *Odbudowa* . . . , pp. 411ff.

on October 10, telegraphed to Trotsky, who was in Kharkov, that in Ioffe's opinion the Poles could not afford a breakdown of negotiations as "they are afraid of a rupture even more than we." The Politburo, therefore, decided to take the risk and transfer some units to the Wrangel front.[102]

The Polish delegates in Riga were equally worried about the prospects of extended negotiations. As Poland was now anxious to concentrate her efforts on her western boundaries where the fate of Upper Silesia was still to be decided, its government suspected that the Soviet government would delay the armistice negotiations at the request of Germany in order to divert Polish attention from the forthcoming plebiscite there. In one of the numerous letters which Dąbski wrote to the Polish Minister of Foreign Affairs, Prince Sapieha, he stated, "Now a few words about the tactics of the Bolsheviks. I do not have the impression that they already have an agreement with Germany to protract the negotiations beyond the date of plebiscite [in Upper Silesia]. . . . Besides, on the basis of the impressions heretofore, everything leads me to conjecture that the Bolsheviks are anxious to sign peace quickly. . . . I will see to it . . . that the negotiations end at the time when the Bolsheviks will have greater interest in reaching an understanding with us than with the Germans." [103]

The armistice and the preliminary peace treaty were signed on October 12, 1920.[104] Neither of the two signatories realized their objectives. Poland acquired more territory than the Entente had been ready to give her but fell short of detaching Belorussia and the Ukraine from Soviet Russia and establishing a federation under Polish leadership. Soviet Russia failed to sovietize Poland and, through the war, spread revolutionary ideas and communism in Germany and in the rest of Europe.

---

[102] *Trotsky Archives,* file A.

[103] Dąbski, *op. cit.,* p. 179.

[104] For the text, see *Soviet Treaty Series.* Compiled and edited by L. Shapiro (2 vols.; Washington, D.C.: The Georgetown University Press, 1950), I, pp. 67–9.

The revolutionary and military phase of Soviet policy toward Poland was over; another phase was soon to begin.

AFTERMATH OF THE WAR

The defeat of the Red army was not only a decisive setback to communist objectives; it also produced a series of recriminations among the communist leaders. Although they all eventually admitted that the Warsaw offensive was a mistake, they did so grudgingly, offering a variety of excuses. Lenin, for example, the man chiefly responsible for the offensive, was slow to characterize it as a blunder. Indeed, in a speech as late as September 22 he continued to emphasize the political importance of reaching the outskirts of Warsaw, "the citadel of capitalism."

A few days later, October 2, he explained the defeat as due to the exhaustion of the Red army, "which lacked strength to pursue the victory . . . [while] the Polish army, supported by the patriotic spirit in Warsaw, sensing the feeling of being in their own country, found assistance, found a new possibility to advance." Nevertheless, Lenin continued, the greatest international significance of the advance to Warsaw was in its effect on the whole structure of the Versailles Treaty in Europe; for "by attacking Poland, we [were] attacking the Entente; by destroying the Polish army, we [were] destroying the Versailles Treaty upon which rests the whole system of present international relations. Had Poland been sovietized . . . the Versailles Treaty would have been brought to an end and the international system built on victory over Germany also would have been destroyed." He spoke in a similar vein on October 15, 1920.

Before the end of the year, however, he admitted the real reason for the defeat as he saw it. "The Polish revolution on which we reckoned failed," he stated privately to Clara Zetkin. "The peasants and the workers . . . defended their class enemies, permitted our brave Red army soldiers to die of starvation and ambushed and killed them." What appears to be

Lenin's last public pronouncement on the Soviet-Polish war, made on March 1, 1921, simply left it to future historians to judge if, in the advance on Warsaw, a strategic or political blunder was committed. At any rate, to him it was a fact that "in the war with Poland we committed a certain mistake." [105]

Zinoviev, on the other hand, was rather forthright. Representing the Communist International at the Second Congress of the Communist Party of Poland, in 1923, he said, "We do not conceal from you, comrades, that at the time of the Russian-Polish war—according to the estimate of our Central Committee, according to the estimate of comrade Lenin, and the Executive [Committee] of the Comintern—we committed a political mistake in regard to the peasants. In the short period of time available, we failed to settle the question of the confiscation of big property in a revolutionary manner. . . . We prevented the plundering of old estates, we failed to understand the demands of the moment to kindle hatred of the classes, of a peasant war against the landlords." [106]

Marchlewski, also, admitted the Polish peasants did not respond to communist propaganda. He thought that the Polish Revolutionary Committee was organized too late; that many Polish communists in Russia were not properly used in the political work; and that the political program was too radical. He also admitted that pillaging had been done by Soviet soldiers. [107]

Another communist writer admitted deficiencies in the political activities and expressed disappointment in the Polish attitude toward the advancing Red army. However, he attributed the defeat primarily to false strategy. [108] In his evaluation he was joined by Tukhachevsky, who maintained, even

---

[105] Lenin, *Sochineniia*, Vol. 31, pp. 251, 278, 281, 301; Vol. 32, p. 149. L. Fischer, *op. cit.*, I (on Clara Zetkin), p. 271.

[106] Regula, *op. cit.*, p. 45.

[107] Marchlewski, *op. cit.*, pp. 20–37.

[108] N. Movchin, *Posledovatel'nye operatsii po opytu Marny i Visly* (Moskva: Gosudarstvennoe izdatel'stvo, 1928), pp. 46–8.

after the debacle, that the time was ripe for revolution in Europe. "The situation in Poland was favorable to a revolution. A powerful movement by the proletariat and an equally menacing movement by the agricultural workers put the Polish *bourgeoisie* in an extremely difficult position. Many Polish communists were of the opinion that once the ethnographic boundary of Poland was reached, the proletarian revolution in Poland was inevitable and absolutely sure," Tukhachevsky stated. He alleged that the Polish workers and later even the peasants welcomed the Red army warmly. Had it not been for errors in strategy, for military defeat, "the revolution's flames would have enveloped the whole European continent. . . . An exported revolution was possible." [109]

On the other hand, Tukhachevsky's subordinate, General J. N. Serghieiev, who was in command in the field, wrote, "Any strategy, based on a revolutionary explosion in Poland, could be considered seriously only in political chancelleries—and in only those, in fact, which are far enough from the front. The troops did not believe in it and . . . the sources of our information were too optimistic as far as the situation in Poland was concerned." [110]

Another Soviet writer was critical of the Polish communist party which he felt was handicapped by the heritage of Rosa Luxemburg, who had been against the idea of an independent Poland. The KPP "continued to reject independence of Poland" and the mistake "was corrected by the Second Party Congress only after the failures of 1920." The Polish communists were convinced, it was stated in one of their declarations in February 1920, that "the overthrow of capitalism in Poland [could not] be accomplished by forces of a foreign army. The advance of such an army would only become a trump in the hands of the Polish *bourgeoisie*. It, therefore,

---

[109] Pilsudski, *L'Année 1920*, pp. 231–32.
[110] J. N. Serghieiev, *De la Dwina à la Vistule*, p. 82, as quoted in Pilsudski's *L'Année 1920*, p. 182.

rejected the idea of overthrowing Poland through the armies of Soviet Russia. . . . One faction of the KPP essentially 'disappeared,' was torn to pieces when the Red units crossed the ethnographic boundary of Poland." The Polish communists failed to understand the revolutionary role of the Red army, wrote the Soviet critic. He was also critical of inadequate political preparation for the war and singled out *Pravda, Izvestiia,* and *Krasnaia Zvezda,* which on May 7 published an appeal to fight for a "united, indivisible Russia." He admitted the complete collapse of political activity due to Polish hostility and Russian fascination with the idea of taking Warsaw, for which, of course, Trotsky was responsible. (The book was written in 1930.) [111]

Kakurin and Melikov, two Soviet military experts, also blamed Trotsky. However, Trotsky at a later period placed the blame for the disaster on Stalin, who was in charge of political affairs on the southern front and, wishing to take Lwów, postponed too long the high command's orders to send reinforcements to the northern flank.[112]

In fact, however, Stalin showed remarkable perspicacity and consistency of thought toward the Soviet-Polish war. As early as May, when the Polish army was still in the Ukraine and in possession of Kiev, he wrote an article in which he equaled the importance of "rear" strength to victory at the front. Denikin and Kolchak, he reasoned, had had no rear "of their own." It was different, however, in the war with Poland. "The rear of the Polish army appears to be homogeneous and nationally welded. Hence its unity and steadfastness. . . . Hence the steadfastness

---

[111] P. V. Suslov, *Politicheskoe obespechenie sovetsko-pol'skoi kampani 1920 goda* (Moskva: Gosudarstvennoe izdatel'stvo, 1930), pp. 17, 18, 29–31, 72ff.

[112] Trotsky, *Stalin,* p. 328. He states that "the chief initiator of the campaign was Lenin. He was supported against me by Zinoviev, Stalin and even by the cautious Kamenev." Rykov and Radek were also opposed to "the Polish adventure." Ruth Fischer confirms Trotsky's position, except that according to her, Radek, Rykov, and Bukharin were also against him; *Stalin and German Communism* (Cambridge: Harvard University Press, 1948), p. 136.

of the Polish army. . . . Surely, the Polish rear is not homogeneous . . . in the class sense; [however] the class conflicts have not reached such intensity as to damage the feeling of the national unity. . . ." He concluded by expressing the expectation that with the Polish army's advance into the Ukraine, it was creating a situation of operating with a rear which was not one "of its own." [113]

When things went well, during the Soviet offensive, Stalin appears to have cautiously approved of Lenin's directives, though no authentic record of his attitude is available. When the news from the Polish front became alarming, however, he declared before two Politburo meetings, August 25 and 30, that these first defeats were due to a lack of reserves for which Trotsky was responsible.[114]

Finally, much later, in March 1923, he warned against attaching exaggerated significance to tactical successes, such as the advance on Warsaw, "when having underestimated the force of nationalism in Poland and impressed by the easy success of our spectacular advance, we took upon ourselves a task which was beyond our strength, to break through Warsaw into Europe, and thus we rallied against the Soviet Army an overwhelming majority of the Polish population. . . ." [115] Still later, however, in April 1923, before the Twelfth Congress of the Party, when defending his thesis that the interest of the proletariat takes preference over the right of national self-determination, Stalin shifted his ground, stating that Soviet Russia, "in order to defend the power of the working class [was] obliged to march on Warsaw." [116]

In retrospect, it seems clear that it was a combination of factors which led to the collapse of the Soviet plan to communize Poland. The Soviet leaders were enamored of the

---

[113] I. Stalin, "Novyi pokhod Antanty na Rossiiu" (*Pravda*, May 25 and 26, 1920).
[114] I. V. Stalin, *Sochineniia* (Moscow: Ogiz, 1947), IV, pp. 346–50.
[115] *Ibid.*, v, p. 167 (an article in *Pravda*, March 14, 1923).
[116] Stalin, *Marxism and the National Question*, p. 158.

Marxist theory of class struggle and class hatred which they expected would sweep the country and release the forces of violence against the despicable landlords and *bourgeoisie*. Nothing of that magnitude happened. The Polish peasant, who represented the majority of the population and who would have been fully justified in hating the big landowner, was for the most part politically apathetic, unconditioned to fiery revolutionary slogans. The Polish workers' movement was split. Its larger segment followed Pilsudski, who, after all, was still considered the leader of the Polish Socialist Party and who was uncompromisingly anticommunist; the smaller part was communist, but its ranks were ideologically confused. Whether peasants or workers, they all "suffered" from the hereditary views of Polish nationalism with very strong anti-Russian attitudes, and in this respect they were unified even with their "exploiters." Obviously, such a situation was not conducive to a successful revolution.

Communism, then, could be brought to Poland only on the bayonets of the Red army. However, the Soviet forces, though growing in number, were weakened by previous battles of the civil war and were spread thinly along the long front from the Baltic to south Russia. The closer they came to Warsaw, the longer became their lines of communication and the larger the hostile area of their operations. In addition, the Soviet rearland, suffering under the drastic policies of war communism, was tired of military expansion. The Polish war was by no means comparable to the massive assault of irresistible Soviet armies some twenty-five years later when Stalin did succeed in exporting communism on bayonets, disregarding, as he did so, any revolutionary potential in Poland. He did learn the lesson of the Soviet-Polish war of 1920.

There is another lesson of the Soviet-Polish war which concerns Soviet historiography. In all the Soviet works on the war which were published in the 1920's and 1930's the chief villains of the scene were the imperialist powers, England and France. They were pulling the strings attached to their puppet, bourgeois Poland. The United States was hardly mentioned.[117] In the publications which appeared after World War II, however, the United States suddenly joined the company of Western imperialists and was held equally responsible for the Polish war on Soviet Russia.[118]

An even more curious twist in writings by Soviet authors appears in their evaluation of the American attitude toward the position of Germany at the time of the Soviet-Polish war. All Soviet leaders had viewed the Versailles Treaty as imperialist shackles on Germany. They and the Polish communists denounced the Polish-German boundary as the product of Western capitalist interests, interests which desired to strengthen capitalist Poland and weaken further the defeated, potentially revolutionary Germany. They were deeply appreciative of the German official policy of neutrality during the Soviet-Polish war and of the help given to Soviet Russia by the German workers who refused to man transports across Germany to Poland. Radek, for instance, wrote in 1922, "The fact that the Allies gave to Poland those areas with mixed German population, that they created the Corridor and gave to Poland both Danzig and Upper Silesia, chained Poland to the victorious chariots of France. . . ." The purpose of the Versailles Treaty,

[117] In addition to the relevant sources mentioned before, see *Bol'shaia Sovetskaia Entsiklopediia,* Vol. 46 (Moscow: Ogiz, 1938), cols. 23–248; *Malaia Sovetskaia Entsiklopediia,* Vol. 6 (Moscow: Ogiz, 1931), cols. 704–705, Vol. 7, col. 335; *Desiat' let kapitalisticheskogo okruzheniia SSSR,* eds. E. Pashukanis and M. Spektator. *Kniga pervaia* (Moscow: Izdatel'stvo Kom. Akademii, 1928).

[118] *Bol'shaia Sovetskaia Entsiklopediia* (2nd ed., Moscow: Gosudarstvennoe nauchnoe izdatel'stvo, 1955), Vol. 36, p. 480; Vol. 39, 1956, pp. 506–509. F. Zuev, *Mezhdunarodnyi imperializm—organizator napadeniia panskoi Pol'shi na Sovetskuiu Rossiiu (1919-1920)* (Moscow: Gosudarstvennoe izdatel'stvo politicheskoi literatury, 1954), pp. 3ff. N. L. Rubinstein, *Vneshniaia politika sovetskogo gosudarstva v 1921-1925 godakh* (Moscow: Gosudarstvennoe izdatel'stvo politicheskoi literatury, 1953).

he pointed out, was to destroy Germany, "and it was Russia which was remedying for Germany the injustices of Versailles." [119]

But post-World War II international developments also changed this interpretation of events. In 1954 Zuev wrote (in connection with the Oder-Neisse boundary between Poland and Germany which runs much further west than the Versailles boundary), "The U.S.A. and England when solving [in 1919] the questions connected with the delimitation of the Polish-German boundary unwaveringly supported German imperialists. They wished to preserve a strong, aggressive Germany, securing for her the usurped Polish territory." [120]

A Polish communist author stated that "the American imperialists always subordinated their relations with Poland to the fundamental needs of the German militarists, whom they treated as pillars of 'order in Europe,' as their chief agents in the war against the social-revolutionary movements. In no case did they wish a weakening of the political and strategic strength of the [German] government and assumed a hostile attitude in respect to our national claims in the west. . . ." They pursued a policy of creating "a state of constant irritation between the two nations [Germany and Poland] and thus made it possible to exploit these conflicts in the interests of the imperialist policy of the United States." [121]

As to German neutrality during the Soviet-Polish war, the official Soviet historiographer, V. P. Potemkin, alleged in 1945

---

[119] Karl Radek, *Likvidatsiia versal'skogo mira* (Petrograd: Izdanie Kommunisticheskogo Internatsionala, 1922), pp. 4, 19, 21.

[120] Zuev, *op. cit.*, p. 12.

[121] Boleslaw Jaworznicki, "Wyprawa Kijowska Pilsudskiego," *Sprawy Międzynarodowe* (Warsaw), VIII, No. 5 (May 1955), p. 45. Similarly, Karol Lapter in "Trzynasty punkt Wilsona" wrote in the same periodical (VII, 1954, pp. 37–53) that Wilson's Fourteen Points were simply a policy of support of German imperialism under the control of American imperialism and their "Polish program" was identical with the program of imperialist Germany, "having not only nothing in common with Poland's independence but was in fact a program of the burial of this independence forever," p. 53.

that in spite of its neutrality the German government offered the German army to the Entente to fight Soviet Russia. Only because Foch feared a revival of German military power was the offer rejected; however, even then Germany did not abandon the idea of joining the common anti-Soviet front, asserted Potemkin.[122] Other communist writers, however, maintained that the neutrality policy had been imposed upon the German government by the working class which, through widespread strikes and agitation of a "Hands off Russia" policy, simply paralyzed any move against the Red army.[123]

One wonders on what occasion in the future Soviet historians will again rewrite the story of the Soviet-Polish war to meet the current needs of a new international policy.

[122] *Istoriia diplomatii*, ed. V. P. Potemkin (Moscow: Ogiz, 1945), III, p. 87.
[123] Albert Norden, *Zwischen Berlin und Moskau* (Berlin: Dietz Verlag, 1954), pp. 322–44. A. S. Erusalimskii, *Germaniia, Antanta i SSSR* (Moscow: Izdatel'stvo Kommunisticheskoi Akademii, 1928), pp. 82–3.

CHAPTER 3

GERMANY VERSUS POLAND

IN THE first three years after the war Germany had neither the strength nor the opportunity to pursue an active foreign policy. Her government had originally refused to sign the Versailles Treaty. Later, when the Social Democrats and the Center Party formed a new government, it accepted the responsibility of submitting to the will of the Allies. In fact, the German people never considered the Versailles Treaty as an obligatory contract into which they had entered voluntarily; however, once signed, Germany had no choice but to accept it as a basis for her foreign policy.

As to the Polish-German boundary, the Treaty gave Poland the Poznań province, as well as Pomerania, the so-called Corridor, in order to allow her access to the sea, thereby separating East Prussia from the rest of Germany. It turned Danzig into a free city and determined that the fate of Upper Silesia and of two less important areas, Marienwerder and Allenstein, would be decided at a later date by a plebiscite.

There was little Germany could do about it. Unreconciled as she was to the terms of the Treaty, for the time being she was powerless to change them. All she could do in the field of foreign policy was attempt to seek some alleviations in the interpretation of the Versailles Treaty. This she did in the protracted negotiations with the Allied Council, using skillfully any sign of British-French disagreement and exploiting the common fear of Western Europe—the nightmare of communist danger. Moving between the Scylla of Allied dictates and the Charybdis of communism, the German governments piloted their unsteady ship of state through the dangerous waters of European chaos.

Out of the political chaos in Germany, one group emerged which represented an element of stability and determined calm. This was a group of military officers, the remnants of the Imperial high command. Defeated on the battlefield, they soon became established as the master operators behind the political scene because the government needed their cooperation in its policy of keeping the extreme elements of the German political scene under control. Their eyes were turned toward Poland, to the lost provinces, and to the lands beyond the boundaries of Poland—to Soviet Russia. The two leading figures in this officers corps were General Wilhelm Groener and General Hans von Seeckt. The first was Minister of Transportation; the latter became the head of the *Truppenamt*. From these positions the two men, both basically conservative and monarchist, exercised decisive power in the frequently changing German governments of the Weimar Republic. However, their plans for regaining Germany's lost territories were markedly different.

GROENER'S PLAN

Groener's design rested on the idea of offering German troops to the Allies in an anticommunist crusade. At the end of December 1918, even before the Versailles Conference started, he had approached Colonel Conger of the American army and "very cautiously raised the question of a common front against Bolshevism." [1]

In the German government he pleaded for a policy of reconquering the province of Poznań and wished to sell high to the Entente German willingness to join forces against Bolshevik Russia. On March 29, 1919, he wrote to Mathias Erzberger, the Undersecretary of State and the delegate at Versailles, "We must make it particularly and most imperatively clear to the Allies that a common front against the Bolsheviks is possible only if we are not bullied on the Polish question. . . . [We]

---

[1] Reginald H. Phelps, "Aus den Groener-Dokumenten," *Deutsche Rundschau,* Vol. 76, No. 8, p. 620.

must therefore struggle politically with the Allies on every occasion for a re-establishment of our eastern boundary as of
1914. . . . If the French take their struggle against Bolshevism
seriously, they cannot shut their eyes to these facts. . . . The
Allies and particularly Marshal Foch need us; our support is
necessary to them." [2]

When the communist revolution broke out in Hungary,
Groener considered it to be an event favorable to the German
position in regard to Versailles. He wrote his wife on March
25, 1919, that at last even the French will see that Germany "is
the last bastion against Bolshevism." He continued to defend
his political concept at the German cabinet session and stated,
on April 24, that the army was ready to win back the lost
Polish provinces. However, declared the general, introducing a
new and significant thought, should Germany not be ready to
defend her own boundaries, the government had better begin
thinking about negotiating with Soviet Russia.

After the peace conditions had been handed over to the German delegation at Versailles on May 7, 1919, Groener felt compelled to recommend their acceptance. He proposed that Germany reach an understanding with Poland in economic affairs
but refuse to weaken her stand on her east boundary. He
warned that should Poland become a viable state as a result of
the Versailles solution, Germany would live to see the day when
the Poles would deprive her of East Prussia and establish themselves on the Oder River.[3] Twenty-five years later, the statement proved to be a correct prophecy.

Then, a few weeks later, in a letter of June 27 to President
Friedrich Ebert, Groener recognized that in the field of foreign policy Germany could do very little overtly. However,
"two things must be pursued immediately and with greatest

[2] Dorothea Groener-Geyer, *General Groener, Soldat und Staatsmann*
(Frankfurt am Main: Societäts-Verlag, 1955), p. 135.
[3] *Ibid.*, pp. 137, 138, 143.

emphasis in foreign affairs—the war-guilt question and the organization of a German irredenta in the detached regions." For such a movement, he believed the German workers to be the best instrument.[4]

In October 1919 the Supreme Council gave the final instructions for the disarmament and disbandment of the German military units in the Baltics, the *Freikorps*—that curious and adventurous product of Germany's defeat which survived for almost a year after the armistice. Its commander, General Rudiger von der Goltz, had entertained the idea, born from the political and military confusion of the times, of joining the White Russian troops to fight Soviet Russia. With their disarmament, however, Groener's last hope of cooperation with the "Russia of the future" to keep Poland in check, disappeared.[5]

SEECKT'S PLAN

While Groener felt that Germany was compelled by the Versailles Treaty to follow, passively, European and world events, General von Seeckt had an entirely opposite conviction—both with respect to the possible dynamics of German foreign policy and to its basic orientation. His views on Poland were identical to Groener's, only more rigorous and determined; his ideas about Soviet Russia were quite different.

General Hans von Seeckt was in some respects a typical representative of the Prussian officers' caste. An ardent soldier, he gloried in the power and prestige of the German Imperial army. He was inaccessible to everyone except his wife and conveyed his sentiments to her through long letters written from

---

[4] *Groener Papers,* Houghton Library, Harvard University, reel 7, *stück* 26.
[5] General A. Niessel, *L'évacuation des Pays Baltiques par les Allemands* (Paris: Charles-Lavauzelle, [1936]); Reginald H. Phelps, "Aus den Groener-Dokumenten. Das Baltikum," *Deutsche Rundschau,* Vol. 76, No. 10, pp. 830–40.

the various locations where his military assignments took him. Unlike many of his colleagues, his brilliant grasp of military affairs was coupled with a realistic political outlook. Though a monarchist, he offered his services to the republican government; as a member of the German delegation he actively opposed the Versailles Treaty, but he adjusted himself, seemingly, to the Versailles Germany. Occupying the key positions as the Head of *Truppenamt,* and since June 1920 the Chief of German Staff, he sought to manipulate the complex forces of German internal and external politics so as to return to Germany all that she had lost in the war—her glory and prestige, her power and her territories. To achieve these goals Russia and Poland were much in his mind.

In a letter of January 31, 1920, he stated that "future political and economic close understanding with Great Russia [must be] an immovable goal of [the German] policy," and continued, "I refuse to support Poland [in the Soviet-Polish dispute] even at the ridiculous risk that Poland will be devoured. On the contrary, I count on it, and if we cannot for the time being help Russia with the re-establishment of the boundaries of her old empire, we should certainly not hamper her." He was strongly of the opinion that Bolshevism, should it reach Germany, should be opposed only at her own boundaries.[6] Opposed to Bolshevism as he was and ready to use his troops against any revolutionary action of the Communist Party of Germany inside the country, he appeared undisturbed by the possibility that communism might spill into Germany once it had reached the German border.

At a lecture in Hamburg on February 20, Seeckt analyzed the military situation of Germany, which he considered, as a result of Versailles, all but hopeless. Should the Red army march against Germany, 100,000 German soldiers (the number permitted by the Entente) could not stop them. He feared the

---

[6] F. Rabenau, *Seeckt. Aus seinem Leben, 1918–1936* (Leipzig: V. Hase & Koehler Verlag, 1941), p. 252.

"Danaidean gift," which the British had indicated they were willing to give Germany in the form of increased armed forces. The only alternative, then, was cooperation with Russia. Concerning Poland, he stated: "To save Poland from Bolshevism—Poland, this mortal enemy of Germany, this creature and ally of France, this thief of German soil, this annihilator of German culture—for that not a single German arm should move. And should Poland go to the devil, we should help her go. Our future lies in union with Russia, whether we like the present situation or not. No other road is open to us." [7]

In a memorandum on the international situation, written February 26, Seeckt evaluated the then current Soviet offers to Poland to negotiate peace. He wrote, "Whether Poland presently is or is not in peace negotiations with Russia is rather immaterial. Such will not lead to the protection of Poland from Russia's external aims. We must count on the probability that Russia will sooner or later, probably this summer, attack Poland. To this attack Poland will succumb. As it happened in the Ukraine and in Siberia, Bolshevism precedes its military plans with propaganda. There is no doubt that Bolshevik feeling has recently grown strong in the former Russian Poland and has also penetrated the army. . . . Polish internal capacity for resistance is to be rated as insignificant."

Seeckt continued, "Poland cannot count on effective support from the Entente. It is certain that neither France, nor England, nor America are in a position to send troops to support Poles against a Soviet attack, nor do they want to. Only support by officers, equipment, and money remains. If such support does not come very soon, it will be too late, particularly if Germany denies to Poland the passage [through her territory] of such help—a decision which is urgently necessary and must be made clear. It should be unquestionably established that Germany deny Poland any help against Russia. In this connection the German policy must steadfastly and uncondi-

[7] *Seeckt Papers,* reel 21, *stück* 111.

tionally disregard all offers from England and all threats from France. Regardless of the necessity of our seeking an understanding with Russia, we still have the compelling duty to encourage every sign which promises damage or even destruction of this most unbearable neighbor of ours. . . . If we cannot now bring it about ourselves, we must in any case view with gratitude the destruction of Poland." [8]

On Seeckt's instruction, his close subordinate, Major Friedrich von Boetticher, wrote another memorandum in much the same vein as Seeckt's. This document, which was dated March 26, 1920, carried Seeckt's ideas a step further. Boetticher considered a Soviet attack on Poland certain. Should the Entente ask Germany to intervene, Germany must resolutely refuse the request. He reasoned logically that the Entente's commitments to Poland prevented her from giving back to Germany her lost territories. In this memorandum he stated the hope that the Soviet army would stop on the 1914 border. However, if that should not be the case, he recommended that Germany's territorial claims be assured by her openly joining Russia as an ally. With the hopeful expectation that the Red army would stop its advance at the prewar boundary, Germany was still duty bound to save the territories which had belonged to her prior to 1914—the implication being that the German army would occupy the former German part of Poland. The memorandum, although approved by Seeckt, was withheld from fur-

---

[8] *Seeckt Papers*, reel 21, *stück* 130. In the light of the evidence based on Seeckt's Papers and the files of the German Ministry of Foreign Affairs, it is difficult to accept Ambassador Dirksen's version of the German Eastern policy at that time. In March 1920 he was appointed First Secretary to the German legation in Warsaw and made preparations for the arrival of Count Oberndorff, the first postwar Minister to Poland. Dirksen wrote of Oberndorff that he was "a Westerner at heart and soul and, abhorring Bolshevism with an almost physical antipathy, he started his political task by offering to the Polish government and his colleagues of the diplomatic corps the collaboration of Germany in the fight against Bolshevism. He met with no response at all." Herbert von Dirksen, *Moscow, Tokyo, London; Twenty Years of German Foreign Policy* (Norman: University of Oklahoma Press, 1952), p. 20.

ther circulation.[9] The course of the Soviet-Polish war and the patriotic stand of the Polish nation proved both Seeckt's and Boetticher's predictions wrong.

Groener's and Seeckt's views, as different as they were on the basic question of the orientation of Germany's external policy, were heard at the sessions of the ministerial council. However, the German government was not able to follow them. Either events ran contrary to the generals' expectations or the government was not given an opportunity to develop their ideas.

MALTZAN'S ALTERNATIVES

Rather, it was the cautious foreign policy concept suggested by Baron Ago von Maltzan which the German government, with some intermittent vacillations, endorsed and tried to implement. Maltzan was at that time the head of the Eastern Division in the German Ministry for Foreign Affairs and a respected expert on Russia. As a German nationalist, suffering from what he considered the humiliation of the Versailles *Diktat,* he looked to Soviet Russia for assistance in the eventual re-establishment of the glory and the power of the German State. As a perceptive diplomat, however, he could not ignore the power of the Allies in whose hands, after all, rested Germany's fate for the first years after the war. Germany could not afford to antagonize them, he reasoned, by cooperating with Soviet Russia openly and too closely. Germany's path must necessarily be determined by her lack of power and she could at best maintain only a tenuous balance between the two camps and exploit their differences as best as she was able. However, he was the chief civilian exponent of the idea of secret cooperation with Soviet Russia.

In spite of this orientation, there is evidence that even Baron Ago von Maltzan was at one time attracted by the possibility of an Entente-German action against the Bolsheviks. As late as

[9] *Seeckt Papers,* reel 22, *stück* 149.

the beginning of 1920, he made "still one secret attempt to bring about an intervention . . . [and] he opened strictly confidential conversations with Englishmen, Americans, and French who were in Berlin. According to the information which leaked out in the Eastern Division [of the German Foreign Office], the conversations with the English representative, General [N.] Malcolm [Chief of the British Military Mission in Berlin], were altogether very promising," wrote the German diplomat, Wipert von Blücher, who at that time served in the Eastern Division in a junior capacity.[10] Blücher also recorded his contacts, acting on Maltzan's instructions, with Russian aristocrats and generals who took refuge in Berlin and participated at many gay and inspiring parties at which the Czarist national anthem and a slightly adjusted German "Deutschland-Russland über alles" were played and sung.[11]

When General Niessel, the French chairman of the Interallied Commission for the Baltics, returned to Berlin from his mission of supervising the disbandment of the Goltz troops, at the beginning of January 1920, Maltzan asked to see him. "The purpose of his visit was, beside other things, to make me accept the principle of using Germany in the struggle against Bolshevism," [12] wrote Niessel.

At about the same time, however, Maltzan engaged in conversations with a prominent Soviet representative in Berlin, Victor Kopp. At the end of October 1919 Kopp, a member of the collegium of the Soviet Commissariat for Foreign Affairs, appeared in Berlin.[13] Soon he was busier in other fields than

[10] Wipert von Blücher, *Deutschlands Weg nach Rapallo* (Wiesbaden: Limes Verlag, 1951), pp. 96–7.

[11] *Ibid.*, pp. 53, 56.

[12] Niessel, *op. cit.*, p. 223.

[13] On March 2, 1920, someone in the German Foreign Office submitted to the German Foreign Minister the following information: "From a confidential informer we are reliably advised that Kopp is by birth a Georgian and is identical with the well-known Damaschwili-Stalin [sic], who in the year 1917 held a leading position in the Georgian government." *St. Antony's Collection,* reel 33. In reality, Kopp had served in the Russian Imperial army during the war, had been taken prisoner by the Germans in

the one to which he had been officially assigned, "the Representative of the Red Cross of Soviet Russia." He paid visits to German Chancellor Hermann Müller on November 1, December 1, and December 27; he began with the modest suggestion of resuming German-Soviet economic relations and later pressed for renewal of political relations. The Chancellor was rather reserved and insisted that as a prerequisite to the consideration of Kopp's suggestion, Russia must stop encouraging communist propaganda in Germany.[14]

Kopp also submitted an official note to Maltzan in which he proposed an immediate regulation of the relations between the two countries. The regulation would consist of a declaration of readiness for immediate resumption of official relations, a declaration of mutual nonintervention in internal affairs, an immediate exchange of goods, exchange of prisoners of war, and the establishment of a trade agency in Berlin and Moscow. Maltzan, reacting to Kopp's note, prepared a memorandum for the German government, dated January 31, 1920, in which he evaluated the international position of Soviet Russia. He did not think that it was in the interest of the two countries to resume diplomatic relations in view of the envisaged hostile reaction of the Entente to such a move. However, "in spite of all hesitations it does not seem wise to me to turn the Soviet offer down bluntly; rather, I propose to accept the trade proposal with qualifications," he concluded.[15]

On February 16, Chancellor Müller received Kopp, but it seems that they discussed nothing but the latter's Red Cross mission. Until then, no official exchange of views on the subject of common interest, Poland, was recorded. However, that same day, the Chancellor spoke before the *Reichstag* Committee on

---

1915 and had remained in Germany until the autumn of 1918. He was released on intervention of the Soviet Embassy in Berlin and joined the Soviet diplomatic service. *Inprecorr*, x, No. 27, June 5, 1930, p. 500; an obituary, published on his death.

[14] *St. Antony's Collection*, reel 103.
[15] *Ibid.*

Foreign Relations. He first dealt with what he termed the hateful policy of Poland toward Germany. Then, with some satisfaction he stated that "Poland stood also in opposition to Russia. She probably will be compelled to conclude peace with Soviet Russia. In case of war, the outcome is doubtful. It is possible that Poland, pierced as she is by Bolshevik ideas, will be easily crushed. Many people are afraid that Germany then, too, will be overrun. [The Chancellor] did not share these fears, as the Russians were much too convinced of the necessity of being on good terms with Germany." [16]

On the eve of the Polish offensive in the Ukraine, the Polish Ministry of Foreign Affairs also evaluated Poland's international position in the light of German-Russian relations. A nine-page document, dated April 15, 1920, stated in the introduction that all political groups in Germany were motivated in their views on Eastern Europe by a desire for revenge; they differed only in regard to tactics. There was one group of the extreme Right, represented by General Hoffmann, who wished an alliance with Soviet Russia for a war against Poland; another right-wing group, which was led by General Ludendorff, pursued the policy of alliance with the Whites. The extreme Left advocated a revolutionary solution in alliance with the Bolsheviks, continued the statement. As to the government itself, it maintained contacts with both Soviet Russia and the Whites.

No other nation, it was further stated in the document, is more hated by Germany than is Poland. Germans are irreconcilable to the existence of Poland as an independent state. They give support to Polish communists, they deliver munitions to Lithuania, and "the Polish soldiers in Lithuania and Belorussia hear from Bolshevik trenches words of command in the German language. . . ." The document concluded by pointing to the importance of Poland as a crossroad of com-

[16] *St. Antony's Collection,* reel 103.

munications between Germany and Russia and said that in this geographical position lies the greatest trump card of Polish policy in its relations with Germany.[17]

It may well be said, however, that Pilsudski badly misplayed his hand. He played his trump, only to discover that he had trumped his own ace. For when he opened his drive into the Ukraine, the only thing he accomplished in his success against Russia was to give Russia and Germany another opportunity to demonstrate their mutual anti-Polish sentiments.

GERMANY AND THE SOVIET-POLISH WAR

The position of Germany during the Soviet-Polish war was, naturally, of cardinal importance to all countries directly concerned with the conflict—Russia, Poland, and the Entente powers.

Throughout the Soviet-Polish war, the Soviet government regarded Germany with both fear and hope. On the one hand, it was coldly calculating the possibility of a communist revolution in Germany, creating wherever possible a revolutionary atmosphere, while the Red army was bringing communism to neighboring Poland on its bayonets. On the other hand, it was worried about the possibility that Germany, influenced by concessions that might possibly be given to her by the Entente, would join forces with them in an anticommunist crusade. To avoid this, the Soviet government maintained friendly contacts with the anticommunist German government, assuaging it with alluring promises.

Soon after the Polish offensive in the Ukraine had started, it was stated at a meeting of the Russian Politburo on June 4, that "the Polish command withdrew from the German frontier fresh divisions and transferred them to our front. This fact makes one think that there was an agreement between the

---

[17] *Ciechanowski Deposit,* Ministerstwo Spraw Zagranicznich, 15 kwietna 1920, No. 30434 D 6293, III/20.

government of Ebert-Bauer-Scheidemann and the Pilsudski government." [18]

At the Second Congress of the Communist International, which noted with jubilation the advance of the Red army into Poland, Marchlewski injected a note of warning. Pointing to various dangers which were still in store for the advancing revolution, he warned that while the Entente powers were unable to send their own armies to Poland they might "send against [Russia] those whom Mr. Noske [the former German Minister of Defense] had already organized for them. . . . It may be that one hundred thousand German volunteers will be sent to the front to suppress the Polish revolution and Soviet Russia." [19] As did other delegates, he appealed for help from the European, and particularly the German, proletariat. Paul Levi, the leader of the German communist party, immediately

---

[18] *Trotsky Archives*, file A. Almost 20 years later, the speculation about German-Polish cooperation in the war against Soviet Russia became a matter of inquiry at another end of this manifold diplomatic maneuver— in Berlin. In connection with Hitler's policy to bring Poland into an anti-Soviet alliance, the German Foreign Ministry sent the following message to Hitler's Chancellery: "According to Polish assertions Marshal Pilsudski inquired in 1919/20 of the Reich government if it wants to support him and Petlura in a march against the Soviet Ukraine. Germany, it is believed, declined." The message asked for information on the subject (*AA*, 1099/2100, 454342). On March 9 the Chancellery answered, "The inquiry concerning Marshal Pilsudski . . . cannot be confirmed in the Chancellery," *ibid.*, 454343. There are two indications which reveal some Polish interest in a common policy with Germany against Russia; both, however, relate to the end of 1920 when the Poles were worried about resumption of Soviet hostilities. One indication points to the visit to Germany of the Archbishop of Warsaw in November 1920. While there, he sounded out the Chancellor, K. Fehrenbach, on the possibility of German-Polish cooperation. (Z. J. Gąsiorowski, "Stresemann and Poland before Locarno," *Journal of Central European Affairs*, XVIII, No. 1, p. 27.) The other indication points to Bavaria. On December 25, 1920, the Bavarian Prime Minister, W. Kahr, wrote to the Foreign Minister in Berlin about a conversation he had had with the Polish Consul in Munich. "The Consul repeatedly expressed the serious will of the Polish government to reach a reconciliation with Germany. Poland would like to enter into trade relations with Germany and strive for a certain common arrangement between Germany and Poland for the purpose of staving off Bolshevism." (*AA*, 1424/2945, 570332-4.)

[19] *Vtoroi Kongress K.I.*, *op. cit.*, pp. 46, 47.

responded and later, in August, advocated in the *Reichstag* a policy of alliance with Soviet Russia, to which the Communist Party of Germany was ready to give full support. "This speech," asserted another prominent former German communist at a later date, "was directly inspired by Radek." [20]

The Soviet-Polish war appeared to Germany as a unique invitation to recover at least some lost territory and prestige; and whatever the Soviet hopes and fears may have been, the German government looked upon this opportunity strictly from the standpoint of German national interest. The paramount question was, however, which side, the Entente or Russia, offered the better chance for the forwarding of those interests. Perhaps the Allies, haunted by the spectre of communism engulfing the whole of Europe, might be induced to see the light and alleviate some of the harsh conditions imposed upon Germany by the Versailles Treaty. As Germany was negotiating with the Entente such problems as reparations obligations, plebiscite plans about Upper Silesia, and the disbandment of German troops, the opportunity was most attractive.

On May 17 the German Ministry of Defense had issued a memorandum requesting the Entente to allow her to maintain an army of 200,000, rather than 100,000 soldiers. The memorandum advanced not only economic but political and military reasons for this request. Though it was written at the height of the Polish offensive in the Ukraine, it argued that "instead of the Polish offensive, should Russia succeed with a Russian-Bolshevik offensive in Poland, the situation would undoubtedly in a very short time be most difficult; it may undergo a complete change." [21] And this same argument was to be used at the conference with the Entente powers as a potent reason for maintaining a larger German army than was envisaged by Versailles.

[20] *Ibid.,* p. 48. Ruth Fischer, *op. cit.,* p. 197.
[21] *Seeckt Papers,* reel 21, p. 3 of the instruction.

The Soviet offensive, unleashed on July 4, lent a ring of reality to the conclusion of the German Defense Ministry's memorandum. The complexity, not only of the issues involved but also of proposed strategies, is well illustrated by the debate on July 5 of the German Council of Ministers. A recommendation had been made by General Hoffmann that the threatening situation should be used by the German delegation, which was debating at Spa with the Supreme Council on this issue of reduction of German forces.

The Ministers, according to the protocol of the meeting, were in agreement "that any support of the Poles against the Bolsheviks was out of the question." Beyond that, however, the views of the ministers took on a variety of hues. "To the question as to what would happen when the Bolsheviks penetrate to the German border, no definite stand was taken," recorded the protocol. "General von Seeckt stated he did not expect this danger in the near future. . . . The Minister for Post and Telegraph, Giesberts, emphasized that in any case any agreement to fight together with the French and English outside the German boundary must in principle be refused. Anyway, the danger is that we nourish a Bolshevik revolution in the country [Germany] the moment we take a stand against Russia."

The Minister of Interior, Koch, "was of the opposite opinion. It is through an understanding with Russian Bolshevism that German Bolshevism will rise. German Bolshevism can be held down by opposing first the Russian brand. . . ." Groener, the Minister of Transportation, then stated he knew the Soviet troops from his own experience and suggested "not to fuss so much about the successes of the Soviet troops." [22]

It was also reported at this Council meeting that there was some encouragement of the idea that Germany might take this opportunity to enlist the Entente's help and gain a generous

---

[22] *AA*, 1680/3617, 800195-6. See also L. Zimmerman, *Deutsche Aussenpolitik in der Ära der Weimarer Republik* (Göttingen: Musterschmidt Verlag, 1958), p. 89.

understanding of Germany's critical needs. "The Freiherr von Eckhardtstein told [the German Vice-Chancellor]," as he now reported to the meeting of the Cabinet, "that he had spoken with the English Ambassador [Lord D'Abernon] about the same questions and about a possible agreement between England and Germany. The latter assured Freiherr von Eckhardtstein of his willingness to bring up these questions and to help us." Another British representative, General Haking, had spoken with the Vice-Chancellor in the same manner.

The German government informed its Foreign Minister at Spa about its discussions. While recommending that the question be treated carefully, the information added that "the military breakdown of Poland and its possible consequences are so evident that nothing should prevent its mention" to the British representatives at Spa.[23]

Lord D'Abernon, the influential British Ambassador in Berlin, whom some German leaders used to call gratefully "the Lord Protector of Germany," ardently advocated the policy of enlisting German cooperation. In a letter written from Warsaw, where he represented Great Britain on the Allied mission in the days of the battle for Warsaw, he stressed "the importance of obtaining German cooperation against the Soviet. News from Paris is to the effect," he continued, "that the German diplomatic representatives there are constantly fishing for an invitation from the Entente to use German military force against the Soviet." [24]

Winston Churchill, the Secretary of State for War and Air, even issued a public invitation to the German government to consider its chance of undoing some of the consequences of its military defeat. He wrote an article for the *Evening News*, July 28, in which he pointed to the dark future should Poland succumb and indicated clearly that Germany could look for-

[23] *AA*, 3462/9125, 242571-2.
[24] Viscount D'Abernon, *The Eighteenth Decisive Battle of the World. Warsaw, 1920* (London: Hodder, Stoughton, 1931), p. 72.

ward to friendly cooperation with England and France if she were willing to render to Europe the service of standing up against the Bolshevik onslaught.[25]

However, the invitation, if it was really contemplated and expected, never came because Marshal Foch was opposed to the risky scheme. After all, France was Poland's ally, and as such was as interested in her continued strength as she was anxious to keep Germany weak and surrounded. She could not have considered a policy of enlisting German military help against Soviet Russia at the expense of Poland. Nor in any case would the proud and militant Poles have evacuated—at anyone's request—the regions which by all rights they considered theirs. Therefore, it was Russia, and only Russia, which was interested in the weakening, if not in the destruction, of an independent Poland. It was from Russia, and only Russia, that Germany could expect help if the German Empire's eastern boundaries of 1914 were to be re-established. The Soviet government was, of course, well aware of this and played the game accordingly.

As early as May 29, when the Red army was suffering defeat in the Ukraine, the Soviet representative in Berlin, Kopp, stated to the press that "neither the Soviet Russian government nor the Russian people nourish any hostile intentions against Germany. . . ." [26] Then, on July 31, when the Red army troops reached the boundaries of East Prussia, the German local authorities established contact with them and were assured that the Soviets "will under any circumstances respect the

---

[25] *D.B.F.P.*, First Series, VIII, p. 742n. The article was widely used by Soviet writers to unmask the British policy. They also alleged that negotiations took place in Berlin between British representatives and General Ludendorff in which Germany was promised revision of the eastern boundaries if she participated in the war against Soviet Russia. *Desiat' let kapitalisticheskogo okruzheniia SSSR*, pp. 83, 84. Zuev, *op. cit.*, p. 136. See also Blücher, *op. cit.*, p. 97, on Churchill's indirect contacts with General Hoffmann.

[26] Norden, *op. cit.*, p. 318 quoting *Die Rote Fahne*, May 30, 1920.

German boundary; they were forbidden, under penalty of death, to cross the border." [27]

If these assurances leave doubts as to which boundaries—those of 1920 or 1914—the Soviet officials had in mind, an instruction of the Soviet Commander-in-Chief of July 23 leaves no room for speculation. His order read: "When the northern wing reaches the *former* [author's italics] Russian-German frontier, it will not cross this border; it will limit itself, in this area, to the task of observation." [28]

It is unthinkable that this Soviet military order, which assumed, of course, the communization of the former Russian Poland, could have implied that the western part of the country was to remain under a bourgeois Polish government. It either expected that German troops would move immediately into this territory and re-establish the old common German-Russian boundary, or it counted on a revolutionary upheaval in Germany herself. The Soviet government was ready for either alternative.

Victor Kopp gave assurances to the German Ministry of Foreign Affairs that the Soviet army would respect the old German-Russian boundary.[29] But on August 2 Trotsky instructed Kopp, in view of the advance of the Red army on the German boundary, to bring about as quickly as possible a close unity and an intensification of the activities of German communists in the area of the boundaries, to prepare public opinion for the arrival of the Red army onto the Reich's territory.[30]

General von Seeckt, the cold-blooded analyst, was not con-

---

[27] *Ibid.*, quoting from *Deutsches Zentralarchiv der DDR*, Zweigstelle Merseburg; Akten des Ministeriums des Innern, Landesgrenzpolizei Osten, Berichterstatung Russland, Bd. II, 16.7. 1920—30.10. 1920.

[28] Kakurin and Melikov, *op. cit.*, p. 211.

[29] Trotsky sent a telegram, August 4, to the Politburo stating, "I consider it unconditionally urgent to entrust the conduct of negotiations with Germany to Ioffe." *Trotsky Archives*, file A. See also Christian Höltje, *Die Weimarer Republik und das Ostlocarno-Problem, 1919–1934* (Würzburg: Holzner-Verlag, 1958), pp. 24–6; Blücher, *op. cit.*, pp. 100–101.

[30] *AA*, 1404/2860, 551923.

fused by the kaleidoscopic colors of the situation. He put small trust in Russian promises. On July 31 he expressed the view in a memorandum which stated that the Red army may well enter the territory of former German Poland. He was, however, opposed to the idea of sending German troops to protect the German minority there as such a move would be considered a severe breach of Versailles and the Entente would intervene. The German government, he proposed, should publicly ask the Russian government to spare the German population the horrors of war. Such a step, in his opinion, would impress the population of the "annexed [German] territory." It would also demonstrate to the world, and particularly to Russia, that Germany felt responsible for these regions. It would establish "the groundwork for the recovery of the land snatched from us."

He further reasoned that should, however, Soviet Russia accept the British proposal for a peace conference in London, Germany should insist on participating at such a conference. Russia herself may, indeed, ask Germany's presence. At the British-Soviet trade negotiations (Lloyd George, Krasin, and Kamenev) "Russia indicated distinctly that she wished economic cooperation with Germany, that she even wanted to have a common boundary with [her]." He hoped for Soviet support "because of her own enmity against Poland, if for no other reasons." Further, as the military situation now had developed so favorably for Russia, he expected that never "in a foreseeable future would Russian and German interests be so parallel as they [were] now." [31]

The following day, August 1, probably in an optimistic mood, General von Seeckt left Berlin for a vacation.

And so, the German government still found itself in a precarious situation. As much as it wished to see Poland beaten, it was most certainly also worried about the threat of communism engulfing Germany. Thus, to facilitate Poland's defeat and also prevent the spread of communism over Germany's

[31] *Seeckt Papers,* reel 21, *stück* 130.

borders, the government decided on a policy of "using Satan to destroy Beelzebub." On July 20 the German cabinet passed the motion "that Germany, through the Herr Reichspresident, declares neutrality" in the Soviet-Polish conflict.[32] This was immediately done, whereupon the government forbade export and transit of war materials "to Russia and Poland." [33]

At the same time, the German Foreign Minister, Walter Simons, resumed the diplomatic conversations with Soviet Russia, which were begun by Kopp's proposals in February. His attitude, under the pressure of military developments, was now markedly changed. On July 22 he wrote a letter to Chicherin, using the opportunity, as he stated, of Kopp's trip to Moscow to inform him that he now considered it an opportune time to negotiate "resumption of normal relations between the two countries." He wanted the Soviet government first to give Germany satisfaction for the assassination of Count Mirbach in Moscow on July 6, 1918. If this was acceptable, he then wanted the Soviet Commissar to suggest the time and place of a meeting to reach speedily an agreement about political and economic relations. The letter continued, "Through the official statement of your representative here I have been informed that the Russian troops in their advance against Poland will respect the old German boundary. Our declaration of neutrality is known to you, Herr Volkskommissar, through our radio statement of the 20th of this month. In order to be able to adhere better to the mutually stated positions and to remove possible complications at the boundaries, I consider it desirable that a German military representative be instructed to join the right wing of the Russian army, so that he could, in direct contact with Russian and German military authorities, settle

---

[32] *AA*, 1669/3438, 745171. The U.S. Commissioner in Berlin, Ellis L. Dresel, urged the State Department to intervene with the Entente powers to enforce full implementation of the German neutrality. Transports to Poland through Germany should be refused "even if it seems that Poland's fate depends entirely" on them; for otherwise "all of Europe would be in a blaze again," he reported. *Foreign Relations Papers*, 1920, VI, p. 388.

[33] *AA*, 1680/3617, 800199.

any such cases immediately. The proposal is justified by the uncertain boundary and sovereignty situations in East and West Prussia. . . ." [34]

Chicherin did not immediately answer Simons' offer. It was nearly two weeks later, August 2—when the Red army was deep in Polish territory and had reached the boundary of East Prussia—that he finally expressed his agreement, in principle, with the Foreign Minister's proposal. He stated that the Soviet government would never subscribe to the policy of foreign occupation of Germany and he stressed the naturalness of friendly ties between Germany and Soviet Russia. He proposed Berlin as a meeting place but was elusive in answering the concrete proposals made by Dr. Simons, stating that as to the "other less important suggestions [he] still must consult with competent authorities and would like to return to them later." One can assume that in expectation of a revolutionary upheaval in Germany, the Soviet government did not wish to tie its hands with a "bourgeois" government. Pointedly, indeed, at the end of his letter, Chicherin spoke about the common interests of the working masses of both nations.[35]

German neutrality was markedly one-sided. Not only did it prevent France from sending armament to Poland by trains, but it also gave direct military help to Soviet Russia. It may be that the German government was ignorant of the contacts between the Soviet and German military; nor is it known that such contacts and military assistance were carried out on orders of General von Seeckt. However, there is little doubt that the Red army did receive some help from Germany.

On July 11 the Commissariat for War answered foreign press accusations that some sectors of the Soviet front were under the command of German officers. It rejected them as pure lies. "In no unit," the statement continued, "is there a single German

[34] *AA*, 1404/2860, 551564–6.
[35] *AA*, 1404/2860, 551574–6.

officer. Needless to say [however], the ranks of the Red army are open to volunteers of all nations who consider it their duty to fight for the cause of communism against imperialist violence." [36]

The Polish government came into possession of documents which told a different story about German contributions to the Soviet forces. According to these sources, some military equipment was sold to Russia as early as March 1920. On the night of May 1 six zeppelins flew over Warsaw in the direction of the northeast, carrying telegraphic and medical supplies to Russia. Units of the Soviet seventh infantry division used German ammunition. At the beginning of July the Soviet government placed orders in Germany for 400,000 rifles and 200 million cartridges. These were transported through Hamburg. Reports from Polish soldiers indicated that Germans were fighting in Soviet lines—allegedly 20,000 soldiers and 80,000 Spartacists. On July 20 Major General von Horn in Breslau signed detailed instructions concerning air communications with Soviet Russia. German officers, some of whose names are listed, served with the fourth Soviet division.

In an article published in *Königsberger Hartungsche Zeitung* on August 10 a reporter described the situation in the boundary town of Prostken. "Here on the border," he wrote, "one can hear the opinion expressed repeatedly that now Germany has the opportunity to free herself, through an alliance with Soviet Russia, from the unbearable burden of the Versailles peace. . . . People are motivated in their sentiments by [their] utter hate of Poland," he continued. "They don't care a nickel about the Bolshevik economic system, [but] they don't see any other way out of Germany's misery. They are ready to sacrifice their lives. Their enthusiasm reminds one of the August days of 1914. Even officers in uniform have gone over, as it has been confirmed to me incontestably from various sides.

[36] Trotsky, *Kak vooruzhalas'* . . . , II, 2nd Book, p. 154.

Every train brings people who, one can surely assume, will disappear in the night as if the land had swallowed them." [37]

In addition, the Polish Ministry of Foreign Affairs had documents relating to preparations by German nationalistic organizations to invade West Prussian and Poznań provinces and describing their secret contacts with Kopp.[38] According to some letters addressed to Kopp, which Polish agents intercepted, he promised Danzig and Upper Silesia to the German government in return for military assistance.[39] An unpublished memorandum by Reibnitz, a confidant of Seeckt, stated that Radek and Kopp reportedly negotiated with Reibnitz on "a plan under which, as soon as the Red army entered Warsaw, German *Freikorps* detachments would advance in West Prussia, Posen [Poznań] and Upper Silesia as far as the old German frontier." [40] At the time of the Soviet advance in Poland, a group of Soviet officers met with some German nationalists at Soldau in East Prussia and promised them liberation of West Prussia and her restoration to Germany.[41]

Kopp's political offers appear to be substantiated by another document, written by none other than Enver Pasha, the Turkish military leader in World War I. An intimate friend of Seeckt, who had been adviser to the Turkish army at that time, Enver Pasha was in Berlin in 1919. Toward the end of the year he left for Moscow and is believed to have brought messages from Seeckt to the Soviet leaders about plans for Soviet-German military cooperation. He appears to have reached the Soviet capital after several months of delay, some time at the height of the Soviet-Polish war. His great idea was to bring about an alliance between Germany, Soviet Russia, and Turkey. In a letter of August 25, addressed to General von Seeckt, his

---

[37] *Ciechanowski Deposit.* A report of the Polish Chief of Staff, General Rozwadowski, August 26, 1920. Ew. 2, No. 38381/11.

[38] *Ibid.,* August 11, 1920.

[39] *Ibid.,* a report of January 20, 1921, No. D.S.P. 93.

[40] E. H. Carr, *The Bolshevik Revolution, 1917–1923* (3 vols.; New York: The Macmillan Company, 1953), III, p. 324.

[41] *Ibid.,* p. 327.

"*lieber Freund,*" he reported with no small satisfaction, that "the Mohammedan units on the Polish front have fought with great brilliance and resoluteness." He wrote that although the situation on the battlefield, according to the Russians themselves, was admittedly bad, "they hope to bring the Polish advance to a stop and pass over to an offensive." The following day he wrote a hurried letter to Seeckt—he was to leave in three hours with Zinoviev for the Third International's Congress of the Peoples of the East at Baku. He had had a conversation with Sklianski who told him that Trotsky and his group "[were] ready to recognize the old German boundary of 1914." However, to win the whole Soviet government to the idea of alliance with Germany and Turkey, Germany should give to Russia some unofficial assistance, "for instance, intelligence [information] about the Polish army and if possible smuggled weapons." [42]

The battle for Warsaw and Pilsudski's smashing victory changed the picture. However, as late as August 18, when the results of the battle could not as yet be fully evaluated, the German Foreign Ministry was still anxious to confirm to Chicherin the German position of neutrality and even to assure him that should the retreating Polish units withdraw onto the disputed plebiscite area of Upper Silesia they would be disarmed and interned.[43] These assurances were wasted.

Germany was disappointed with the outcome of the war. With Pilsudski's victory, "Poland was saved and the Bolshevik threat to mid-Europe warded off; however, the German east boundary, dictated at Versailles, was again stabilized, too," wrote a German specialist in East European affairs.[44]

There was a by-product of the Soviet retreat which offered a flicker of hope to the disappointed German government. The

[42] *Seeckt Papers,* reel 24, *stück* 202f. Later, Trotsky's contacts with Seeckt were presented as espionage to which the traitor Trotsky lent himself. Rubinstein, *op. cit.,* p. 34.
[43] *Vneshniaia Politika,* I, pp. 487–88. See also Höltje, *op. cit.,* pp. 29–30.
[44] Blücher, *op. cit.,* p. 101.

authorities in East Prussia were unable to execute an orderly internment of the retreating Soviet units. For a short period Berlin pressed for concessions from the Entente, asking for permission to send military reinforcements to East Prussia.[45] But even that faint hope was extinguished when the Soviet and the Polish governments signed the preliminary peace treaty in Riga on October 12, 1920.

The German attitude toward the Soviet-Polish war taught, or rather should have taught, all participants in the theatre of European politics the lesson that Germany was ready to move in any direction that promised a loosening of the shackles of Versailles. She was willing to consider an association with France and Britain against Soviet Russia and when that proved unpromising she at least indirectly supported the Soviet forces in the war against Poland.

However, the Soviet government conducted its policy toward Poland always with an eye on developments in Germany. Should a communist Germany emerge from the postwar chaos, Poland, barring an armed intervention by the Allied powers, would be unable to resist the pressure from her two communist neighbors and would succumb to communism. Should Germany succeed in withstanding the revolutionary efforts of the communist party, still, as the Soviet leaders knew, even a non-communist German government could be counted on to share Russia's hostility toward Poland. Soviet Russia, therefore, kept both irons in the fire, maintaining close contacts with the German government even as she fanned the flames of revolution.

Let Germany become communist or democratic, let the Soviet government stand or fall—the common target of both sides would remain always the same: Poland. The ruins of a terrible war still could be seen all over Europe; the situation in Germany and Russia still was far from stabilized, but the old pattern, the old mutual design of placing the Polish neck in a noose already had become apparent.

[45] *AA*, 3623/9855, 317281–516.

The British and the French appeared to have misread this lesson of history. They did little to prevent its recurrence. In fact, their policy indirectly encouraged this trend. First, they differed among themselves on the settlement of the Soviet-Polish conflict and their attitude was, therefore, one of vacillation. Second, neither of them considered the idea of drawing Germany away from a Soviet-oriented policy by giving support to the fragile structure of German democracy; sentiments of hatred against Germany were still too strong in France and Britain to permit such a policy. Nor, in the third place, did they give any decisive assistance to Poland in her war against Russia which might have affected the political outcome of the conflict. This particular attitude helped to plant the seeds of bitterness against the West which at a later date played a significant role in Polish foreign policy.

As to Poland, the experience of singlehandedly fighting a successful war against Soviet Russia and at the same time successfully maintaining a posture of hostility toward Germany led to the false and dangerous conclusion that she could long endure the simultaneous enmity of both.

These, then, were the factors which established a solid foundation for cooperation between Russia and Germany in the postwar period. However, with the cessation of hostilities on the battlefront, the period of bold ideas and adventurous combinations also came to an end. A period of diplomacy, first equally adventurous though later somewhat pedestrian, had begun. Yet, the common goal of somehow bringing proud and independent Poland to her knees continued to be one of the primary links in the strange and frequently strained friendship of Weimar Germany and communist Soviet Russia.

PART II. 1921–1925

YEARS OF DIPLOMATIC
CAMPAIGNS

CHAPTER 4

SETTING THE SCENE — 2

IN THE first half of the 1920's powerful internal and external forces compelled both Soviet Russia and Germany not only to reconsider their approach to Poland but also to change their attitude toward the principal European powers.

The revolution in Germany, which the Soviet leaders had expected with great hope, if not with certainty, failed to materialize; it was within Russia that critical problems appeared. In March 1921 the Kronstadt sailors' rebellion served as an ominous warning of the disaffection of the rank-and-file soldiers of the revolution. Famine spread throughout the country and peasants revolted against the severe strictures of continued communist war-economy. To save the revolution, Lenin introduced the New Economic Policy, releasing agriculture and the distribution system from the grip of communist control. Credits and foreign trade continued to be the order of the day.

Nevertheless, the Soviet revolution had survived the most crucial period of its infancy and the notion that socialism could exist in one country, despite its bourgeois surroundings, began to attract and influence the thinking of the Soviet government. While the Third International, by repeated revolutionary appeals, provided some cover for this ideological retreat, the government itself endeavored to seek the stabilization of its relations with the outside world.

The Soviet-British Trade Agreement, signed in March 1921, represented a significant break in the ring of isolation which the victorious powers had thrown around Russia. It did not yield important practical results in trade, however, because the relations between the two countries continued to be plagued

97

by communist-led and Soviet-supported revolutionary activities in British India, Persia, and Afghanistan. The Labor Party, favorably impressed by the socialist experiment in Russia, formed a government in autumn 1923 and less than half a year later, in February 1924, Britain became the first major power to grant diplomatic recognition to Soviet Russia. Other powers followed suit in speedy succession, even though by October of 1924 the Labor Party was swept out of power and Soviet-British relations took a turn for the worse. Even so, the Soviet place in the international arena was by that time assured.

Though the Western powers were seemingly unwilling to normalize their trade relations with Soviet Russia without receiving in return her obligation to honor the Czarist debts and indemnify them for confiscated property, Germany's economic interests were such as to pull her toward Moscow. Since the Versailles Treaty assured Russia of participation in German reparations should she sign the Treaty, here obviously was a situation open to a favorable bargaining on both sides. When the Genoa Conference met in the spring of 1922 to renew the whole gamut of conditions of economic contacts with Russia, the Soviet and German delegates, ostracized by the Allied powers, worked out together and signed at Rapallo an agreement which renounced reparations, indemnification, and old debts claims and opened an avenue for close political and economic relations between the two countries.

There were several other reasons which made close cooperation between Germany and Soviet Russia desirable. Compelled by the Versailles Treaty to maintain only a small army and to produce only light arms, Germany found in Soviet Russia an eager accomplice who would allow her military experts to pursue on Russian soil experimentation with, and production of, modern weapons. Such an arrangement served well the interests of both countries as it not only strengthened the Red army but also allowed German officers to keep up with the progress of military science. Moreover, it permitted Germany secretly to receive Soviet produced armaments. This military cooperation between Soviet Russia and Germany continued almost uninterruptedly until Hitler's rise to power in 1933.

The fate of Upper Silesia was another factor which influenced German orientation toward Moscow. When, in the long-awaited plebiscite of March 1921, the majority of the voters expressed a desire to rejoin Germany, the whole country lived in the jubilant expectation that it would be permitted to do so. Needless to say, the shock and chagrin was great when the League of Nations in October recommended the division of this disputed province. As a reaction to the shock, almost all political parties clamored for closer cooperation with Russia.

The problem of reparations gave still another impetus to this development in German foreign policy. Toward the end of April, the Allies informed Germany that the reparation bill would amount to 132 billion gold marks. In response, the German government resigned; but just before doing so, it hastily signed an agreement with Soviet Russia calling for a resumption of trade relations. An Allied ultimatum that the Ruhr would be occupied if Germany did not accept the reparations terms brought the responsible political leadership to its senses and a new government, under Joseph Wirth, was formed. However, the government's decision to accept the terms threw the country into a turmoil of violence and agitation. Under the influence of extremists of the Left and Right, Germany was brought to the brink of civil war. Even political assassinations occurred; that of the Foreign Minister, Walther Rathenau, was the most widely known. Inflation, which the government did not desire to halt, threatened the basic economic structure of the country. Germany became insolvent and soon was in default in paying the required reparations. France and Belgium responded with the occupation of the Ruhr in January 1923. Germany reacted with passive resistance. Inflation now reached calamitous dimensions: in August, 500,000 marks sold for one dollar; in October, 25 billion marks sold for one dollar. Disruptive forces were everywhere at work; the Rhineland and the Palatinate, encouraged by the French, declared their separation from Germany; in Saxony and Thuringia communist attempts at seizure of power were suppressed only by intervention; in Bavaria, Hitler staged a *putsch.*

However, in these moments of supreme crisis the reasonable elements of German politics again prevailed. They called a halt to the senseless policy of passive resistance, brought about a currency reform and thus created a favorable atmosphere for renegotiating the reparations. The Dawes Plan laid down new, more realistic, foundations for German reparation obligations and opened a new era in German internal and external affairs. It was an era of political and economic consolidation and of Germany's re-entrance into world affairs. It culminated in October of 1925 when she signed the Locarno Pact. Germany rejoined the circle of big powers and established close cooperation with the West but did not give up her collaboration with Soviet Russia.

Not only the internal politics of Russia and Germany but also their relations with the outside world inevitably affected their policy toward Poland. This country, too, passed through a period of severe political and economic strain. Poland's political system, though democratic in the first seven years of the country's independence, showed all of the characteristics of an unstable, frequently irresponsible administration. In this short period the government, exposed to the vagaries of a constantly feuding parliament, changed thirteen times. Finally, in May of 1923, Marshal Pilsudski, that granite figure of Polish politics, publicly demonstrated his disgust with this type of democratic practice by withdrawing into private life.

Economic and financial problems were of staggering proportions, multiplied as they were by an economically unbearable rate of population growth. Poverty was widespread and inflation choked both industry and agriculture. In 1924 the original 120 Polish marks to one dollar dropped to six and a half million marks to the dollar and it was not until 1927 that currency reforms and foreign loans led to some stabilization. The traditional Russian market was denied to Poland for political reasons and the most attractive German market for Polish agricultural products was completely sealed in 1926 when the two countries began a damaging tariff war.

Having extended her boundaries at the expense of Russia and Germany, Poland had to cope with the difficult problem of minorities. Of 32 million inhabitants, some 10 million belonged to non-Polish nationalities. Five million Ukrainians, unreconciled to their fate and following orders from exiled leaders, organized terrorist activities which the Polish government answered with brutal repression. One and a half million Belorussians, poverty-stricken and underdeveloped politically and culturally, were more of a burden than an asset. Three quarters of a million Germans, economically solid and with feelings of superiority, undermined the structural foundations of the country by well-organized irredentist activities. Two and three quarter million Jews could find no real security in a country where intense anti-Semitism flourished among the conservative elements of the population. The Polish government's policy toward the minorities was a matter of constant discussion before the League of Nations; in the period between 1920 and 1931 no less than 155 minority complaints were brought up before this forum. (It should be added that population statistics differ and that only estimates are given here.)

Yet, strangely enough, none of these serious problems of Poland's internal developments appears to have affected her foreign policy. Basing her international position on an alliance with France and Rumania and on her work in the League of Nations, Poland continued to defy both her neighbors, Germany and Soviet Russia, never giving consideration, as far as it is known, to the thought that accommodation with at least one of them might strengthen her security and her posture toward the other. But perhaps even at that time she felt as a

Polish colonel did during World War II when he was asked why Poland had not in the past sought an understanding with Russia or Germany. He answered, ". . . if we had there would be no Poland."

CHAPTER 5

CURRENTS AND
CROSSCURRENTS

WITH the end of the Soviet-Polish war a new era in East Europe seemed to have begun—a period of relative realism and stability in the relationship of the political triangle, Moscow, Berlin, and Warsaw. Poland and the Soviet Union to all appearances took cognizance of their political regimes and tried to settle the most pressing problems of their more elementary international contacts. Germany and Poland also appeared to have accepted the necessity of coexistence and established a semblance of peace on their common border.

However, beneath the ashes there smoldered the fires of national mistrust, contempt, ideological hostility, and territorial claims—ineradicable conflicts of emotions, ideas, and interests that threatened to erupt at any moment. And always there persisted the ebb and flow of diplomatic maneuvering, each party seeking to strengthen its position against the other.

SEMBLANCE OF CONSOLIDATION

On October 12, 1920, in Riga the preliminary peace treaty and armistice was signed between Soviet Russia, the Ukraine, and Poland.[1] In addition to the clauses concerning boundaries, abstention from intervention in the internal affairs of the signatories, and the procedures to be used in solving complex economic problems, the two countries agreed to the highly significant commitment not to lend support to any organization which would promote armed action against the other con-

[1] For the text see *Soviet Treaty Series*, I, pp. 67–9.

103

tracting party or propagate a change of its regime. Moreover, they agreed on a kind of neutrality by promising to undertake "to support no foreign military action against the other Party." The first of these clauses was obviously meant to eliminate the activities of the numerous Russian refugees in Poland against Russia and of the Polish communists in Russia against Poland; the latter "neutrality" clause was included to alleviate Soviet suspicions that Poland might join in a military action against Soviet Russia. The Riga Peace Treaty was finally signed on March 18, 1921.[2] Subsequently, several agreements were reached to implement the Riga Treaty; also, provisions were made for local railroad traffic across the frontier.

For a while it appeared that Soviet Russia and Poland might indeed reach agreements, even on political matters of importance. The Western powers were negotiating the question of economic reconstruction of Russia, the problem of Czarist debts, and the question of indemnities for confiscated foreign properties. Had the Soviet government accepted the old Czarist obligations, Poland and the Baltic States, as successor states, would have been partly responsible for their respective shares of these debts. The problem was expected to be settled at what later became the Genoa Conference.

In their preparation for this Conference, the Baltic States and Poland came to the realization that these issues might indeed be of as much interest to them as to Soviet Russia. To coordinate their policies, insofar as it was possible, representatives of Poland, Latvia, Estonia, and Soviet Russia met at Riga on March 29 and 30, 1922. Here they signed a protocol, the significance of which appeared even to transcend the common financial involvement in the old Russian debts. The protocol expressed the desirability of coordinating their actions at Genoa in economic questions of common interest and, more significantly, of combining their efforts to achieve recognition *de jure* of Soviet Russia by other powers. Second, the docu-

[2] *Soviet Treaty Series*, I, pp. 105–116.

ment confirmed the wish of the signatories to solve all disputes by peaceful means, expressed support for the policy of limitation of armament and suggested a partial demilitarization and neutralization of boundary zones.[3] These were hopeful signs; and two prominent Soviet diplomats, Leo Karakhan and Ivan Maiskii, felt justified in stating that the Soviet-Polish relations showed a marked improvement.[4]

REALITY OF HOSTILITY

Such official appearances were misleading, however. At no time did the Soviet Union view the Riga Treaty as a final settlement for its boundary with Poland and, moreover, it was constantly disturbed by the thought that Great Britain and France might start a war against Russia with Poland serving as the springboard for the attack.

Shortly after the Riga Treaty had been signed, leading Soviet statesmen developed the thesis that it did not satisfy their "interpretation of the principle" of self-determination, that it was an "imperialist peace." They stated that at the end it "will turn against Poland," because she "will never be able to assimilate" the acquired territories, and, at any rate, "in an epoch of class struggle and civil war the significance of boundaries [was] illusory." Radek stated openly that the Riga Treaty did not provide a definite settlement of Soviet-Polish problems and pointed to the danger of a new war. A Polish communist leader, Max Walecki, promised on behalf of the Communist Party of Poland that in the "not too distant future [it] will in open struggle, in a civil war, seize the power and proclaim a Soviet Poland."[5] Lenin himself on two occasions

---

[3] Narodnyi Komissariat po inostrannym delam, *Materialy Genuezskoi Konferentsii*, Moscow, 1922, pp. 51–3.

[4] Karakhan's interview, *Pravda*, February 19, 1922. I. Maiskii, *Vneshniaia politika R.S.F.S.R., 1917–1922* (Moscow: Izdatel'stvo "Krasnaia Nov.," 1923), pp. 92–3.

[5] I. Steklov in *Izvestiia*, October 14, 1920; K. Radek in *Pravda*, October 15, 1920; *Izvestiia*, October 20, 1920; J. Markhlevskii in *Kommunisticheskii Internatsional*, II, No. 14, November 6, 1920, cols. 2751–54; D. Manuilskii

warned of the danger of a resumption of hostilities. He was particularly bitter about the Russian *émigrés* in Poland who, he asserted, continued their counterrevolutionary activities.[6] Lenin's accusation was not without justification. It is true that Boris Savinkov, the audacious Russian revolutionary and the political leader of Russian *émigrés* in Poland, wrote to General Wrangel three days after the Polish government had signed the Riga Treaty that the counterrevolutionary units— some 20,000 soldiers—had decided, following Marshal Pilsudski's proposal, to abandon Polish territory and "continue independently in an armed struggle with the Bolsheviks." [7] However, this move never occurred and continued activities of the Russian *émigrés* in Poland, contrary to the obligations of the Riga Treaty, became a matter of repeated Soviet complaints for years to come.

It was not until six months after the Treaty had been signed that diplomatic relations were established between Poland and Russia. In May 1921 when Chicherin asked Prince Sapieha, the Polish Foreign Minister, whether Karakhan, the Deputy Foreign Minister, could come to Warsaw to open the Soviet legation, the Polish government, after a six-week delay, answered that it wished simultaneously to send its own representative to Moscow. Therefore the government asked for "reasons of purely technical nature" for a postponement of the exchange of diplomatic representatives for a few weeks.[8]

At last, on August 3, 1921, at a border station Karakhan and Tytus Filipowicz, the Polish representative, formally changed

in *ibid.*, No. 15, December 20, 1920, cols. 3076–82. K. Radek, *Die Auswärtige Politik Sowjet-Russlands*, pp. 66ff. *Protokoly S'ezdov i Konferentsii Vsesoiuznoi Kommunisticheskoi Partii (b)*. Desiatyi S'ezd RKP (b), Mart 1921g (Moscow: Partiinoe Izdatel'stvo, 1933).

[6] Lenin, *Sochineniia*, Vol. 32, pp. 93–4, 125–26.

[7] *Archives, B. V. Savinkov*, Hoover Institution. See also, *Trial of Boris Victorovich Savinkov*, English translation of the stenographic report, published in *Pravda*, August 30, 1924; "Vrangelevshchina," *Krasnyi Arkhiv*, Vol. 2, 1930, pp. 3–46; Vol. 3, 1930, pp. 3–40.

[8] *Sovetskaia Rossiia i Pol'sha* (Moscow: Izdanie Narodnogo Komissariata po inostrannym delam, 1921), pp. 72–3.

special trains which took them to the capitals of their respective appointments.

Meanwhile, the two governments exchanged sharp verbal encounters accusing each other of repeated violations of the Riga Treaty. Chicherin, in a series of notes, pointed to the activities of the Russian *émigré* organizations, particularly the one led by Boris Savinkov, which were plotting against the Soviet regime, crossing the Soviet borders with the alleged assistance of Polish authorities. The Polish Foreign Ministers —Sapieha and his successor, K. Skirmunt—rejected resolutely such Soviet accusations; but they themselves protested against the assaults of Bolshevik bands operating in the border area "under the authority of the Military Council of the West Front" of the Soviet Union. Equally bitter were the diplomatic notes which were concerned with the lack of progress by Soviet-Polish commissions entrusted with problems of evacuation, reconstruction, and rehabilitation.[9] The Soviet government saw in almost every move preparation for a new war.

In effect, the same threat-of-war psychosis which the Soviet leaders have cultivated to this day permeated the atmosphere in the early 1920's, never permitting a modicum of mutual trust to become established. True, the Soviets at that time had serious reason to remain worried about the goals of the Western powers in regard to Russia. None of these powers had as yet recognized the Soviet government, and the catastrophic famine in 1921 and 1922 prompted the West to use an economic blockade as an effective weapon against Russia. Most countries still expected an early fall of the communist regime.

International acts designed to assure Eastern Europe of a *status quo* based on peace treaties were interpreted by Moscow as first steps toward armed intervention. The pacts of alliance between France and Poland, of February 19, 1921, and be-

---

[9] *Ibid.*, pp. 15–35, 79–121. *Dokumenty dotyczące akcji delegacyj Polskich w Komisjach Mieszanych Reewakuacyjnej i Specjalnej w Moskwie* (Warsaw, 1922, 1923).

tween Rumania and Poland, of March 3, 1921, were viewed in Russia with alarm. However, the first simply defined the obligations of the signatories in a rather vague fashion and was directed principally against German revisionist plans; the latter provided for common defense against unprovoked aggression on "the present eastern boundaries." [10] Even the recognition of the Baltic States in January 1921 by the Entente powers was attacked by the Soviet government as an imperialist move, despite the fact that it had granted them recognition the preceding year. It was perhaps the timing, rather than the substance of such diplomatic moves which intensified Soviet apprehension.

By the autumn of 1921 these tensions appeared to have become critical. On September 13 the People's Commissariat for Foreign Affairs issued a statement asserting that it was in possession of documents proving that on September 3 France had suggested to Poland and Rumania that they exploit the famine in Russia and that they present to Moscow in the form of an ultimatum, including the threat of military action, their maximum claims. Though the Polish government had declined the French proposal, the statement continued, it did decide to continue to pursue a policy of threats. The statement went so far as to assert that "at the same time the Polish government had inquired of Germany what concessions she would expect in the Upper Silesian question for the price of a benevolent German neutrality in case of a Polish-Russian war." [11]

The Polish government rejected the Soviet accusations. Nevertheless, lending some credence to Soviet claims, Poland, on

---

[10] For the text, see *British and Foreign State Papers, 1923*, Part II, Vol. 118, pp. 342–43, and *ibid. 1921*, Vol. 114, pp. 916–17. The post-World War II Soviet literature ascribed these pacts to the American pressure. See T. K. Kobliakov, *Ot Bresta do Rapallo* (Moscow: Gosudarstvennoe izdatel'stvo politicheskoi literatury, 1954), p. 130.

[11] *Sovetskaia Rossiia i Pol'sha*, p. 50. Though there is no hint in accessible documents confirming either of the Soviet accusations, they were repeated in the post-World War II publications; see Rubinshtein, *op. cit.*, pp. 163–64, 172.

September 14 and 18, requested the Soviet government to implement the most pressing provisions of the Riga Treaty before October 1—otherwise the Polish government would consider "further presence of its representative in Moscow superfluous."

The Soviet government, answering the Polish note, considered it "unacceptable in form and unsatisfactory in content." Once more, it protested against the partisan war being waged in the Polish boundary areas "with the assistance of the Polish military authorities" and asked the Polish government to put an end to these activities. Expressing willingness to examine the Polish complaints, the Soviet government then put before the Polish government a list of its own demands and pointed to the gravity of the planned withdrawal of the Polish representative from Moscow.[12]

Although the Polish diplomatic mission was not recalled, mutual accusations continued. The Soviet government accompanied them with the appeals of the Executive Committee of the Communist International, with a resolution passed by the Ninth All-Russian Congress of Soviets, and with the usual "war-scare" propaganda barrage, fired by the press. Radek, however, revealed that Soviet communists did not in fact believe their own propaganda when he wrote, with his characteristic bluntness, "Poland is as able to fight as a paralytic is able to dance."[13]

SIMILARITY ON THE WESTERN BORDER

Meanwhile, German-Polish relations were developing in much the same manner as those between Poland and Russia. Outwardly, there was some semblance of a desire to solve

---

[12] For the text of the notes, see Kliuchnikov and Sabanin, *op. cit.*, III, I, pp. 131–32, 132–35, 135–37.

[13] *Pravda*, September 10, 1921. For the Soviet press campaign and appeals, see *Pravda*, October 20, November 9, December 17, 23, 1921 and *Izvestiia*, October 14, November 13, 1921. Degras, *The Communist International*, I, pp. 297–99. Kliuchnikov and Sabanin, *op. cit.*, III, I, pp. 157–60.

mutual problems in a peaceful manner. In reality, however, deep-seated hatreds born of fear and frustration dominated the scene.

In the period between the autumn of 1920 and the spring of 1921 the two governments signed agreements dealing with such matters as the transfer of judicial administration in the territory ceded to Poland, restitution of German ships, exchange of prisoners of war, return of interned persons, and execution of some articles of the Versailles Treaty. Even the thorny problem of the free city of Danzig seemed to have found its solution in a series of constitutional arrangements and agreements signed by Poland, Germany, and the Danzig authorities. The plebiscites in Allenstein and Marienwerder, which resulted in a union with Germany, encouraged the Germans to hope that the envisaged plebiscite in Upper Silesia, by far the most important territory in dispute, would also result in reunification.

Before long, however, a deep disappointment set in, which stimulated German orientation toward Soviet Russia. For some time, Germany had hoped to extract concessions from the Allies by an attitude of opposition to Russia. She had seen in the defeat of the Red army at the hands of Poland a convincing and deeply disappointing proof of Russian weakness. Now that her hope of a Russian conquest of Poland was gone, it would indeed be unwise to overemphasize any common interests between the two countries. Moreover, from her constant negotiations with the Allied powers about the implementation of the economic and military clauses of the Versailles Treaty, even the most unreconciled statesmen in Berlin must have been convinced of Germany's utter helplessness and complete dependence on the West. This, then, was certainly not the time to seek open cooperation with "the outlaw," Soviet Russia, and in particular, an open alliance against the French *"enfant protégé,"* Poland.

The time seemed opportune to picture Germany as the only

safe wall against communism and thus possibly secure a more lenient attitude from the West toward Versailles obligations. According to a Soviet source, German Foreign Minister Dr. Walther Simons sent a note to the Allied Control Commission on November 9, 1920, asking them to reconsider the order of dissolving the German irregular military units, the Home Guard (*Einwohnerwehr*). In this same note he stated, "Recent events have diminished considerably the hope for an early end of the conflict between Poland and Russia," and that "the Soviet government now prepares a new attack on the Lithuanian border." [14] He pleaded also with the British Ambassador, Lord D'Abernon, in the same manner, presenting Germany as "the barrier against Bolshevism and disorder." When the Ambassador pointedly remarked that "Poland was usually regarded as the barrier and that they had achieved recently a notable victory," Simons insisted that Germany was "the real barrier. Poland was far too weak. . . ." Two other German statesmen, the conservative Prime Minister of Bavaria, Gustav von Kahr, and the Social Democratic President of the Reichstag, Paul Loebe, also warned Lord D'Abernon of the danger of the Soviet attack on Poland.[15]

Exploiting the widespread communist scare, the German government urged the Allies not to proceed with the reduction of German military forces to an army of 100,000 men as prescribed by the Versailles Treaty. Maltzan was in possession of strictly secret information "from a reliable informer, not a paid agent," according to which Germany, in case of a Soviet-Polish conflict, would be allowed to put some 500,000 soldiers into the field against Russia. England was reportedly ready to

[14] N. Rubinshtein, *Sovetskaia Rossiia i kapitalisticheskie gosudarstva v gody perekhoda ot voiny k miru (1921–1922 g)* (Moscow: Ogiz, 1948), p. 37 quoting from *Vestnik NKID*, No. 3-4, 1921, p. 59. (The note could not be located in the files of *AA*.)

[15] Viscount D'Abernon, *Versailles to Rapallo* (Garden City, N.Y.: Doubleday, Doran, 1929), pp. 83, 84, 100–101, 104. See also the letter of von Kahr to Simons, January 3, 1921, *AA,* 1405/2860, 552074-8.

give Upper Silesia to Germany without a plebiscite and France would be ready to follow English policy.[16]

This information proved to be entirely wrong. The result of the plebiscite held on March 20, 1921, first encouraged German hopes for the retention of Upper Silesia. However, the German majority of 228,246 votes failed to impress the Allies. The Ambassadors' Conference on October 20 accepted the recommendation of the League of Nations that Upper Silesia be divided between Germany and Poland. Neither of the two countries was satisfied with this solution; and Germany was now worried that Poland might try to annex the German part of Upper Silesia by force.

"THE POLISH CARD"

Thus it was that Germany, reluctantly, sought a position of some strength in cooperation with Soviet Russia. Common interests of subduing Poland and of opposing the West's dominant position were stronger than Germany's fear of communism. Past Soviet pronouncements, whether by the government, the party, or the Third International, had frequently condemned the Versailles Treaty and the "injustice" of depriving Germany of territory in favor of Poland. Lenin pointed to the "monstrosity" of Poland dividing Germany in two parts and separating her from Soviet communism.[17]

Now, after the Ambassadors' Conference had returned their verdict on Upper Silesia the Soviet press denounced it as a machination of the Anglo-French imperialism which wished to weaken Germany further.[18] Such an attitude was bound to

[16] *AA*, 1405/2860, 552008–9.

[17] Lenin, *Sochineniia*, Vol. 31, p. 280.

[18] *Pravda*, October 22, November 11, 1921. See also the resolution of the Fourth Congress of the Communist International, December 5, 1922. *Kommunisticheskii Internatsional v Dokumentakh . . .* , ed. Bela Kun (Moscow: Partiinoe izdatel'stvo, 1933), p. 341. The Polish communists shared, of course, the views of the Soviet government on the Upper Silesia question. After World War II, however, they made a radical turnabout and presented its final solution as a plot of international finance and Western imperialism to help Germany and weaken Poland.

find an appreciative reception in Berlin. Otto Gessler, the Minister of Defense, spoke in the closed sessions of the *Reichstag* Committee on Foreign Affairs, for a close German-Soviet cooperation and "expanded freely, particularly on his favorite theme, the Polish danger," records the prominent witness, Ruth Fischer. "Against the Poles," she continued, "all nuances of German nationalism were united; even those nationalists who rejected any compromise with Bolshevism on domestic issues recognized the worth of Gessler's argument that against the new Polish state, against this French stronghold in Eastern Europe, German interest could be best served by a German-Russian alliance." [19]

While Gessler fought in the political arena, his subordinates worked out concrete plans. General von Seeckt, according to his biographer, as early as December 1919 had prepared a strategical plan for action against Poland as "for him only an aggressive solution . . . should be considered; a solution which—if one set one's hopes high enough—could have as a goal the reconquest of Poland." [20]

If such offensive plans were ever prepared, they remained as mere blueprints. Seeckt was as aware as anyone of Germany's military weakness, but he did anticipate the possibility of a defensive conflict with Poland. He expected Poland to attack Upper Silesia and urged Dr. Simons to prepare the German people, through the press, for "vigorous resistance," since Germany "must expect to have to oppose this State within a short time with arms in hand." It was possibly at Seeckt's insistence that on January 25, 1921, a fortnight after his conversation with Simons, the German cabinet decided to stand up against "a Polish assault with force of arms." [21]

See Franciszek Ryszka, "Kulisy decyzji w sprawie Śląska w r. 1921," *Kwartalnik historyczny* (Warsaw), LX, No. 1, 1953, pp. 127–67.

[19] R. Fischer, *op. cit.*, pp. 533–34.

[20] F. Rabenau, *op. cit.*, p. 297.

[21] *AA*, 1424/2945, 570345 (Dr. Simons' memorandum on his conversation with Seeckt, January 11, 1921); Rabenau, *op. cit.*, p. 298.

Toward the end of 1920 the Soviet representatives, Radek and Krasin, indirectly approached Seeckt through Major Kurt von Schleicher and proposed that "the Soviet Union and Germany should join forces to wipe out Poland"; Seeckt rejected the idea because of Germany's weakness. However, these contacts opened the avenue to a close, secret military cooperation between the two countries, a cooperation which despite mutual fears and suspicions was maintained by their common hatred of Poland.[22] In September 1921 when certain German industrial circles hesitated to enter into concrete arrangements with the Soviet government, the latter was advised to "play the Polish card"—an argument certain to secure a favorable reaction in Berlin.[23] Later in the year, probably in the last days of December, Colonel Otto Hasse went to Moscow and discussed with P. Lebedev, the Soviet Chief of Staff, the action of the two countries "in the event of a Polish war." The Soviet officer told him "that the Red army would attack Poland in the spring of 1922 if Germany made all-out efforts to rebuild Russia's war industry." Seeckt, however, aware that Lebedev was playing "the Polish card," rejected the idea of a Soviet-German war against Poland but recommended to his government a policy of "benevolent neutrality in case of Russian-Polish conflict."[24] When in September 1921 Soviet-Polish relations once again reached what appeared to be the breaking point, the German Foreign Office instructed its representative in Moscow, Kurt Wiedenfeld, to "state secretly to Chicherin that in case of a Russian-Polish conflict the Reich's government will assume the same position [of neutrality] as last year."[25]

[22] H. R. Berndorff, *General Zwischen Ost und West* (Hamburg: Hoffmann und Campe [n.d.]), pp. 76, 78. Rabenau, *op. cit.*, p. 309. See also G. Freund, *Unholy Alliance* (New York: Harcourt, Brace, 1957), pp. 84ff. Also Hans W. Gatzke, "Russo-German Military Collaboration during the Weimar Republic," *American Historical Review*, LXIII, No. 3, pp. 565–97.
[23] Carr, *op. cit.*, III, pp. 363–64.
[24] *Ibid.*, p. 364. Freund, *op. cit.*, p. 99; Rabenau, *op. cit.*, p. 309. See also the Memorandum of Major Fritz Tschunke in Julius Epstein, "Der Seeckt Plan," *Der Monat.* Vol. 1, No. 2, November 1948, p. 49.
[25] *AA*, 785/1563, 378170.

History of the preceding year, then, was being replayed: Germany was too weak and too dependent on the West to think of an active intervention against Poland, but she did give Russia encouragement to try her hand again. This time, however, Russia resisted the temptation; rather, her efforts were directed toward her own economic plight.

THE GENOA-RAPALLO TANGLE

On the other hand, in view of the approaching Genoa Conference, Soviet Russia was also anxious to prevent any *rapprochement* between Germany and the Western powers. With that in mind she was determined to exploit quickly and completely Germany's bitterness against the West.

In January 1922 Radek came to Berlin secretly. The following month he was joined by two other leading Soviet communists, Leonid Krasin and Khristian Rakovsky. The three men played for high stakes. In conversation with members of the German government and of the Foreign Office they intimated that France was ready to make major concessions to Russia if the Soviet government would recognize the Versailles Treaty as binding upon Germany. "The French were even prepared 'to drop the Poles,' if Russia would help France hold Germany down," related Radek. At the same time, Radek is reported to have urged General von Seeckt to deliver military equipment to Russia as she wished "to launch an attack on Poland in the spring." [26] The German government, alarmed by the spectre of complete isolation, agreed to examine a draft treaty, which was prepared during Radek's visit, to put Soviet-German relations on a formal and more solid foundation.

At the Genoa Conference (April 10 to May 19, 1922) the Allies failed to achieve their objective of settling their economic problems with Russia. Instead, their policy accelerated the process of German-Soviet *rapprochement*. On April 16 these two powers signed the Rapallo Treaty, an event that not

[26] Freund, *op. cit.*, pp. 109, 112. D'Abernon, *op. cit.*, pp. 261–62, 273.

only affected the development of European affairs but also produced another immediate crisis between Poland and Soviet Russia. Their delegations at Genoa accused each other of having violated their respective commitments. The Polish Foreign Minister, Skirmunt, protested against the right of Russia to enter into any agreement with Germany which prejudiced the Polish claims on German reparations; Chicherin defended the sovereign position of Soviet Russia against any attempt of Polish intervention and reminded the Polish Foreign Minister of his country's obligation to cooperate at the Genoa Conference and work toward a *de jure* recognition of Russia. Skirmunt, answering the note, gave Chicherin a lesson in the meaning of terminology used in international law and diplomacy, making it clear that only a protocol had been signed in Riga on March 30—an act not binding upon the signatories.[27]

The Rapallo Treaty, which laid the foundation for German-Soviet diplomatic relations and the development of close economic cooperation, had far-reaching consequences in European politics. However, more important than its contents was "the Rapallo spirit" to which Berlin and Moscow frequently referred in years to come. It signified not only German-Soviet cooperation in East European affairs but implied also a common anti-Western attitude. As to their specific position toward Poland, Herbert von Dirksen, the first German diplomat in Warsaw in 1920, probably represented the feelings of the German Foreign Office when he testified that he "was rather enthusiastic" about Rapallo, "for [he] looked at this treaty . . . as the only means of impressing the Poles." [28]

Official Polish opinion was divided in its evaluation of the Rapallo Treaty. The Foreign Ministry, though publicly engaging in strong protests, stated in a confidential memorandum

---

[27] For the text of diplomatic notes see *Materialy Genuezskoi Konferentsii,* pp. 314–22. The Soviet delegation did not fail to keep the German delegation in Genoa informed about these diplomatic exchanges. *AA,* 1429/2945, 570501–2.

[28] Dirksen, *op. cit.,* p. 31.

that the belief that Rapallo represented any great danger to Poland was entirely unfounded. The Polish general staff, on the other hand, considered it extremely dangerous.[29]

Subsequent events left little doubt that the Rapallo Treaty had weakened Poland's position vis-à-vis her neighbors. Though no secret protocol accompanied the Treaty, as many observers at that time suspected, Rapallo soon led to an intimate exchange of views about Poland between Moscow and Berlin. To this day, the ghost of Rapallo haunts many Poles, reminding them of the fearful possibility, even under new political circumstances, of a Soviet-German understanding at the expense of Poland.

UNITY IN DIVERSITY

The Rapallo Treaty clearly revealed the direction of German foreign policy. An intensive exchange of views took place in the summer of 1922 between three leading personalities: the Prime Minister, Joseph Wirth; the Chief of Staff, General von Seeckt; and the candidate for the post of the first German Ambassador to Soviet Russia, Rantzau. They were all united in the view that the hostility between France and Germany was irreconcilable and that Germany must struggle to shake off the heavy burdens of the Versailles Treaty. They differed sharply, however, on political strategy. Wirth argued for a policy of temporization, doing only as much as necessary—seemingly to fulfill the Treaty obligations. However, when the inflation of the summer of 1922 reached catastrophic dimensions and the Ruhr was threatened with invasion, he threw his weight fully behind the policy of open cooperation with Russia. Seeckt pronounced himself as favoring a Soviet-German military al-

[29] *Ciechanowski Deposit.* A report of the Polish Ministry of Foreign Affairs, 569-T, May 25, 1922. The current Polish political literature stresses, for obvious political reasons, that Poland has no reason to be haunted by the "ghost" of Rapallo and it defends Rapallo. See Boleslaw Jaworznicki, "Rapallo i polityka rapallska," *Sprawy Miedzynarodowe* (Warsaw), VIII, No. 11, November 1955, pp. 40–50.

liance. Rantzau warned against such a step which in his opinion invited the wrath of the West, perhaps even an intervention against helpless Germany. He expressed himself as in favor principally of economic and possibly also political cooperation with Russia. The controversy between Seeckt and him led to heated arguments which were set out in memoranda written by the two men and exchanged through the office of the Prime Minister.[30]

The three statesmen were in complete accord on one subject: their hatred and contempt for Poland. Wirth, on July 24, discussing with Rantzau his eventual appointment, stated that Germany could rise to a position of great power only through close cooperation with Russia. He rejected the slogan "no more war" and added, "There is one thing I can tell you point-blank: Poland has to be destroyed. My policy is directed at this goal. . . . On this point I am in complete accord with the military, especially with General von Seeckt." [31]

Rantzau, as early as July 1920, had rejected any policy of revenge, which he had then considered "a madness," and had warned against any pact with Bolsheviks. "Break Poland down," he had written at that time, "and Bolshevik Russia stands on our border." [32] Now, however, he was "convinced" that Germany would not have lost Upper Silesia had she "previously established direct relations with Russia." [33]

As time went by, he saw in cooperation with Russia the only hope for an active German foreign policy; he hoped as well to

[30] For the text of Rantzau *Pro Memoria* of August 15, 1922, see H. Helbig, *Die Moskauer Mission des Grafen Brockdorff-Rantzau. Forschungen zur Osteuropäischen Geschichte* (Berlin, 1955), II, pp. 331ff., and Freund, *op. cit.*, pp. 130–34. For the text of Seeckt's answer, September 11, see *Seeckt Papers, Heeresarchiv*, reel 24, *stück* 213. The Soviet-German relations at the period are extensively treated in: Freund, *op. cit.*, Chapter v; Carr, *op. cit.*, III, pp. 434–39; Gatzke, *op. cit.*, pp. 569–71; Helbig, *Die Träger der Rapallo-Politik* (Göttingen: Vandenhoeck & Ruprecht, 1958).
[31] Freund, *op. cit.*, p. 129.
[32] *AA*, 1013/1690, 397295.
[33] Helbig, *Die Träger der Rapallo-Politik,* p. 104, quoting from a letter of Rantzau to Schlesinger, January 5, 1922.

be able to convince Moscow that it was in Soviet interest not to weaken Germany. "This conviction," he wrote on July 17, 1922, "must be strengthened in Moscow to the point that Russia, even without being allied with us, would march immediately should France, or her political monstrosity, Poland, attack us." [34]

However, gravely concerned with the Wirth-Seeckt idea of a German-Soviet military alliance and their bellicose attitude, Rantzau expounded, in his *Pro Memoria* of August 15, 1922, his views on the consequences of a war between Poland and Russia. Rejecting a military alliance which would throw Germany into the hands of the "unscrupulous" Soviet government, he wrote, "The policy is hopeless because, in the event of Russia attacking Poland—and this is the only serious consideration—we would be almost defenseless in the West against a French invasion.

"Even if the Russians were to succeed in overrunning Poland, we would be surrendering Germany as a battleground for the conflict between the East and the West. . . .

"If it should come to war, our leading statesmen will have to labour diligently to keep us out of the conflict. If we succeed in remaining neutral, then, in the event Poland collapses, there is a chance that we shall win back Upper Silesia and perhaps also other territories in the East that were torn away from the Reich. If the Soviet Army is defeated—which is by no means out of the question if the Polish forces are led by outstanding French staff officers—then Russia will be faced with further serious internal disruptions which would bring a change of regime well within the bounds of possibility." [35]

Eventually, as time progressed, Rantzau moved closer to Seeckt's views. He was convinced of the necessity for a close cooperation with Russia and advocated a policy of an "aggressive diplomacy" of both countries toward Poland. In 1922,

[34] *AA*, 1013/1690, 397402.
[35] Freund, *op. cit.*, pp. 133–34.

however, Seeckt still condemned Rantzau's policy as passive and defeatist. Answering Rantzau's memorandum, Seeckt wrote, "Poland is the crux of the Eastern problem. The existence of Poland is unbearable and incompatible with vital interests of Germany. She must vanish and shall vanish through her own internal weakness and through Russia—with our assistance. Poland is even more unbearable for Russia than for us; no Russian government can ever reach a settlement with Poland. With Poland falls one of the strongest pillars of the Versailles peace, the power outpost of France. To achieve this goal must be one of the most fundamental drives of German policy since it can be achieved. But it can be achieved only through Russia or with her help. Poland can never offer any advantage to Germany; not economic, as she is not capable of development, nor political, as she is France's vassal. The restoration of common boundaries between Russia and Germany is a precondition of this mutual strengthening. A Russia and Germany with 1914 boundaries should be the basis of their understanding.

"This attitude of Germany toward Poland does not need to be a timidly guarded secret. A clearly stated position can create only confidence with Russia. Poland's hostility toward Germany cannot be increased. To threaten her on both sides will in the long run increasingly affect her [Poland's] stability. Above all, however, one could hardly overestimate Germany's advantage should Poland be sure that in case she should join with France in a war against Germany she would have to face Russia. The Rapallo Treaty, which only suggested the possibility of military implications, had already favorably influenced the Polish policy." [36]

As time went by, Seeckt's views were pushed into the background. With the progressive political consolidation in Germany, his role was gradually being limited to the conduct of military affairs; and the German government, entangled in

[36] *Seeckt Papers, Heeresarchiv,* reel 24, *stück* 213.

intricate negotiations with West European powers, could no longer follow his advice of an exclusive reliance on Soviet Russia. Now it was Rantzau who took the leading role in the direction of Soviet-German relations and whose concept of diplomatic strategy toward Poland influenced, for at least two years, the thinking of the German Foreign Office.

RANTZAU

To any superficial observer, sending Rantzau to Bolshevik Moscow must have appeared to be an act of diplomatic and political folly. Coming from an old aristocratic family, he had developed a supersensitive belief in the exclusivity of his class. He abhorred what he considered the vulgarity of the masses and looked down upon all persons of low origin. He was an aristocrat not by blood alone but also in the manner of his living—artistically, intellectually, gastronomically. He enjoyed a small and scrupulously selected circle of friends whom he considered to be his equals. He did not trouble to conceal his hatreds and did not spare his criticism, even of his superiors; he excelled in sarcastic remarks and sharp verbal sorties. The unshakeable conviction of both his natural and intellectual superiority found frequent expression in arrogant outbursts. Yet, he commanded complete loyalty and even devotion from his subordinates, who were fascinated by this strange, complex personality.

Nevertheless, professionally, Rantzau was well qualified for his Moscow assignment. He had served at various diplomatic posts before the war; and during the war he was located at that important international crossroad of political currents, Copenhagen. In February 1919 he had accepted the most ungrateful task of representing defeated Germany as her Foreign Minister at the Versailles Peace Conference. There, he answered the Allies' condescending attitude with equal scorn and personified his country's traditional disdain for France.

Politically, his perceptive mind came to realize long before the war had ended that democratic reforms in Germany could not be indefinitely postponed and because he made these views known in the highest imperial circles he was disliked and suspected. To him, with its defeat, the old Germany was dead; and though he rejected everything that suggested people's rights, he decided to serve, in his own way, the Weimar Republic. He fought against those military men whose Prussian heritage sought to find in a revitalized military might a revival of Germany's glorious past. He was, on the one hand, realistic enough to be aware of the impossibility of achieving this goal as long as Germany was chained by the limitations imposed by Versailles, but on the other, he also distrusted the political talents of the military and saw that the proper road to German rehabilitation was through economic growth. Probably this was the main reason that the governmental parties agreed to his choice as Germany's representative in Soviet Russia, though even as they made their choice, these same party leaders must have sensed that his conservative and aristocratic mind despised them all, whether they were socialists, businessmen, or industrialists.

Rantzau reported from his post in Soviet Russia directly to the President, whom he recognized as the only authority above him. He tolerated the German Minister of Foreign Affairs only as an inevitable fact of political practice and whenever he disagreed with him on a serious issue (which was the case more frequently than not), he would come to Berlin for prolonged periods, attempting personally to force his opinion upon the government.

Rantzau's appointment to Moscow, the seat of a revolutionary government, must have seemed as out of place as directing a general manager of an industrial concern to join a trade union. His anti-communist views, his aristocratic manner, made him appear to defy everything for which the Soviet government stood. However, the assignment was of his own choice, for he was motivated by his grand design to bring Germany, this enforced outlaw of Western society, back to glory through cooperation with another outlaw, Soviet Russia.[37]

CHICHERIN

In Moscow Rantzau found an eager listener and congenial conversationalist in the person of the People's Commissar for Foreign Affairs, George V. Chicherin. The two statesmen were at opposite poles in their ideological outlook; yet, as men, they soon established a close relationship which over a period of six years of almost daily contact evolved, according to direct observers, into an intimate friendship.

Chicherin also came from an aristocratic family, though he could not claim as glorious a past as his German counterpart could and did. He, too, had served in the diplomatic service, though only in a minor capacity in the archives of the Czarist Foreign Ministry. However, this was only a temporary step in Chicherin's career.

In 1904 he left Russia, unable to breathe the politically suffocating atmosphere, an atmosphere repugnant to his sensitive, already socialist, mind. In Western Europe he established contact with German and other socialists and joined the Menshevik wing of the Russian Social Democratic Party. During the revolution in Russia, he joined in communist agitation in London and was promptly arrested by the police. After his return to Russia, at the beginning of 1918, he joined the Bolsheviks; Lenin, quickly recognizing his brilliant mind, his experience and contacts with the outside world, and his skill in negotiations, appointed him as People's Commissar for Foreign Affairs. He remained at this post until 1930 but exercised only nominal influence over the conduct of Soviet foreign af-

[37] The brief sketch of Count Brockdorff-Rantzau's life is based on: *The Diplomats, 1919–1939*, eds. Gordon A. Craig and Felix Gilbert (Princeton: Princeton University Press, 1953), pp. 132–48. Dirksen, *op. cit.*, pp. 48–9. Helbig, *Die Träger der Rapallo-Politik.* Gustav Hilger and A. G. Meyer, *Incompatible Allies* (New York: The Macmillan Company, 1953), pp. 84–125.

fairs. It was not until 1925 that he was admitted to the Party Central Committee, only to lose this position five years later. Other members of the Soviet diplomatic service, such as Litvinov, Karakhan, Ioffe, Rakovski, and Krestinski probably had more influence than their minister. At any rate, the Soviet foreign policy was determined by the Politburo, and Chicherin was its eloquent spokesman.

Chicherin found in Rantzau not only an equally lucid mind but also a man of similar interests. He, too, enjoyed a good conversation, a glass of old wine, the arts, and music. They were both ill and Rantzau was the only diplomat in Moscow to whom Chicherin revealed his sickness, diabetes. Chicherin gave his life to work, escaping the drudgery of politics only from time to time by shutting himself in his room and playing the music of Mozart on the piano. Much of his precious time was wasted by such petty practices as personally addressing his letters. He spent nearly every day and most of the nights in his office. In this respect he differed from Rantzau who never, during his six years in Moscow, entered the official premises of the German Embassy. Rantzau started his working day in the afternoon and stayed up long into the night, but always remained in his private quarters. Chicherin also differed from the meticulously dressed German diplomat in his shoddy appearance. He was absent-minded, fidgety and nervous, his shoulders bent; only his spirit was alert and sharp.

However, more things pulled the two men together than separated them. It was particularly their common belief in the necessity of German-Soviet cooperation which established a lasting foundation for close cooperation; it was their rejection of the League of Nations, their mutual dislike of France, their utter contempt for Poland which brought them closest together.[38]

[38] The brief sketch of Chicherin's life is based on: Craig and Gilbert, *The Diplomats, 1919–1939*, pp. 234–81. Louis Fischer, *Men and Politics* (New York: Duell, Sloan and Pearce, 1941), pp. 85–147. Louis Fischer,

RANTZAU'S FIRST EXPERIENCE

Rantzau's major objective, upon his arrival in Moscow, of course was not concerned with Poland per se; rather, it was to free Germany from the chains of the Versailles Treaty and see her re-established as a great power—within the old boundaries. To him, France was the chief obstacle on the road to his goals. He expected Russia's help in removing this obstacle but at the same time was not willing to commit his own country too closely or too far. England was, in his view, bound to lend assistance in due time and he therefore did not wish to antagonize her by overt political cooperation with Moscow, though he was in full accord with the secret military contacts.

In this broad context of Germany's policy and goals Poland figured prominently in Rantzau's mind. Here was a subject on which he thought he could reach an agreement with Soviet Russia almost without qualification. To eliminate Poland as an important power would inevitably increase Germany's political stature and weaken France's international position. Also, of course, any move against Poland would give some satisfactory expression to his contempt for the Polish nation.

It was with these thoughts in mind that this aristocrat came to Moscow in early November 1922. Diligently, and far beyond the normal limits of his diplomatic assignment, he worked for close German-Soviet relationships. It appears, however, that he tended to interpret various successful developments as his own personal successes, misunderstanding frequently the motives, tactics, and immediate goals of Soviet foreign policy.

After Rantzau had reached Moscow, he witnessed, undoubtedly with satisfaction, one of the frequent duels between the Soviet and Polish governments. On November 9, the People's Commissariat for Foreign Affairs announced that Pil-

The Soviets in World Affairs, pp. vi–xiv. George F. Kennan, *The Decision to Intervene* (Princeton: Princeton University Press, 1958), pp. 297–99. Helbig, *Die Träger der Rapallo-Politik.*

sudski had refused to receive the newly appointed Soviet Envoy, Obolenskii, and that the Soviet government was therefore giving the same treatment to the Polish representative, Roman Knoll. The two diplomats returned to their respective countries.[39]

Equally pleasing to the new German Ambassador must have been the slashing attacks on Poland delivered by delegates to the Fourth Congress of the Communist International, held in November and December 1922. Bukharin stated that Soviet Russia had grown so big "that [she was] in a position to conclude a military alliance with a bourgeois state [alluding most probably to Germany] for the purpose of destroying some other bourgeois state [meaning undoubtedly Poland] with the help of the bourgeois ally." In a debate on the consequences of the Versailles Treaty a Polish communist, Keller, pointed to "Upper Silesia, Danzig, East Galicia, Teschen and Vilna" as "new areas of conflict." Finally, the Congress carried a resolution condemning Poland which "received vast regions inhabited by populations of foreign languages. . . ." [40]

As the Comintern Congress was brought to an end, another international gathering convened in Moscow, the proceedings of which were first followed in Berlin with considerable apprehension. This was the disarmament conference, called by the Soviet government.

On June 12, 1922, M. Litvinov, the Soviet Deputy Foreign Commissar, had sent out invitations to the governments of Poland, Estonia, Latvia, and Finland to participate in a conference in Moscow on reduction of armaments. He pointed to the failure of the Genoa Conference to deal with the chief source of economic difficulties in Europe—armament—and expressed the wish of the Soviet government to reach an agree-

[39] *Vneshniaia Politika,* II, pp. 652–54.
[40] *Fourth Congress of the Communist International.* Abridged Report of Meetings held at Petrograd, Moscow, November 7–December 3, 1922 (London: Communist Party of Great Britain [n.d.]), pp. 171, 162. Kun, *op. cit.,* p. 341.

ment with Russia's neighbors in Europe. Later, Lithuania and Rumania were also extended an invitation. After a prolonged exchange of views, the conference opened December 2, 1922. Only Rumania was absent. She had made her participation dependent on Russia's recognition of the Rumanian-Soviet boundary, an act which the latter had repeatedly rejected.

At the opening session Litvinov proposed the establishment of a "precise plan for reciprocal reduction of land armed forces," whereby the existing Red army would be reduced to one quarter, i.e., to 200,000 men and the armies of the other participants to a corresponding figure. He proposed also a "financial disarmament," which would determine maximum sums for military expenditures, a liquidation of irregular military formations, and the establishment of mutual neutral zones along the frontiers.

Other delegates, except the representative of Lithuania, insisted that the "technicality" of reduction of forces must be preceded by a political agreement to give to the countries concerned a sense of security. Poland presented a draft treaty on nonaggression and arbitration, which the conference, after Litvinov had made some procedural concessions, discussed, amended, and even, with some exceptions, adopted. When it turned to the study of military disarmament, it ran into all manner of technical difficulties. During the conference, Estonia, Latvia, and Finland followed Polish leadership, while Lithuania, demonstrating on every occasion her territorial claim against the Polish Vilna, sided with Russia on most questions. It soon became apparent that any agreement was impossible, due to a feeling of deep mistrust. The neighbors of Russia could hardly attach much credibility to a Soviet desire for peace at a time when their governments were being subjected to incessant vituperation and their respective communist parties were responding to the Third International's appeals with acts of violence. They considered the conference as a continuation of Genoa, as another forum for Soviet propaganda. The Soviet government, on the other hand, professed to live in fear of an outside aggression—a mood which was not conducive to a policy of disarmament. On December 12, the conference adjourned in failure.[41]

After the conference, Rantzau reported to Berlin that to him "the Russian government's love for peace seemed quite sincere." When the Polish delegation spread the news that the Soviet government, in spite of the failure of the conference, wished to cooperate with Poland in economic affairs, Rantzau hastened to assure his government that any Soviet cooperation was entirely dependent upon a Polish understanding with Germany.[42]

Before long, Soviet-German relations and their common concern over Poland were to be put to a crucial test.

[41] *Conférence de Moscow pour la limitation des armaments* (Moscow: Édition du Commissariat du Peuple aux Affaires Étrangères, 1923).

[42] *AA*, 1425/2945, 570828; 1405, 2860, 552353-4.

CHAPTER 6

THE RUHR CRISIS

❧ ON January 11, 1923, France and Belgium, in response to German default in the payment of reparations, occupied the Ruhr. Immediately, the question arose as to what Poland's position would be. The German government was seriously concerned with the possibility of a Polish invasion of the German part of Upper Silesia or of East Prussia. Soviet Russia, expecting the occupation of the Ruhr to ignite the flames of revolution in Germany, was anxious to prevent any Polish intervention in German affairs. Moreover, always fearful that Poland, under orders from Paris, might well be willing to entertain expansionist moves against Russia, the Soviets saw in an eventual Polish march into East Prussia the clear danger of a general war against their country. It was, therefore, in the common interest of Russia and Germany to keep Poland in check during the Ruhr crisis.

THE SOVIET GAME

Even before the Ruhr was occupied, the German government had been anxious to know the Soviet attitude toward the possibility of French military action when and if Germany should stop paying reparations. On December 22, 1922, Rantzau, acting at his government's instructions, had a long conversation with Trotsky, the Commissar for War. Rantzau informed him that in the middle of January the German government would resolutely refuse to meet its obligations. He wished to know the Soviet position in such a situation. Trotsky's answer, Rantzau reported, was fully satisfactory. Though he could not recommend German armed resistance to any French military move, he did promise, "Should Poland, at the order of France, at the same time invade Silesia then under no circumstances would we look at it passively; we cannot permit it and we shall intervene." [1]

When, subsequently, the Ruhr was occupied, Russia's political action appeared to be as Trotsky had outlined it to Rantzau, though certainly with different goals in mind than those suggested to the German Ambassador. The day of the occupation, Bukharin sent an open letter to the French communist, Souvarine, in which he stated, "Should a revolution break out in Germany and should Poland attack Germany from the east, Russia would in all probability march against Poland. The workers the world over must then support the German revolution as well as Russia's war against Poland. Should bourgeois Lithuania use this opportunity to march against Poland, then a military-political agreement of Russia with Lithuania would be altogether permissible." [2]

The Soviet press now opened a vigorous campaign against the occupation of the Ruhr. Poland inevitably shared the brunt of these attacks. January 13, the All-Russian Central Executive Committee issued a statement in which Poland was once more reminded that "several regions . . . were taken away from Germany by force." [3]

In the diplomatic field, the Soviet government made it known in Warsaw that it would not regard passively any Polish intervention in the German situation. It kept the German government informed about these diplomatic moves and the German government, in return, expressed its gratification to Moscow.[4] Nevertheless, not quite everything in the Soviet attitude rang true. In diplomatic conversations Litvinov indicated his belief that Poland would not intervene and was

---

[1] *AA*, 1405/2860, 552734.
[2] *AA*, 1405/2860, 552719.
[3] Kliuchnikov and Sabanin, *op. cit.*, III, I, p. 228; see also *Izvestiia*, January 24, 1923.
[4] *AA*, 1405/2860, 552746.

somehow too optimistic about the outcome of the crisis. Trotsky had a conversation with Fridtjof Nansen, the High Commissioner of the League of Nations for Prisoners of War and Refugees, and assured him of the Soviet government's firm intent to remain peaceful. Only if Poland should attack Germany, with the obvious intent to turn against Russia later, would the Soviet Union have to react to such a direct attack. This conversation created some consternation in Berlin, where Rantzau was spending a few days to get better acquainted with the position of his government. Upon his return to Moscow, at the beginning of February, he was assured that the information about the Nansen-Trotsky conversation did in no way correspond to the truth.[5]

There is no evidence that Poland seriously planned any aggressive action against Germany during the Ruhr crisis. On the contrary, on January 18 the Polish Minister of Foreign Affairs declared in the *Sejm*'s Foreign Affairs Committee that no one had asked Poland to participate in sanctions against Germany; a few days later, on January 22, he assured the German Minister to Warsaw, Ulrich Rauscher, "that Poland [was] resolved to remain passive." He was, however, "worried about the Russian attitude." Simultaneously, the Polish Minister to Berlin declared to the German Foreign Minister "on behalf of his government that Poland will under all circumstances maintain peace and did not intend in any way to step out of her present position." He admitted, however, that "alleged Russian military preparations made the Poles very nervous" and that Rantzau's presence in Berlin was indicative of a common Soviet-German plan concerning Poland.[6]

Poland, indeed, was in no position to strike. Marshal Pilsudski had retired in protest against constant conflicts among political parties and the country was on the verge of economic collapse. General Sikorski, the new Prime Minister, in a series

---

[5] *AA*, 1405/2860, 552755, 552769; see also, Blücher, *op. cit.*, p. 173.
[6] *AA*, 1425/2945, 570834–5, 570836–7.

of public speeches pleaded for unity, for a strong Poland which would be able to defend herself against the revengeful policy of Germany and prevent the revival of Russian dreams of the acquisition of old Russian territories. The Ruhr crisis gave Germany, he asserted, an opportunity to accuse Poland of provocative actions. However, the country would remain calm and on guard, he promised.[7]

In May 1923 Marshal Foch was to pay an official visit to Poland. Both Berlin and Moscow considered the visit a symbol of French plans to provoke Germany into a war which would also drag Poland into conflict with Germany and, eventually, with Russia. Movement of Polish troops in Upper Silesia was reported and numerous telegrams from Danzig spoke about Polish preparations to annex the free city. *Izvestiia* on May 4 denounced Foch's visit as an anti-German and anti-Russian imperialist demonstration. Radek, in the presence of Rantzau, proudly proclaimed his authorship of the article. Rantzau took Radek into his confidence and suggested that "the gentlemen [the Poles] from now on be told the bitter truth. Radek immediately expressed his readiness and promised to use the Polish national holiday and Foch's visit for a sharper campaign against Poland."[8] Radek kept his word. The campaign against Poland was intensified during the spring months of 1923. No occasion was left unexploited in the effort to keep the Soviet-Polish relations tense.

At the beginning of 1923 the protracted mediatory efforts of the League of Nations to settle the Polish-Lithuanian conflict over the territory of Vilna reached a deadlock. On March

---

[7] Władyslaw Sikorski, *O Polską Politykę Państwową*. Mowy i Deklaracje (Cracow: Nakl. Krakowskiej spółki wydawniczej, 1923), pp. 23–4, 41–2, 112–13, 127. Nevertheless, it was later admitted in Polish circles that the French and Polish military laid the foundations for a plan of common operation in case of war against Germany. Hans Roos, *Polen und Europa* (Tübingen: J. B. C. Mohr, 1957), p. 6, quoting from *Polskie Siły Zbroine w drugiej woinie swiatowej* (London: Historical Commission of the Polish General Staff, 1951), pp. 112–14.

[8] *AA*, 1406/2860, 552913–4, 552922–3; 1425/2945, 570875–6, 570910.

15 the Ambassadors' Conference awarded the territory to Poland. The Lithuanian government refused to accept the verdict.

The Soviet government, which had openly supported the Lithuanian claim on Vilna since 1920, now offered its services to Poland and Lithuania as mediator. The Polish government condemned the Russian move as an intervention, incompatible with Soviet international obligations, and rejected emphatically the offer of mediation; the Lithuanian government, on the other hand, naturally favored the Soviet offer. An exchange of sharp diplomatic notes between Warsaw and Moscow ensued in which the Soviet government did not fail to stress repeatedly its grave concern over the possible consequences of the dispute; nor did it fail to keep the German Embassy informed about such steps.[9] Thus, during the Ruhr crisis Poland was kept busy on her Lithuanian border.

During this same period, Russia revived the issue of East Galicia. The Ukrainian and Russian governments addressed to Poland briskly worded protests stating that East Galicia had been occupied and annexed by Poland through violent means and that, in spite of the Riga Treaty, Russia could not remain indifferent to the fate of their fellow countrymen and of this territory.[10] These two major diplomatic steps were also accompanied by an exchange of attacks in which Warsaw insisted on the implementation of the Riga Treaty, while Moscow accused Poland of a deliberate delay in recognizing the new constitutional government of Russia (the Union of Soviet Socialist Republics) and of denying elementary rights to the Belorussian and Ukrainian peoples in Poland.[11]

All these Soviet moves were understood by Berlin as an

---

[9] For the text of the Soviet and Polish notes see Kliuchnikov and Sabanin, *op. cit.*, III, I, pp. 229–33. *AA*, 1425/2945, 570857.

[10] Kliuchnikov and Sabanin, *op. cit.*, III, I, pp. 235–37.

[11] *Godovoi otchet za 1923 g. Narodnogo Komissariata po inostrannym delam.* II S'ezdu Sovetov SSSR. Moscow, 1924, pp. 61–7. *Vneshniaia Politika*, II, pp. 804–810.

important service to German policy at a time of supreme crisis and Rantzau and the German Foreign Office expressed their gratitude to Moscow on frequent occasions. Yet, in spite of these reassuring signs of solidarity, Moscow was full of rumors about an impending political understanding between the Soviet government and Germany's chief enemies—France and Poland—rumors which Chicherin denied emphatically. Rantzau, reporting these speculations, excluded any chance of Russia and France reaching an agreement and summed up his convictions about Poland in one sentence: "The attitude of Russia towards us in the Polish question remains unalterably loyal." [12]

Rantzau seems to have failed to grasp that Soviet loyalty was and would always be dictated by Soviet national interests and ideological goals; or, at least, he misunderstood the significance and value of assurances which he received frequently from Foreign Affairs Commissar Chicherin. Facts which came to light many years later confirmed some of the rumors of the 1920's and revealed the duplicity of Soviet policy. Officially, Moscow supported the German government during the Ruhr crisis; however, it constantly fanned the flames of a communist revolution within Germany and, at the same time, secretly explored the possibility of an understanding with Poland at the expense of Germany.

During the first months of the Ruhr crisis, the Soviet government gave official support to the German government's policy. The Third International instructed the Communist Party of Germany to defend Germany against the French, even at the price of not exploiting the current explosive situation through a concerted attack on the German government.

---

[12] *AA*, 1405/2860, 552778–80, 1406/2860, 552813, 552836–7, 1425/2945, 570953. It is of interest to note that D'Abernon predicted at about the same time, in 1922, on several occasions that in ten years Russia and France would reach an understanding; France, he wrote, would abandon Poland which might join Germany. D'Abernon, *op. cit.*, II, pp. 106–107, 115.

When, however, the summer months of 1923 brought further chaos, further calamitous inflation, strikes, and the fall of the government, the Third International asked the German communist party to establish a common front with the extreme German Right against the newly formed government of Gustav Stresemann. Then, in October, the German communists formed a government with the socialists in Saxony and Thuringia, and Hamburg witnessed a communist rebellion. All these happenings were to the communists unmistakable signs of another cyclical crisis in the bourgeois world, another case of "objective conditions" for a revolutionary seizure of power. "Revolution in Germany is ripe," was the daily slogan of Soviet leaders and writers.

The paramount task now was to coordinate the activities of the Third International with Soviet diplomacy. The Third International sent to the Communist Party of Germany instructions, money, and agents; it also revitalized the activities of the Communist Party of Poland to ready its members for action when the revolution in Germany reached its peak. The Soviet government had the task of covering the illegal activities of the Comintern by maintaining correct contacts with the German government, and thus keeping open a road of retreat should the revolution fail.

Radek, the chief spokesman for the Comintern and the Soviet expert on Germany and Poland, wrote a number of articles pointing to the favorable revolutionary conditions in Germany. At the same time, he accused Poland of planning to seize East Prussia, to invade Lithuania, and even to intervene in a communist revolution in Germany. He warned the West and Poland to keep "hands off Germany." He reminded his own party, the Communist Party of the Soviet Union, of its publicly stated commitments "not to permit a German revolution to be throttled by the Entente . . ." and though he warned against overestimating the strength of other communist parties, he reasoned that "the strength of the Communist Party of Poland would be of great importance to the German revolution." [13]

Zinoviev, the chairman of the Third International, was equally prolific and eloquent in encouraging revolution and threatening "bourgeois" Poland. In September 1923, the days when the crisis in Germany was quickly moving toward its culmination, he attended the Second Congress of the Communist Party of Poland, held in Moscow. A resolution, passed by the meeting, stated that the Soviet Union would of necessity lend all its strength to a German communist revolution and that the Polish proletariat, in case of a Polish official action against the revolution, would have to "step onto the arena of historical events not only as an agent representing the interests of its own class but also as a leader and speaker for the interests of the whole nation." The resolution continued, "A lasting independence of Poland is possible only under the rule of workers and peasants, only in an alliance with the workers'-peasants' republics of Russia and Germany and other neighboring governments. Only a victorious revolution in Germany will remove once and forever the danger of the strangulation of Poland by the German *bourgeoisie*. Only the dictatorship of the proletariat in Russia protects [Poland] against the return of Czarism." [14]

As late as December 1923, when the chances of a successful revolution in Germany were very slim, Zinoviev was still convinced that it was inevitable, its importance surpassing even that of the Russian revolution. He relied on the revolutionary spirit of other communist parties to paralyze any attempts by other countries to intervene in the German revolution. Concerning Poland, he wrote, "If the more adventurous section of the Polish *bourgeoisie* decided to assume the role of the

---

[13] *Inprecorr*, Vol. 3, No. 57, August 23, 1923, pp. 612–13; No. 59, September 6, 1923, pp. 687–88; *Izvestiia*, August 31, 1923, September 4, 1923.

[14] Regula, *op. cit.*, p. 77. KPP. *Uchwały i rezolucje* (2 vols.; Warsaw: Książka i Wiedza, 1953, 1955), I, pp. 66, 73.

executioners of the German revolution, they would thereby be signing their own death warrant," and assured the German revolutionaries they had behind them "the experience—and not only the experience—of the Soviet Socialist Republics. . . ." [15]

As the German government was in possession of documents which proved Moscow's support of German communists, Ambassador Rantzau was kept busy in those critical months of the autumn of 1923, lodging vigorous protests in the Soviet Commissariat for Foreign Affairs. However, neither Radek nor Zinoviev held positions in the Soviet government; they spoke in the name of the Comintern. If necessary, the Soviet government could always say that they were not responsible to it, nor was the Soviet government responsible for their views and actions. It was Chicherin who was assigned the task of covering up the extreme attitude of the Radeks and the Zinovievs. In his role of the diplomat untainted by illegal activities against the German government (with which the Soviet Union continued to maintain close relations), he always expressed sorrow in response to the protests. Once this was done, the subversive contacts and the press campaigns continued. At an exciting meeting on December 11, 1923, between Rantzau, Radek, and Chicherin, Radek simply stated that he would not accept instructions from the Soviet government which would contradict the policy of the Third International, rather than do so, he would resign his position on the Executive Committee of the Soviet party. Chicherin tried to lessen the tense atmosphere of the meeting and explained again that the Soviet government was not responsible for the Comintern. Rantzau retorted that in German-Soviet relations there were only two possibilities, either complete and open cooperation, or no cooperation at all. He himself believed in cooperation, but to do his part, he must have both influence

[15] G. Zinoviev, "Problems of the German Revolution," *The Communist International*, No. 29, December 1923, pp. 38, 36.

with the German government (which he knew he had) and full confidence in Moscow which he must assume he had. Otherwise, he threatened, he would not stay for one more hour at his post. Radek generously conceded that the Soviet government could well work with a reactionary German government. Rantzau stayed—and Chicherin was obviously relieved.[16]

Gustav Hilger, who witnessed the critical official relations between Germany and Russia in the autumn of 1923, stated that Chicherin regarded the communist maneuvers in Germany "as a terrible personal embarrassment." To alleviate it, "he would never let [Germany] forget that Soviet-Russian declarations had prevented the Poles from invading Germany's eastern provinces." [17]

Soviet Russia was, of course, playing a risky game, formally assisting the German government on the one hand and fostering its overthrow on the other. The height of such duplicity was the Soviets' secret approach to the Polish government to find out whether it would be willing to offer its transit facilities to Russia should she support a German revolution. And the price she was willing to pay—at least according to some Polish sources—was to permit Poland to take some territory from Germany.

In October 1923 the Soviet Commissariat for Foreign Affairs sent the prominent member of its collegium, Victor Kopp, who had been very active in Berlin in the years immediately following World War I, to Warsaw to negotiate minimum Soviet plans: Polish neutrality toward events in Germany and an unhampered transit of Soviet goods through Poland.

Before going to Warsaw, Kopp stopped in the Latvian capital, Riga. According to German sources, he offered the Latvian

---

[16] *AA*, 1406/2860, 553270-2, 279-83, 292; 1425/2945, 571121-2. Gustav Hilger describes briefly the conversation of December 11, 1923 in *Incompatible Allies*, p. 125. The members of the German Embassy, Hilger among them, who were present wrote and signed a detailed memorandum about the conversation. For the text see *AA*, 3036/6698, 11754-63.

[17] Hilger and Meyer, *op. cit.*, p. 124.

government a "guarantee pact," which Latvia was ready to sign, though she wished to couple the negotiations with parallel Polish-Soviet negotiations.[18] According to the Polish sources, however, Kopp's diplomatic activities went much further. He was reported to have stated that Soviet Russia would "support morally and materially the communist uprising in Germany." He asked—indeed, it was reportedly presented as an ultimatum—that the proposed pact include a declaration of Latvian disinterest in German affairs as well as an obligation on Latvia's part to allow Russia free transit. Finally, Latvia was to sign a treaty of nonaggression with the Soviet Union.[19]

Kopp then proceeded to Kaunas; with the Lithuanian government he could speak more freely. The Lithuanian Foreign Minister revealed to the German Minister to Kaunas that, "Kopp wanted to find out the attitude of the Lithuanian government in case a communist government comes to power in Germany, and Russia then intervenes in Poland in order to establish common boundaries with a communist Germany." He added that Lithuania, in such a case, would remain neutral.[20]

Kopp reached the main city of his diplomatic mission, Warsaw, toward the end of October. Although he was presumably on an inspection trip to the Soviet Legation in the Polish capital, he used the occasion of his presence to state to the press that Soviet Russia would remain neutral toward happenings in Germany as long as Europe maintained the same attitude. However, he also made it clear that European intervention in German affairs would be understood by Russia as equivalent to an intervention in Russian affairs.

Subsequently, he met the Polish Deputy Foreign Minister, Marjan Seyda. Polish official sources disclose that the chief

[18] *AA*, 1406/2860, 553344–6.
[19] *Ciechanowski Deposit*. A *pro memoria* of the Polish Legation in London, October 26, 1923.
[20] *AA*, 1406/2860, 553295.

request made by Kopp was directed toward obtaining un-controlled and unlimited transport between the Soviet Union and Germany and that "this problem was viewed in the light of possible further political developments in Germany." The Polish government took the attitude that "the matter of transit [was] a purely economic issue from which all political factors should be eliminated." It wished to limit the question of transit to areas covered by Article 22 of the Riga Treaty, which gave Poland the right to determine the nature of such transits and excluded the transport of war materials. Poland had no intention of interfering in the affairs in Germany, declared Mr. Seyda before the *Sejm's* Committee on Foreign Affairs, but she considered a specific declaration in this respect as superfluous. And the Minister for Foreign Affairs, Roman Dmowski, added, "The purpose of Kopp's visit was other [than to negotiate a trade agreement]. Once he failed to achieve an agreement on political matters, he became in-different to other problems."

After Kopp's return, the Soviet government in an official statement blamed the Polish government for the breakdown of negotiations, accusing it of deliberate vagueness, of avoiding the real issues, and thus aggravating the already grave situa-tion in Central and East Europe. The statement made it clear that the Soviets wished to sign an agreement with Poland on mutual neutrality regarding events in Germany.[21]

Kopp's travels and visits were shrouded in mystery. Al-though Moscow created in Berlin the impression that Kopp's mission was meant to help the German government,[22] in fact his visit in Poland pursued an entirely different purpose. An official Polish memorandum, for example, stated "that in the last two months agents of the Soviet government tried to sug-

[21] For the text of the official Polish statement on Kopp's visit see Kumaniecki, *Odbudowa* . . . , pp. 728–33. For the Soviet statement see *Pravda*, November 17, 1923, Kliuchnikov and Sabanin, *op. cit.*, III, 1, pp. 291–93.

[22] *AA*, 1425/2945, 571090–1, 571076–82; 1406/2860, 553295.

gest to the Polish government an agreement relating to matters of certain developments in Germany." Accordingly, it asked for a free transport of food supplies and in return, "the Soviet government would be ready to assure the integrity of the Polish boundary." Moreover, "Poland and Russia could enlarge this agreement to permit Poland to be interested in a more particular manner in Danzig and in East Prussia while the Soviets would find their compensation in the Baltics." However, "the Soviet government would be obligated to consider any Polish intervention in German Silesia as a *casus belli*." The memorandum concluded with the statement that the "Polish government did not give any consideration to these suggestions." [23]

Louis Fischer, who was in contact with Chicherin and other Soviet leaders, adds credibility to this extraordinary testimony, though he ascribes the initiative in the planned Soviet-Polish deal to Poland, rather than to Russia. "In the latter half of 1923," writes Fischer, "Roman Knoll, the Polish chargé d'affaires in Moscow . . . came to Radek and declared that his Government would not interfere with a Communist Germany provided Poland could annex East Prussia." [24]

Before the year of 1923 came to a close, it became clear that communist revolutionary efforts in Germany were a failure. Neither the Soviet propaganda campaign, nor the money sent to German communists, nor the Comintern's agents were able to transform local agitation and disorders into revolutionary action on a national scale. If there was any marked trend in German politics it was toward the Right and

---

[23] *Ciechanowski Deposit.* An aide-memoire of the Polish Embassy in Paris, 1461/245/23, October 27, 1923.

[24] L. Fischer, *op. cit.,* I, p. 451. When in the following year rumors circulated in East European capitals about the Soviet-Polish deal, Moscow denied officially the part concerning East Prussia. *Izvestiia,* June 27, 1924. However, Kamenev had previously admitted Kopp's efforts concerning "free transit between the USSR and Central Europe" to help the German revolution. *Vtoroi S'ezd Sovetov SSSR. Stenograficheskii otchet* (Moscow: Izdanie TsIK SSSR, 1924), p. 66.

the Communist Party of Germany had no chance, in absence of direct military assistance from Soviet Russia, to seize power.

The developments which accompanied the Ruhr crisis gave Soviet leaders final proof that an era of communist revolution in Europe had come to an end, that an era of stabilization had set in; the ebb had inevitably followed the flow, as indeed communist theoreticians had always taught. This experience, however, had a profound impact on Soviet policy. Though the duplicity in officially supporting the German government while fomenting a revolution and simultaneously threatening and making overtures to Poland, were undoubtedly deliberately calculated as a division of labor between the Third International and the Soviet government, the discouraging result of these efforts left their mark on the internal struggle for leadership. Lenin was incapacitated by serious illness and such leaders as Trotsky, Zinoviev, Bukharin, and Radek were, through their public statements, compromised by the failure in Germany. However, Stalin, working cautiously but steadily toward personal victory in the Politburo's struggle for primacy, was not tainted by the collapse of communist hopes. On the contrary, he did not appear to believe in a successful revolution in Germany and emerged from the crisis with a strengthened hand. Thus, his policy of concentrating on Soviet internal problems and of establishing normal relations with the outside world at the expense of revolutionary adventures gained strength, too.

However, in the case of Germany, it was exactly this policy of good relations which suffered most from the double-dealing to which the German government was exposed during the Ruhr crisis. Soviet-German relations by the end of 1923 were severely strained and were never fully to recover. Moreover, the conduct of German foreign affairs passed into the hands of a strong man whose political strategy fundamentally differed

from that of his predecessors. The man was Gustav Stresemann.

STRESEMANN

Gustav Stresemann was a curious and complex mixture of
views and inclinations which taken by themselves would appear
to contradict each other; yet, outwardly and in practical politics
he gave the impression of a well-integrated, remarkable personality.

Born of a middle-class family of beer merchants, he carried
a grudge against the German aristocracy which would not admit him to its close circle. But in his later years he did succeed in turning not a few of them into friends and even
winning their respect.

Growing up during the last thirty years of the German Empire and witnessing its power and prestige, he was deeply impressed by its qualities and became a devout and ardent
monarchist. After the war, when the Kaiser exiled himself to
Holland, Stresemann, in January 1919, sent him a birthday
message of devotion and loyalty. However, when the Kaiser's
return to Germany clearly became impossible, he buried his
monarchist sentiments and resolutely served the Weimar Republic.

As the youngest member of the German parliament he delivered fiery speeches with chauvinistic intonations; during the
war, he identified himself with the military group advocating
an unlimited submarine warfare. He was an annexationist
and condemned any mention of Poland's independence, shar-
ing with other German nationalists a feeling of superiority
over the Slavic nations. He ridiculed Wilson's enunciation
of the principle of self-determination and denounced the idea
of the League of Nations. He was against Germany's signing
the Versailles Peace Treaty. But it was this same Stresemann
who was instrumental in reorganizing his party, the National

Liberals. Despite its former nationalistic, monarchist, expansionist nature, he changed it into the German People's Party—a party which, from 1923 until his death, was one of the solid pillars of the Weimar coalition governments. No less nationalistic than in his youth, his sentiments were nevertheless subdued by the realities of political life. As far as Poland was concerned, though he struggled incessantly for the revision of her boundaries, he was at least reconciled to her national existence.

His policy was subjected to attacks from both the radical Left and Right and not infrequently criticized by members of his own party. Against his inner convictions, he advocated Germany's close cooperation with France and her entry into the League of Nations. A conservative man, defending the interests of industry, he found the most consistent support for his foreign policy in the Social Democratic Party, whether it was in or out of the government, though its socialist program was as unacceptable to him as were his economic views to them.

Stresemann enjoyed good things in life: good company, good beer, a good cigar, good theatre. He had an enormous capacity for work, though he was the despair of the bureaucrats. Impressed by the company of devoted officials (often of aristocratic origin), by Geneva and other international conferences, and by the power of the position he occupied, he never was a true democrat given to the principle of equality. However, he was one of the few politicians of his kind who understood the value of public opinion; he wrote numerous articles (both signed and anonymous), held press conferences and used his convincing oratory to influence the great issues debated in the *Reichstag.*

A man with such a past and now in charge of German foreign policy, limited as it was by certain inexorable realities, must have had a unique capacity for adjustment. He was a Faustian figure, with "two souls dwelling in his breast." He was a realist—perhaps even an opportunist—but he never put the realization of personal goals ahead of the interests of his country. Always he kept the vision before him of a powerful Germany, free from the shackles of Versailles, once again imperial, respected and feared by the rest of the world. Among his numerous political battles, probably the most complex was his battle with the romantic and, at the same time, bitter spirit of his own nation. He found it difficult, as he himself once put it, to conduct foreign policy for a people which prayed not only for its daily bread but also for its daily illusion. He wanted ardently to turn this illusion of greatness and power into reality as time and opportunity arose.[25]

With Gustav Stresemann, German foreign policy acquired a new dimension which had remained totally unexplored by his predecessors, namely, an apparent policy of sincere reconciliation with France. Today we know this to have been not so much a new policy as a new strategy in the conduct of German foreign affairs; the goals remained unchanged.

Indeed, Stresemann differed not at all from other German statesmen or, in fact, all Germans, in his bitter convictions about the grave injustice of the Versailles Treaty. Whether it was the "guilt clause," which made Germany responsible for the outbreak of World War I, the enforced disarmament, the reparations burden, the occupation of the Rhineland, the loss of colonies, or, above all, the loss of territory in East Europe, Stresemann's goal was identical with that of all Germans: to do away with these impositions. But his policies did differ. In contrast to most other political and military figures, he intended to reach his goal, not through stubborn opposition to France, the chief guarantor of peace in Europe, or through exclusive cooperation with the Soviet Union, but rather through establishing cooperative relationships with France,

---

[25] The brief sketch of Gustav Stresemann's life is based on: Henry L. Bretton, *Stresemann and the Revision of Versailles* (Stanford: Stanford University Press, 1953). Dirksen, *op. cit.*, pp. 45–6. Annelise Thimme, *Gustav Stresemann* (Hannover: Norddeutsche Verlagsanstalt O. Goedel, 1957).

while at the same time maintaining the precious collaboration with Russia.

Therefore, he set about to accomplish several goals: to give to France a sense of security on the Rhine, to get for Germany a seat among the big powers in the League of Nations and thus acquire again a decisive role in European and world affairs. With equal determination he worked toward the broadening and deepening of German-Soviet relations, beyond those of the general intent of Rapallo, always, however, on guard against Soviet support of communist subversion and propaganda in Germany. With such formidable diplomatic weapons in her hands, Germany would then be able, he reasoned, to concentrate her efforts on her goal of first priority—Polish Upper Silesia and the Corridor.[26] Stresemann followed this policy till his death in October 1929, in spite of intense opposition from the extreme Left and Right in parliament, in spite of tremendous pressure from the Soviet Union, in spite of disagreements with General von Seeckt and certain outstanding German diplomats, the foremost among them being the Soviet oriented and anti-French Ambassador to Russia, Rantzau.

The day after Stresemann was appointed Prime Minister and Foreign Minister, August 13, 1923, Rantzau sent him a telegram from Schleswig where he was vacationing, warning against Germany's entrance into the League of Nations. Such a step, he said, would destroy present friendly relations with

---

[26] With the release of Stresemann's unedited personal papers, *Nachlass*, and of the documents of the German Foreign Office, after World War II, there has been a steady growth of literature reassessing Stresemann's policy. See *Nachlass des Reichsministers Dr. Gustav Stresemann* (Washington, D.C.: National Archives). Hans W. Gatzke, *Stresemann and the Rearmament of Germany* (Baltimore: The Johns Hopkins University Press, 1954). ———, "Von Rapallo nach Berlin: Stresemann und die deutsche Russlands Politik," *Vierteljahrshefte für Zeitgeschichte*, IV, No. 1, pp. 1–29. Zygmunt J. Gąsiorowski, "Stresemann and Poland before Locarno," *Journal of Central European Affairs*, XVIII, No. 1, pp. 25–47. ———, "Stresemann and Poland after Locarno," *Journal of Central European Affairs*, XVIII, No. 3, pp. 292–317. Helbig, *Die Träger der Rapallo Politik*.

Russia and would mean the end of any hope for a successful German policy in East Europe.[27] He defended this conviction through more than two years of strenuous negotiation, in scores of dispatches from Moscow and during his frequent visits in Berlin. However, when he discussed the problem with Chicherin or Litvinov, though he loyally advanced Stresemann's arguments, his own doubts rendered them unconvincing.

Stresemann, however, would not be deterred from his plan. After having called off the policy of passive resistance to the occupation of the Ruhr and having introduced a currency reform, he readily entered into negotiations concerning details of German reparations. In August 1924 the fruit of these negotiations, the Dawes Plan, was finally approved.

Now the ground had been prepared for Stresemann's grand design: to win the friendship of France, and to isolate Poland, thus exposing her to concerted Soviet-German pressure. However, the road to his distant goal was perilous, full of twists and unpredictable obstacles. Though his untimely death precluded the accomplishment of his goal, he did live to see the withdrawal of the Allied Control Commission from Germany, the evacuation of the Rhineland, the participation of Germany in European politics as a great power, and the weakening of Franco-Polish ties.

As early as February 1924 Stresemann had sounded out the French government concerning the possibility of some kind of guarantee for peace on the French-German border. Assuming that France would immediately tie the security of her own boundaries to that of Poland, he contemplated an arbitration treaty with Poland which would leave the boundary dispute open but would assure the Poles of Germany's peaceful intent in bringing about its change. The German Foreign Office meanwhile directed their attention to the British and French Ambassadors in Berlin, arguing that the French commitments

[27] *AA*, 1406/2860, 553189.

to Poland made a *rapprochement* with Germany difficult and aroused Soviet hostility as well. Assuming, correctly, that his efforts toward reconciliation with France would meet with Moscow's opposition and might provoke the Soviet government itself to seek closer contacts with France, Stresemann spared no effort in stating repeatedly to the Russians his intense desire to remain on the friendliest of terms with them.[28]

Then, at the beginning of May 1924, the German police searched the premises of the Soviet Trade Mission in Berlin and thus clouded Soviet-German relations; for three months all political contacts between the two countries were limited to the exchange of recriminatory notes.[29] Germany used this period for furthering negotiations with France, without keeping Russia informed of her actions.

A LOST OPPORTUNITY

It would have seemed understandable had the Soviet government attempted to strengthen its bargaining position by seeking a *rapprochement* with Poland. After all, Poland had reasons to be equally apprehensive about the possible consequences of any Franco-German friendship. However, Poland had too many irons in the fire and as a result worked none of them well. Unalterably hostile to both Germany and the Soviet Union, she opposed any improvement in either French-German or French-Soviet relations. "It is in the interests of Poland as well as in the interests of peace to oppose the growth of Soviet influence in the international field," stated a June 1924 report of the Polish Ministry of Foreign Affairs. Though the Polish government welcomed the current Soviet-German tensions, it saw in them the possibility, as a by-product, of a dangerous Soviet-French understanding. It therefore instructed its diplomatic representatives in the seven most important

---

[28] Freund, *op. cit.*, pp. 190–92. Gąsiorowski, "Stresemann and Poland before Locarno," pp. 28–31.

[29] Freund, *op. cit.*, pp. 191–200.

foreign posts systematically to inform the outside world of
the true nature of the Soviet regime in order to discourage
any thought the Western powers might have of seeking closer
cooperation with Russia.[30]

Under such circumstances neither the Soviet Union nor
Poland was able or anxious to use the temporary deterioration in German-Soviet relations to establish a better atmosphere between themselves. True, some progress was made, as
had been the case in the preceding years, in regularizing a few
less important matters, such as the signing of a railroad convention in April 1924, or the agreement, in May, for exchange
of the remaining prisoners of war; and indeed, a consular
convention was reached in July. But even these agreements
were either not fully implemented or were ratified after almost
two years of delay. More important, however, they were overshadowed by the frequent and familiar accusations concerning the treatment of minorities or attacks by armed bands.
One particular diplomatic furor accompanied a Soviet organized raid on the Polish frontier station of Stolpce on the
night of August 3, 1924. On another occasion, the Soviet
Legation in Warsaw was accused of dispensing illegal communist propaganda and six Soviet employees were asked to
leave the country. One of them was caught distributing
leaflets in Upper Silesia.

The diplomatic battle over East Galicia was revived in
August 1924. The Soviet officials continued to maintain the
thesis that the territory remained an international problem.
They put forward the rather strange theory that despite the
fact that the Soviet Union, by the terms of the Riga Treaty,
had renounced its rights to East Galicia, this did not mean
"that the fate of the people of East Galicia—seventy per cent
of whom are Ukrainians—can be indifferent to the Soviet
Ukrainians"; nor did it mean "that the Soviet government
recognized the Polish Republic's right of annexing East

[30] *Ciechanowski Deposit,* D.V. 2543/24, June 1924.

Galicia, the population of which repeatedly and in various ways expressed its opposition to its incorporation in Poland." [31] This, of course, was true, but it did not imply the wish of Ukrainians in Poland to exchange the Polish shackles for Soviet chains; nor was it plausible for the Soviet government to obviate its signature and obligations to the Riga Treaty.

Soviet diplomatic actions were accompanied by the usual salvos from the Third International. Its Fifth Congress, which was in session from June 17 to July 8, 1924, carried several resolutions aimed against Poland. One, "Against the White Terror," branded Poland as a country of mass executions without trial, "reminiscent of the worst era of the Middle Ages." Another replayed the old tune of Polish annexation of foreign territories and asked "a national separation of oppressed people in Poland." Another, on the "Upper Silesian Question," condemned the division of Upper Silesia and asked the communist parties in both parts of the territory to turn it into "a natural bridge between the maturing revolutions in Poland and Germany." Still another resolution, "On the Ukrainian Question," termed the Polish Ukraine, Subcarpathian Russia in Czechoslovakia, and Rumanian Bessarabia and Bukovina as annexed territories which had the right to independence and to join the Soviet Ukraine.[32]

In October 1924 the atmosphere between Warsaw and Moscow improved somewhat—indeed, rumors even circulated about a possible meeting between Chicherin and the Polish Foreign Minister, Skrzyński. However, it was too late for the two countries to exploit the Soviet-German impasse, for by that time Berlin and Moscow were anxious to renew their close political contacts. Berlin, of course, wished to maintain Soviet

---

[31] *Vneshniaia Politika*, vol. II, pp. 889–94, 918–21. *Godovoi otchet Narodnogo Komissariata po inostrannym delam za 1924 g. k III s'ezdu Sovetov SSSR.* Moscow, 1925, pp. 76–85.

[32] *Ve Congrès de l'Internationale communiste.* Compte rendu analytique (Paris: Librairie de l'Humanité, 1924), pp. 10, 428, 430, 432–33.

friendship, both in spite of and because of its new policy of cooperation with the West; Moscow sought to renew German contacts in order to develop all possible efforts to prevent such a development. By October 21, 1924, the German Embassy could report that, according to Litvinov, there was no thought of a meeting with the Polish Foreign Minister and that, at any rate, it would not take place without an understanding with Germany.[33] In addition, pressing economic problems in both countries contributed to the mutual desire to bury the memories of the May incident. Germany was in need of the vast Russian purchasing power, always worried that Great Britain might invade her markets; and Soviet Russia was in desperate need of German credits.

[33] *AA,* 1425/2945, 571317.

CHAPTER 7

SHIFTS IN POWER

❧ WHILE Germany negotiated with France and England
for eventual membership in the League of Nations and
the Soviet Union opened its diplomatic offensive to forestall
this step, Poland became once more an important diplomatic
battleground. All these moves heralded a new era in the European balance of power.

A PRELUDE

As a prelude to attack, the Soviet government made preliminary overtures to Germany concerning a general political
understanding with her. On September 13, 1924, the chargé
d'affaires of the German Embassy in Moscow, Radowitz, reported to Berlin that Litvinov had intimated to him Soviet desires for closer contacts with Germany, at least to the extent
of a confidential exchange of views in regard to certain individual international questions.[1] On November 4, 1924,
Chicherin repeated Litvinov's suggestion to Rantzau, who had
just returned to Moscow from a vacation.[2]

It became increasingly apparent that the Soviet government, having no alternative to a policy of cooperation with
Germany, wished to eliminate from German policy any alternative save cooperation with the Soviet Union. When, however, there was no reaction from Berlin to the Soviet proposals,
the Soviet government decided on a more devious way to
achieve its goal, a way which it hoped could always be counted
on to attract Germany. That way, of course, led through Poland.

[1] *AA*, 1407/2860, 554349–50.
[2] *AA*, 1408/2860, 554491–2, 554500.

THE POLISH BAIT

On December 4, 1924, Rantzau had a highly interesting conversation with Victor Kopp, who in the course of their remarks indicated that "an understanding" with Germany on the most important question of Poland was "urgently desirable." He wished to know, therefore, if Germany was still determined not to give up her territorial claim against Poland. The Poles, he said, had addressed to Moscow certain wishes concerning Galicia, but Russia did not intend to meet them. Indeed, if "Germany does not give up her claims on Upper Silesia and the Corridor, a common German-Russian pressure on Poland can be exercised," Kopp told him.

Rantzau assured Kopp that quite obviously Germany would never waive her claim against Poland, though he considered the use of force at the present time as hopeless, an act of "madness." Then, always worried about the possibility of a Soviet-French understanding, he expressed to Kopp the expectation that with the forthcoming arrival of the French Ambassador in Moscow the Polish question would be discussed. He therefore wanted to make it clear that Germany would regard any Soviet recognition of the Polish western boundary as an unfriendly act. Kopp replied with a counter-question. How, he asked, should Russia view Germany's entry into the League of Nations, an act which would imply her recognition of Poland's eastern boundary.

Reporting the conversation, Rantzau urged his government "to enter into a confidential exchange of views with the Soviet government particularly about the *Polish* question and to do it *before* the arrival of the French Ambassador who is expected here in about one week." [3]

A few days later, on December 13, Maltzan, on behalf of the German Foreign Office and undoubtedly at Stresemann's instruction, gave Rantzau permission to open a "confidential

[3] *AA,* 2313/4562, 154862–5.

exchange of views . . . over the Polish question." He suggested that the following line of reasoning be explored in conversations with Chicherin: "Theoretically, it is quite correct that Germany, after entering the League of Nations, will have to respect, according to Article X, the territorial integrity of Poland. However, such an obligation is in no way a guarantee, and as far as the Polish east boundary is concerned it has hardly any practical meaning. . . . The only article which in a practical sense may come into consideration for Germany is Article XVI. In this connection Germany is decided, in case of her entry into the League of Nations, to maintain her reservation that she has the right of neutrality and that she would not participate in the execution of her obligations toward the League of Nations. A recognition of the German right of neutrality would represent a strong support for Russia as it would make League of Nations' sanctions little more than an illusion. The prerequisite [for an agreement with Russia] would be, of course, that Russia would support the German position in regard to the Polish western boundary."

Maltzan further stressed that Poland's problem with her neighbors was that her boundaries extended far beyond her ethnographic lines. In this respect, he pointed out, Soviet and German interests were parallel. "I leave it to your judgment, according to the development of the conversation," concluded Maltzan, "as to whether it is opportune to mention at this moment that it is in the interests of both Germany and Russia to seek a solution of the Polish question by pushing Poland back toward her ethnographic boundary." [4] In plain language, Maltzan's instruction implied that Germany would remain neutral in case of a war between the Soviet Union and Poland and that she would refuse the League of Nations' request to apply sanctions. In addition, the two countries would act together to acquire the ethnically non-Polish territories.

[4] *AA*, 1425/2945, 571338-40.

Always eager to strengthen Soviet-German ties, particularly if they worked to the disadvantage of Poland, Rantzau, on December 20, informed Chicherin that Berlin welcomed the idea of cooperation. However, Chicherin listened to him with "a kind of nervousness." The Soviet Union, Chicherin indicated, wished continuous cooperation on all political questions, but now Berlin wanted to discuss common procedure in regard only to Poland.

Rantzau was confused by Chicherin's reaction. In bewilderment he answered that his "statement represented the answer of the German government to the precise questions which had been brought up by Kopp in a detailed conversation; Kopp had mentioned the Polish question first, and only in connection with this question had he raised that of the League of Nations." But, he added, Germany was not opposed to discussing general political questions. Obviously, Rantzau failed to understand that Kopp's remark about Poland had been meant only to lure Germany into the necessity of a broad understanding on all important problems, a development which might well prevent her from reaching a *rapprochement* with France and from entering the League.

As the tense conversation proceeded, Chicherin pointed to the disproportionate nature of the obligations which supposedly the two countries would undertake toward the Polish problem. Germany, he pointed out, promised only neutrality in regard to the Polish eastern boundary but expected from Russia active support in regard to the Polish western boundary. Rantzau now considered it opportune to follow Maltzan's suggestion and using his good judgment stated "that a solution of the Polish question on the part of Germany and Russia [lay] entirely in pushing Poland back within her ethnographic boundaries."

Chicherin was cordial to this suggestion but then belabored in detail the obligations which Germany would assume by joining the League, jeopardizing by such an act both her professed neutrality and her refusal to recognize Poland's frontiers. Both statesmen agreed to consult their respective governments on what Chicherin termed "significant differences of opinion." [5] Obviously, this diplomatic battle, of which this was only the first round, was the product of certain mutually exclusive interests: Germany planned to enter the League of Nations and Soviet Russia was determined to dissuade her from such a step. Their common desire to leave the question of Polish boundaries open and to support each other on this particular question was at this moment relegated to secondary place and used only as a weapon to achieving their major goals.

A FRONTAL ATTACK

After receiving instructions from "decisive persons" in the Soviet government, Chicherin met Rantzau on the night of December 26. He first expressed appreciation for the openness with which the German government had stated its views on the Polish question. Then, however, he began a blunt frontal attack. He stated he "would consider it desirable before entering into any consideration of the Polish question to establish a basis for an exchange of opinion over all concrete political and general questions." He did not wish this suggestion to be considered as an "ultimatum. However, should the German government decline his proposal, although present-day relations would, of course, continue to be maintained, the opinion of the Soviet government was that the treatment of the Polish question as proposed by Berlin would not be possible."

When Rantzau interjected that the suggestion "after all, came from Kopp," Chicherin calmly and undoubtedly hypocritically answered that Kopp had spoken as a private individual and had overstepped his authority. He then stated bluntly the proposal that had been at the heart of Soviet official opinion ever since Litvinov had vaguely suggested it to

[5] *AA,* 1425/2945, 571344–6.

Radowitz in the middle of September 1924; namely, that before any common front in regard to the Polish question was possible, "the German and the Russian governments [should] commit each other not to enter into any political or economic alliance or understanding with a third party which was directed against the other." Rantzau expressed the view that such an agreement was rather extreme and asked whether it would also affect Germany's entrance into the League of Nations. Chicherin's reply was that he wished to make another proposal, a proposal "which he would like to consider as another condition for the common solution of the Polish question." This proposal was that the two governments should coordinate their action toward the League of Nations; and the "ideal solution" would be to treat in concert the question of either entering the League or sending their observers to Geneva.

This was, of course, the crux of the whole dispute. Moscow wished to make Germany's entrance into the League dependent on Russia's approval. In other words, the Soviets wished to prevent it. There was no chance that Soviet Russia would join the League, that "imperialist-capitalist institution" as it was constantly called; at any rate, her application for membership would in all probability have been rejected. Moreover, the Soviet government was genuinely worried lest Germany's membership in the League expose Russia to isolation and eventually, under British and French influence, turn her friends in Berlin into enemies. Hence the stakes of Soviet diplomacy were high, indeed. Equally high were those of Germany, for her compliance with the Soviet wish not to enter the League would ruin Stresemann's basic strategy.

Both sides were aware of this clash of interests, but they ardently desired not to antagonize each other. Rantzau, therefore, in the course of further conversation tried to assuage the Soviet Commissar by suggesting a nonaggression agreement as a supplement to a general understanding. Chicherin thought such a supplement was not necessary. Rantzau, however, pointed to the experience of the preceding year, 1923, when the rumors circulated—he diplomatically blamed the Poles for spreading them—that Russia, during the revolutionary disorders in Germany, had attempted to secure for the Red army the right to march through Poland. Germany, he said, must defend herself against such eventualities.[6]

In a letter to Stresemann marked "strictly secret," Rantzau pleaded for full confidence in Chicherin who, Rantzau repeated, wished to reach an understanding with Germany on all questions before there was any agreement on the solution of the Polish question. He added that Chicherin also had promised "to make no agreements with France which would be directed against Germany if Germany would agree to assume the same position toward England." "We shall do nothing with Herbette [the French Ambassador to Moscow] if you do nothing with Chamberlain," stated Chicherin.[7] He knew that to Rantzau the possibility of a Russian-French understanding was a nightmare; yet Chicherin was equally worried that the current tense British-Soviet relations might well bring Britain closer to Germany, for, in fact, both London and Berlin desired closer contacts. As it turned out, Soviet Russia "did nothing" with France, aware as she was of France's greater interest in cooperation with Germany than with Russia. Germany, however, "did a lot" with Chamberlain who was the prime mover in the negotiations which were meant to pull Germany closer to the West and away from Russia.

The German Foreign Office was, or gave the appearance of being, puzzled by Chicherin's attitude. A few days later, on December 29, the Undersecretary of State, Karl von Schubert, telegraphed to Rantzau (and it will be well to keep in mind that the message went under his signature) that he did not "quite understand why Chicherin [took] exception to the dis-

[6] *AA*, 2313/4562, 154926–30.
[7] *Ibid.*, 154923.

cussion of the Polish question," which, after all, was posed by Kopp himself. The German government was naturally ready at any time to exchange views on general political questions, but Poland was a good place to begin as it was of equal interest to both countries. Schubert continued, "Your indication of our intent to join with Russia and push Poland back toward her ethnographic boundary corresponds with our conception. It is a general goal which, however, requires intimate and detailed negotiation. The choice of means must, of course, be left to the developments." Discussing further Soviet objection to Germany's intentions of joining the League, Schubert wished the Soviets to be assured that there was no question of Germany's participation in a war against Russia and to remember that even in 1920, when Germany was really weak, neither the Allies nor the League attempted to violate German neutrality.[8]

Obviously, the German government held fast to its determination not to make its negotiations with the West dependent on Soviet consent. Thus, although Chicherin's frontal attack had failed, the diplomatic battle was far from over.

THE TUG OF WAR

The year of 1925 saw one of the most intricate and strenuous diplomatic tugs of war in modern history. After the rejection of the Geneva Protocol, Stresemann's idea of securing the tranquility of Western Europe by a regional arrangement received new impetus. France, encouraged by England, was now more willing to negotiate with Germany. Not only would such an arrangement hopefully assure France of security against another German invasion, it would also, it was hoped, detach Germany from Russia. However, both France and Germany were fully aware that the position of Poland might prove to be a serious obstacle to an agreement. She was France's most important ally and Germany's most implacable enemy;

[8] *AA*, 1408/2860, 554677-8.

France was interested in strengthening Poland's position and Germany was equally interested in weakening it.

The Soviet Union, faced with the grave prospect of a reorientation of German foreign policy and having failed to commit Germany to cooperation through a plan of common action against Poland, now tried to achieve its goal by indicating the possibility of Soviet cooperation with Poland. Stresemann set himself to walk the tightrope. His goal was to win France without losing Russia and to undermine Poland's position at the same time.

At the beginning of 1925 Stresemann submitted to France and England a proposal for a pact. He made it clear, however, that Germany would not guarantee the present boundary with Poland and Czechoslovakia, that all she was willing to sign was an arbitration treaty with these two countries covering nonpolitical matters only. On this, as well as on subsequent occasions, to the British and French governments, before the parliament and to the press, he declared that Germany would never be reconciled with the present Polish boundary but would attempt to achieve its revision peacefully.[9]

Stresemann informed the Soviet government in a general way about his negotiations with Paris and London and was particularly anxious to demonstrate that the envisaged Western pact would not in any way affect Soviet-German relations or Germany's Eastern policy.[10] He only wished to settle first his relationships with France, then resume negotiations with Russia.[11]

However, on March 16, in a conversation with the French Ambassador, Stresemann assured him that Germany had no intention of attempting to solve the problem of Polish bound-

[9] Gustav Stresemann, *Vermächtnis* (3 vols.; Berlin: Ullstein Verlag, 1932), II, pp. 69ff.

[10] *AA*, 1408/2860, 554907–10; March 6, 1925.

[11] Gąsiorowski, "The Russian Overture to Germany of December 1924," *The Journal of Modern History*, XXX, June 1958, No. 2, pp. 110–11.

aries by war; that if there was "the danger of a war it [did] not come from [Germany] but from Russia. A consolidated Russia will hardly accept the present border and an impoverished Russia will, perhaps out of misery, seek a solution in a war," he stated.[12] The conversation leaked out. A Polish newspaper, *Rzeczpospolita,* probably adding some substantial color to it, reported that Stresemann had stated that Germany would be ready to ally herself with the West and, for the price of regaining Silesia and the Corridor, even sign an anti-Bolshevik pact with Poland. The Polish paper was engaged in a transparent maneuver to create some strain in Soviet-German relations—a development which was naturally always most welcomed in Warsaw.

The report was, of course, promptly denied by the German government.[13] On March 19 Stresemann sent a long message to the Soviet government, restating the German position, explaining that the envisaged arbitration treaty with Poland was merely a "façade" for France's benefit and in no way an obstacle to German policy toward the eastern boundary. In fact, he continued, Germany will be able, as member of the Council of the League of Nations, "to hinder any action of the League directed against Russia." He admitted that membership in the League would hamper any active German intervention "to push Poland back to her ethnographic frontiers" but reiterated that Germany would preserve neutrality toward Russia in case of a conflict with Poland.[14]

A similar diplomatic battle went on in Berlin between Stresemann and the Soviet Ambassador, Krestinski. There, the German Minister defended much more forcefully his government's policy than did his Ambassador in Moscow. Insisting on his desire to maintain friendly relations with Russia but to postpone any treaty with her until a Western

[12] Stresemann, *Vermächtnis,* II, p. 84.
[13] *AA,* 1425/2945, 571548–50, 571590, 571593.
[14] *AA,* 2313/4562, 155072, 155081, 155084.

treaty was signed, he assured Krestinski, on April 15, 1925, that Germany would never "go with Poland against Russia," that, on the contrary, she wished "to create a stable situation in the West while keeping a weather eye on developments in the East . . . and preserving . . . freedom of action there." On April 25 Stresemann assured Krestinski in a memorandum that though Germany's entry into the League would prevent her from starting a military offensive against Poland, she could, however, "never be forced to brand Russia the aggressor in the event of another Russo-Polish conflict." This was a real German service to Russia, Stresemann maintained; for it implied that Germany was in a position to prevent military sanctions from the League.[15]

Stresemann's messages to Chicherin remained unknown to the rest of the world. Though they did not satisfy the Soviet government, they did speak eloquently, however, of Stresemann's real goals in regard to Poland, of his lack of sincerity toward France, as well as of his readiness to keep in mind Soviet interests in Europe.

Meanwhile, the Soviet government issued in effect a warning to Germany that it, too, was in a position to consider a change of policy. On March 4 Chicherin sent up a trial balloon. He stated publicly that Polish-Soviet relations were of great importance to the Soviet Union. "The Polish government," he said, "has expressed a desire to reach an agreement with us." Then, invitingly, he added, "These expressions [however] of the Polish Minister are as a rule of such a nature that a little bitterness (and there is a great deal of it) spoils much sweetness." Soviet policy, he insisted, was one of peace, but regular frontier incidents and the attempts to organize a Baltic anti-Soviet bloc prevented better relations with Poland.[16]

---

[15] Freund, *op. cit.*, pp. 221, 222, quoting from Stresemann's *Nachlass*, 7129H/H147779/80.
[16] *Soiuz Sovetskikh Sotsialisticheskikh Respublik. 2. sozyv, 2. sessiia.*

Radek accompanied Chicherin's statement with the editorial, "About Polish Boundaries." He was, he said, only stating publicly what officials in some European capitals kept to themselves. Stressing Germany's refusal to recognize her frontier with Poland, he asserted that this question, in the last analysis, was a matter of power and that Poland's power position was declining while Germany was gaining in strength. France, continued Radek, was unable to give full support to Poland due to her negotiations with Germany; he concluded with the alluring remark that Russia was ready to cooperate with Poland if she seriously desired it, though not "on the grounds of cunning and illusion." [17] This time he pointedly omitted mentioning the question of the Soviet-Polish boundary which was a matter of frequent discussion between Rantzau and Chicherin.

In the wake of such statements Rantzau sent to Berlin a member of his Embassy, Andor Hencke, to convey to the German Foreign Office a message which he did not wish to put into writing. The Ambassador was dubious about the wisdom of even an arbitration treaty between Germany and Poland and expressed the opinion "that there [was] a danger of an agreement between Russia and Poland." [18]

This impression was supported by the Moscow correspondent of *Berliner Tageblatt,* Paul Scheffer, who enjoyed a privileged position of close contact with Soviet officials. One of them, Rothstein, frankly explained the improved Soviet-Polish relations as a move on the part of Russia to counterbalance French and British negotiations with Germany. "The wish to achieve some bearable relations with Poland has existed for a long period," he stated, adding—by way of not too subtle pressure—that the Soviet government was "convinced that any clarification of relations with Poland must be preceded by a

Tsentral'nyi Ispolnitel'nyi Komitet. Stenograficheskii otchet (Moscow, 1925), pp. 47-8.

[17] *Pravda,* March 8, 1925.

[18] *AA,* 2313/4562, 155052-3; March 13, 1925.

strong and lasting clarification of relations with Germany."
Scheffer did not fail to inform the Foreign Office in Berlin of
this highly confidential conversation.[19]

Then, at a session of the Third Congress of the USSR, two
delegates criticized the Soviet government's failure to implement the Riga Treaty. Chicherin, answering the criticism,
asked them to understand the Soviet foreign policy "as a
whole." The Soviet Union was for peace, he stated, and there
were also in Poland "powerful forces in favor of a stable agreement with [Russia]. . . . Our aim is to conclude a lasting
agreement with Poland." [20] This speech prompted Berlin,
toward the end of May, to send instructions to its diplomatic
representatives in Warsaw and Moscow to inquire as to
whether current trade negotiations between the Soviet Union
and Poland could be expected to lead to a broader cooperation
between them.[21]

The answers came but with some delay. Rantzau had been
in Berlin since April, expressing freely his opposition to Germany's negotiations with the West. In his absence Counselor
Hey answered the inquiry. He explained the envisaged Soviet-
Polish cooperation as a consequence of German negotiations
with France. So far, only general contact had been established
in the economic field and the process of political negotiations
would depend on the German attitude to the West. Moreover,
the report continued, the Soviet Union wished to achieve
some guarantees concerning its 1400-kilometer-long boundaries with Poland. Indeed, a few weeks ago, Chicherin was
reported to have offered the Poles a nonaggression pact but
Poland had rejected the proposal.[22]

The German Minister in Warsaw, Rauscher, answered Ber-

[19] *AA*, 2313/4562, 155063–6.
[20] *Tretii S'ezd Sovietov Soiuza SSR*. Stenograficheskii otchet (Moscow: Izdanie TsIK SSSR, 1925), pp. 83, 89.
[21] *AA*, 1426/2945, 571758.
[22] *Ibid.*, 571778–9; June 26, 1925.

lin's question on June 30.[23] Though his contacts with Polish officials were limited strictly to day-to-day business matters and did not allow him access to inside information, his answer to the Berlin inquiry reveals an analytical and logical mind. He expected some closer cooperation between Poland and Russia in trade. As to the political relations, however, he pointed to repeated border incidents, to the Soviet-organized raids into the Polish territory, espionage affairs, and finally a complete boycott of the Soviet diplomatic mission in Warsaw by Polish official circles. He maintained that a closer Russian-Polish relationship, if it did come, would amount to little more than speeches and articles. A real *rapprochement* was preconditioned by the revision of the Riga Treaty, a move which Poland could not make because it would open a host of other problems, particularly the problem of Poland's boundary with Lithuania and Germany. Any such move would create, Rauscher continued, "the ghost of a fourth partition of Poland, and the historical parallels come only too quickly to the Poles' attention." He therefore did not believe in any lasting *rapprochement* and expressed his unchanged conviction that "in spite of all the bluffing, Poland and Russia remain in a latent state of struggle which will one day explode into war." [24]

Rauscher's analysis proved correct. Poland remained deaf to Soviet overtures and Moscow, therefore, had little opportunity to play "the Polish card." Nevertheless, the Soviet government continued to gamble. Litvinov, in another attempt to exert pressure, told the German Ambassador on April 7 that he did not see "the possibility of achieving any positive results on the most important questions, such as that of the ethno-

[23] In the numerous messages concerning Germany's negotiations with France and Britain—negotiations which directly involved Poland to whom Germany was willing to offer an arbitration treaty—there is no indication that Warsaw and Berlin negotiated the arbitration proposal directly.

[24] *AA*, 2314/4562, 155517-21.

graphic boundaries of Poland," before a general agreement on policy between Germany and the Soviet Union had been reached. He repeated the argument that Germany's entry into the League would not only turn the country against Russia but would also tie her hands insofar as any revision of the Polish border was concerned. To prove this point, he handed to Rantzau a secret French document which supposedly proved that Paris and London had agreed to exclude any discussion about the revision of the Versailles boundaries, once Germany entered the League.[25] On June 2, a Soviet note was delivered to the German government repeating once more Moscow's objections to Germany's intention of joining the League and adding the warning that "the Soviet Union might be forced to seek other ways of gaining sufficient guarantees for herself." [26]

On June 13 Litvinov himself appeared in Berlin and said bluntly to Stresemann that Poland might "try to get in touch with Russia." If so, Russia could not but react to the new situation. He added that "France also might seek a *rapprochement* with Russia." [27]

Neither the Soviet pressure, nor the danger—if there really was one—of a Soviet-Polish *rapprochement* deterred Stresemann from his plan. He either did not believe in the possibility of a changed relationship between such stubborn enemies, or he reasoned that if he could not keep Poland isolated from the Soviet Union, her consequent isolation from France would be of inestimably greater value to Germany's eastern policy. This was his real goal, though at the same time he sincerely wished—when the proper time came—to re-establish himself in Moscow's good graces.

[25] *AA*, 1408/2860, 555070–4.

[26] Freund, *op. cit.*, p. 224, quoting from Stresemann's *Nachlass*, 7415H/H175580/7. The text of the notes exchanged on the subject is in Theodor Schieder, *Die Probleme des Rapallo-Vertrags* (Köln: Westdeutscher Verlag, 1956), pp. 75–91.

[27] Gąsiorowski, "Stresemann and Poland before Locarno," p. 39, quoting from *Nachlass*, 3113/7129/147856–59; see also Schieder, *op. cit.*, pp. 61–2.

As the diplomatic tug of war continued, it became clear to the participants that its result would entail significant shifts in the balance of power throughout Europe. A Soviet success would not only strengthen her international position but would also sharpen the differences between Germany and the Western European powers, with the additional advantage of strengthening the Communist Party of Germany. It would also bolster the Soviet posture toward Poland and toward the Baltic States, which the Polish government had coveted for years and had tried to bring into an alliance against the Soviet Union. Moreover, if the Soviets succeeded Germany would have to pay respectful attention to Soviet policies.

Should, however, the diplomatic struggle result in a German victory, the Soviet Union would be isolated from European politics and Germany would emerge as a central power, a key figure in a new balance of power, with freedom to lean to the East or the West as her national interests might demand. The League of Nations would provide her with a platform and a meeting place to foster her plans of revising the Treaty of Versailles, particularly her boundary with Poland.

As the battle proceeded, the issues at stake came sharply into focus; it became increasingly clear as well that Germany's strategy seemed to move steadfastly toward a successful end.

Before long, messages started to reach the German Foreign Office which could only encourage Stresemann to continue to follow his path. Whenever the French government, in connection with the negotiations on the Western pact, mentioned the need for a guarantee of the Polish-German as well as the French-German boundaries, Britain steadfastly refused even to consider such a guarantee for Poland. But now, the German Ambassador in London learned that England's views extended even further, that Austen Chamberlain had stated recently in a memorandum, presented to the cabinet, that "the German-Polish boundary in its present form, particularly in connection with the Corridor and Upper Silesia, [could not] remain as it is." [28]

France at first insisted on the same guarantees for Poland as she asked for herself, but this Stresemann resolutely refused. In various confidential statements he explained that the security treaty with the West was "above all an instrument to achieve a revision of the Eastern boundaries" and the French idea would forestall the very thing for which he was ready to sign a Western pact.[29]

However, the French attitude soon changed. The German Ambassadors in London and Paris informed Stresemann in frequent reports that there were many indications of France's retreat from her position of guarantees to Poland. To encourage this promising trend, Stresemann was careful to conceal his real reason for negotiating a security treaty with the West. In a circular telegram to German diplomatic missions, dated June 30, he acknowledged the untenability of the German boundary with Poland, but for the time being declined to pursue any active revisionist campaign. On the contrary, he instructed his diplomats to stress "that German initiative for a security pact in no way aimed at opening the question of the modification of the German eastern frontiers." In the same breath, however, he stated that he was looking forward to a situation when pressure could be exercised on Poland to make her amenable to a boundary revision; and this pressure, he maintained, could be applied particularly with Russian cooperation.[30]

Even the chief representative of the French foreign policy, Aristide Briand, indicated to Stresemann that France would not support Poland at all costs; and he offered Stresemann advice as to the method of achieving Germany's goals. On August 6 the French Foreign Minister spoke at some length

[28] *AA*, 1425/2945, 571579; March 23, 1925.
[29] Freund, *op. cit.*, p. 226.
[30] Gąsiorowski, "Stresemann and Poland before Locarno," p. 42, quoting *AA*, 2301/4556H/E149414-34.

with the German Ambassador, Leopold Hoesch, about the necessity for Germany and France to reach an agreement; otherwise, he stated, the United States and Great Britain would refuse to give them credit. If the Polish problem was the chief stumbling block, Germany would have the right to pursue, by peaceful means, a policy of attempting to secure a change of boundaries according to Article XIX of the Covenant. Briand felt "he would be lying if he suggested that there [were] at this moment any inclinations on the part of Poland to accept such modifications. Poland suffers from a psychosis which does not always create a favorable impression," he stated, and expressed further the conviction that "there will be the possibility of solving other questions" once Germany sits "as an equal partner" in the League of Nations. "Chamberlain and Beneš share this opinion and France will certainly not stand in the road of such solutions, once they offer themselves," he remarked. Then, in the light of this possibly promising development, Briand gently appealed to the Ambassador that, "Germany, therefore, may perhaps give up the phantom policy of close cooperation with Russia. Bismarck's ideas about German-Russian cooperation, as they appear to be represented by Count Brockdorff-Rantzau, have now been proved by events to be untimely. Nobody insists that Germany break up with Russia, and France herself, since she wants to treat her own relations with Russia in a cautious way, does not contemplate any hostile attitude toward the Soviet government. However, Germany should not chain herself to Russia, if she does not want to damage her own world position; nor should she forget that Russia is the carrier of bacteria which could infect the whole world and Germany first of all." [31]

Germany, under Stresemann, had no intention of chaining herself to Russia. Yet she needed Soviet cooperation to balance Western pressure and the assurance of the Soviet's support of her policy toward Poland. Stresemann, therefore, was ready—

[31] *AA*, 1406/2945, 571872–6.

now that negotiations with France were proceeding satisfactorily—to temper Soviet antagonism and meet certain Soviet demands, though much less than halfway. On the occasion of Litvinov's visit to Berlin, Stresemann suggested that in the preamble to the long-negotiated trade treaty with the Soviet Union they embody a pledge by the two signatories to maintain, in a Rapallo spirit, "a lasting friendly contact." However, he said, such declaration would be signed and made public only after the completion of Germany's negotiations with the West.[32] This proposal, however, was much too vague to interest the Soviet government. Stresemann, therefore, seemingly made another concession and expressed readiness to enter into negotiations on the basis of the Soviet proposal of December 1924.[33]

As the next step, Rantzau presented to Chicherin on July 3 a draft proposal stipulating in general terms continued friendly relations between Germany and Russia. Chicherin immediately noted that the December Soviet proposition went much further and included a mutual obligation of the partners not to enter into any economic or political combination which would be directed against either of the two powers.[34]

In another conversation with Rantzau, on July 18, Chicherin remarked scornfully that the German proposal sounded like "an introduction to a veterinary agreement" and, in turn, submitted a Soviet draft containing a neutrality declaration. He also stated that, according to the Soviet proposal, the Soviet government's obligations would in a way be greater than those of Germany as the Soviet Union "would be bound not to reach, under any circumstances, an agreement with France or Poland." Rantzau did not consider the mention of Poland as a real concession because as far as he could "recall from history, Poland, with her megalomaniac ambitions, for cen-

---

[32] Gąsiorowski, "Stresemann and Poland before Locarno," p. 40.
[33] *AA,* 1409/2860, 555357–60; June 29, 1925.
[34] *Ibid.,* 555393–5.

turies has been the most reliable reason for a common German-Russian policy." [35]

As time went by, and Stresemann's confidence in a successful outcome of his negotiations with the West grew, he felt himself ready to open negotiations with Russia in regard to a neutrality pact.[36] Immediately, the question emerged as to the neutrality position of Germany in case Russia should be involved in a war, particularly in a war with Poland. In one of his frequent sharp exchanges of views with Rantzau, Litvinov wished to know whether Germany's obligations toward the League of Nations would not be incompatible with her obligations toward Russia. When Rantzau avoided a direct answer, Litvinov stated gravely, though diplomatically, that "in such a situation it would be a question of 'priority' obligations." He expressed fear, however, that Germany might give priority consideration to the League. Rantzau answered that his government wished to avoid such a situation, to have the relations between the two countries clear, because *"clara pacta, boni amici."* [37]

The Soviet government now passed over to its last, somewhat desperate, diplomatic offensive. Again Poland was to be —or so at least it seemed—the decisive weapon. It soon proved to be ineffective. The German newspaper, *Vossische Zeitung,* reported on September 15, 1925, that, on his way to Germany, Chicherin was planning to stop in Warsaw on September 20 for two days to enter into consultations with the Polish Foreign Minister, Skrzyński. The news was followed by a report on September 18 in the distinguished daily, *Berliner Tageblatt,* "from allegedly reliable sources," that French-Soviet negotiations were nearing successful completion. Naturally enough, the German Foreign Office became nervous and asked Moscow for information because "the Soviet Embassy in Ber-

[35] *Ibid.,* 555484–5, 555494–7.
[36] *Ibid.,* 555656 ff.
[37] *Ibid.,* 555743–8; August 27, 1925.

lin had answered [its] inquiry [saying] that it [knew] nothing about Chicherin's travel plans." [38] Rantzau reassured Berlin that the newspapers' reports were "false"; that Chicherin would indeed, for reasons of health, travel to Germany, however "not through Warsaw but through Riga." [39]

Nevertheless, a few days later, September 24, Rantzau reported that Chicherin had asked him to see him "at the usual hour (1 a.m.)" and had told him that the doctors had urged him to take a cure as soon as possible. He was, therefore, to leave the next day for Germany—via Warsaw.[40] Two days later the Soviet chargé d'affaires, Brodovski, assured German Undersecretary of State Schubert that Chicherin's visit to Warsaw was "in no way of political significance." [41] Such a statement could hardly satisfy the German Foreign Office. After all, there was considerable import in the mere fact that the Soviet Commissar would even stop in the capital of Poland. On many previous occasions, members of the Soviet government, who were traveling to Germany had studiously avoided taking the shortest route—through Poland.

Rantzau appeared undisturbed by Chicherin's trip to Warsaw, even though the fact itself must have been highly embarrassing to him personally, for he had denied such a development only a few days before. While Chicherin was in Warsaw, Rantzau conveyed to Berlin that so far as he could discover, he had not been misled about the purpose of Chicherin's trip. As bitterly as he opposed German negotiations with the West, however, Rantzau used this opportunity to restate Soviet mistrust of German policy and to stress that without doubt the improved Russian-Polish relations were a by-product of these Soviet suspicions. But he concluded that there was still no reason to doubt the sincerity of the Soviet foreign policy toward Germany or the loyalty of the People's

[38] *AA,* 1426/2945, 571919; 1409/2860, 555837.
[39] *AA,* 1409/2860, 555840.
[40] *Ibid.,* 555873-5.
[41] *Ibid.,* 555876.

Commissar, who since December 1924 had urged a secret exchange of views between Berlin and Moscow.[42]

For a few days the German Foreign Office was not informed about the purpose and the success or failure of Chicherin's mysterious visit to Warsaw. Karl Radek wrote an editorial titled "Poland and the USSR" on the day of Chicherin's arrival in the Polish capital. He noted first the change in the Polish press of its treatment of the Soviet Union and reminded his readers—among whom he counted, of course, Polish officials—that Poland owed her independence to the defeat of Germany which was the result, not of the Entente victory but of the October Revolution. His distortion of the historical truth is as obvious as its purpose. It allowed Radek to proceed to state that Polish public opinion was misled in being grateful to the Entente, which, in any case, was now "no more." American interest in Poland was more or less Platonic, he continued; England was becoming less and less interested in Poland as she concentrated increasingly on cooperation with Germany to outbalance France and Russia. France, once ready to back up Poland, was, over the last few years, losing her power. Thus it was, he argued, that the very basis of former Polish foreign policy was disappearing; Poland had begun to realize the serious danger to her security and to consider a possible change of attitude toward Russia. In conclusion, he assured Poland that Russia had no hostile intentions toward her, that she did not wish nor need Polish territory. With Germany moving toward the West, "Soviet diplomacy [had] no reason whatsoever to weaken Poland." [43]

Radek's analysis of the attitude of the major Western powers toward Poland was not without foundation. She was unquestionably losing ground in the international arena as the West became increasingly eager to reach an agreement with

[42] *Ibid.*, 555883–5.
[43] *Izvestiia*, September 27, 1925. See also *Izvestiia*, September 30 and October 1, 1925.

Germany and as her own financial bankruptcy and her policy of oppression of minorities provoked both serious concern and resentment in financial and political circles. However, Radek was completely wrong in his assertion that Poland was considering a change in her attitude toward the Soviet Union. Whatever may have been the position of Poland on the shifting scales of European power politics, nothing could affect her attitude toward her perennial enemy, Russia. This, Chicherin was soon to discover for himself when he embarked upon his pilgrimage to Warsaw.

Chicherin, as the official representative of the Soviet Union, had, of course, to be considerably more careful in his approach than did the volatile Radek. When he was in Warsaw on September 28, 1925, he expressed to the press his pleasure at having personal contacts with the Polish leaders, for these would enable him to "help to remove certain misunderstandings and establish a firm base for further diplomatic conversations, which would lead toward an enduring *rapprochement*" between the two countries. He felt that "the friendly sentiments" with which the Polish government received him were "a political fact of real importance." [44]

As it later transpired, Chicherin, in confidential negotiations with the Polish government, proposed a treaty of nonaggression. The Polish government, however, always bold and sometimes shortsighted, refused.[45] It is perhaps futile to speculate what would have ensued had Poland accepted the Soviet proposal. It is probable that the Soviet Union would in any case have invaded her territory, pact or no pact, whenever the circumstances seemed propitious, as they were fourteen years later. But one may be allowed to advance the thesis that such a pact of nonaggression, signed in this period of crucial reorientation of European forces, would at least have strengthened the position of Poland toward Germany and weakened

---

[44] Degras, *Soviet Documents on Foreign Policy*, ii, pp. 55–6.
[45] Gąsiorowski, "Stresemann and Poland before Locarno," pp. 44–5.

Soviet-German relations—a development much desired by the Polish government.

A CRITICAL CONVERSATION

On the eve of Stresemann's departure for the historic Locarno Conference, where the negotiations on the security pact were to be brought to a successful conclusion, Chicherin reached Berlin. Twice the two men met for long and dramatic discussions, Chicherin striving mightily to swing Stresemann away from the West and back toward Russia. The first meeting took place on September 30, 1925; it began at 10:30 p.m. and lasted until 1:30 a.m. Stresemann, anticipating Chicherin's bold offensive, launched the conversation by voicing strong complaints against the Soviet-supported communist propaganda in Germany. Chicherin brushed the statement aside, saying that he was on vacation but would transmit Stresemann's statement to Moscow. He would, nevertheless, continue to stand on his frequently repeated statements that the Soviet government was not responsible for the Third International, the source of such propaganda. Stresemann retorted sharply that he could put small credence in the thought that the Soviet government was not responsible for comrade Zinoviev, the President of the Comintern.

Then, for a short while, the conversation took a more quiet course. Stresemann announced that he was now ready to sign the long-negotiated trade agreement with Russia. He hoped Chicherin could see in this further proof that the German government was not dilatory in its relations toward the Soviet Union and there was not a word of truth in the allegations concerning a new orientation of German foreign policy. He wanted to assure Chicherin that Germany would under no circumstances pursue an anti-Soviet policy and invited Chicherin to explain to him the reasons for Soviet complaints. Chicherin's answer brought the conversation to the point of a diplomatic explosion.

He first spoke about the Rapallo Treaty, which had developed into what was called "the Rapallo spirit," which, in turn, was to have been implemented through the development of a common Soviet-German policy. He was, therefore, at a loss to understand present German policy in seeking a Western security pact. Then, according to Stresemann's memorandum concerning the conversation, Chicherin said that, "in December of last year, Count Brockdorff-Rantzau visited him and proposed a concerted action of Russia and Germany against Poland. He [Rantzau] set forth as the goal of this Russian-German concerted action, that Poland be pushed back to her ethnographic boundary. He [Chicherin] considered this proposal of the German government of such importance that he convened immediately a session of the Russian Ministerial Council. As a result of this session there followed the [Soviet] December proposals which were based upon the idea of defining first of all exactly the relations between Russia and Germany and then to reach an agreement on mutual neutrality—in case one of the two states would be attacked—and on renouncing any mutually hostile activities. Though last December Germany had taken initiative in the question of Poland, in February she invited the Western powers to sign a security pact. Germany's answer to the Russian proposal [on a treaty of neutrality] was of such a nature that it was perhaps appropriate for a toast but not for a state treaty." [46]

Stresemann's memorandum continues, "I was so astonished over this statement of Mr. Chicherin, since I had no knowledge about a German proposal of an alliance with Russia for the partition of Poland, that I asked him twice during his statement to give me an opportunity to be better informed about what he had just said. I then called—it was already after midnight—the Undersecretary of State Schubert on the telephone and asked him if he knew anything about a German

[46] *AA*, 1409/2860, 555904.

declaration of that sort. This he resolutely denied, but he did tell me that it was Mr. Kopp who had asked Count Brockdorff-Rantzau for information as to how Germany looked at the Polish question and if it would be possible to enter into an exchange of views on Poland. It may be that Count Brockdorff-Rantzau, in his conversations, spoke about Poland's existence being justified only within her [ethnographic] boundaries but no German offer of an alliance for that purpose was ever made." [47]

After having made the telephone call, Stresemann returned to the meeting with Chicherin to express again "amazement" about his statement. Then, in an attempt to set the position straight, he relayed to him Schubert's explanation. Chicherin was now obviously on the defensive and denounced Kopp for acting without instructions. Stresemann retorted that Kopp was an official of the Foreign Affairs Commissariat and suggested "some drastic steps . . . against Mr. Kopp's highhandedness." [48] Stresemann then assured Chicherin that there was no possibility of German acceptance, at the forthcoming Locarno Conference, of the present Polish boundaries which Germany "will never recognize." [49]

The discussion then took another peaceful turn and the two statesmen spoke about the necessity of close and friendly relations between the two countries. As it was getting late and the third participant, Ambassador Krestinski, had fallen asleep, Stresemann suggested another meeting for the next day.[50] There is a human and significant quality in this vignette of the old Bolshevik, Krestinski, who in the midst of these important conversations did not mind giving way to physical exhaustion in the presence of his Foreign Minister.

When the three statesmen met again, on October 1, Stresemann resumed the offensive on the controversy about Poland

[47] *Ibid.*
[48] *Ibid.*, 555906.
[49] *Ibid.*, 555907.
[50] *Ibid.*, 555910.

and read to Chicherin from the telegram which Rantzau had sent Stresemann on December 5, 1924, concerning his conversation with Kopp. This proved that the initiative had come from the Soviet government. Stresemann then reminded Chicherin of the conversation Rantzau had had with the Soviet Foreign Affairs Commissar on December 22 (during which—as Stresemann alleged—Chicherin had failed to disavow Kopp as he had the previous day before Stresemann). "Herr Chicherin could not answer these statements with one single statement," remarks Stresemann in his memorandum.[51]

But Chicherin had his dossier handy, too. He read from a memorandum about the conversations which he had had with Rantzau on the subject of "pushing Poland back" as suggested by Baron von Maltzan. Stresemann remarked that Maltzan's statement was indicative only of the German policy toward Poland in the future. "Yesterday [Stresemann] had had the feeling that [Chicherin] was thinking of a kind of an offer of a military alliance between Germany and Russia, as he had used constantly the phrase, 'pushing back.'"[52] The fact is that these words were used first by Maltzan, Schubert, and Rantzau; but Stresemann conveniently overlooked this detail.

The next day, October 2, Stresemann left for Locarno. Chicherin thus had suffered within a few days a double diplomatic defeat. In Warsaw he had failed to convince the Poles of the usefulness of signing a nonaggression pact; in Berlin he had failed to turn the tables in his attempt to revitalize the idea of a common action against Poland.

Then, surely more as an illustration of the extreme flexibility of Soviet policy than from any realistic assessment of the situation, Chicherin moved further west. After taking a diabetic cure in Germany, in December 1925 he paid a visit to Paris. At press conferences on December 15 and 17 he ex-

---

[51] *AA*, 1409/2860, 555913. The truth of the matter is that Chicherin did disavow Kopp.
[52] *Ibid.*

pressed great satisfaction about his conversations with French statesmen. He noted a new spirit in France in regard to relations toward Russia.[53]

However, according to a report from the German Embassy in London, quoting a "reliable" source, Chicherin failed to convince Briand that Locarno would not bring France security but would rather make her dependent on England. He supposedly told Briand that "a political understanding between France and Soviet Russia, strengthened by a Russian-Polish treaty, would give France and Europe much greater security and would assure France of freedom of movement." He offered France close Russian cooperation if she gave the Soviet Union urgently needed financial assistance. He also indicated Soviet willingness to abandon "the Rapallo spirit" of friendship with Germany if an understanding with France could be achieved. It is difficult to see in Chicherin's radical proposition anything other than a last act of desperation, an attempt to extricate the Soviet Union from the isolation into which it had been forced by the Locarno Pact. According to this same report, Briand brushed aside Chicherin's remarks and insisted that Locarno was a guarantee of security and the best way to achieve European peace.[54] Thus ended in failure a series of Soviet efforts, extending over a period of almost two years, to prevent German cooperation with the West.

Germany's remarkable success at the Locarno Conference stood in direct contrast to Soviet Russia's failure. Though Germany eventually became a member of the League of Nations, she was freed from obligations to participate in a League action, or even to facilitate its action, against Soviet aggression. She avoided giving boundary guarantees to her eastern neighbors, Poland and Czechoslovakia, and the resulting treaties of French-Polish and French-Czechoslovak alliance were an insufficient substitute. Stresemann declared openly a few

---

[53] Degras, *Soviet Documents on Foreign Policy*, II, pp. 66–8.
[54] *AA*, 1410/2860, 556141–3, 556478–85, 556517–9.

days after Locarno that these treaties "defined exactly France's right to help Poland to the extent to which the League of Nations' Covenant permits it. . . . [However] they are not an alliance any more." [55] The treaties of arbitration which Germany signed with Poland and Czechoslovakia were politically ineffective and confirmed, rather than eliminated, German revisionist intentions.

Locarno gave Germany a highly strategic position in the East-West struggle. She could look toward Moscow without fearing the West's intervention; she could cast her eyes on Paris and London unafraid of estrangement from the Soviet Union. Germany would be able to cooperate with East and West, for now both needed German good will. She thus acquired that unique prerequisite of successful diplomacy, the freedom of multiple choices. The same cannot be said about her partners. As the Soviets' relations with France failed to improve and the relations with England began to deteriorate seriously, France and England became more interested in establishing friendly relations with Germany. Therefore, the Soviet Union was left with no choice save the cultivation of cooperation with Germany. Moreover, Locarno brought Germany closer to her unchangeable goal of revision of the boundaries with Poland. She could be assured of Russia's continued encouragement and, in addition, she had now weakened France's bonds with this primary target country. Germany emerged from the Locarno negotiations exactly as Stresemann had planned. This was, indeed, a unique diplomatic achievement if one does not forget the treatment she had received only a few years before from her erstwhile enemies and the limitations which the Versailles Treaty continued to impose on her military posture.

[55] Stresemann, *Vermächtnis*, II, p. 213.

PART III. 1926–1933

YEARS OF PRECARIOUS
BALANCE

CHAPTER 8

SETTING THE SCENE—3

THE Locarno Pact appeared to be a good omen for European politics for the second half of the 1920's. Germany agreed voluntarily, not under duress as in the Versailles settlement, to the *status quo* of her boundaries with France and Belgium. The deep-seated hostility between her and France seemed to have given way to a spirit of friendly co-operation and she looked forward to the promised day when the Inter-Allied Control Commission would be withdrawn from her territory and the Allied Army would leave the Rhineland. Germany entered the League of Nations in September 1926 and she was regarded in the Geneva forum as an equal.

Great Britain, through her signature of the Locarno Pact, became committed to a guarantee of peaceful policies in Western Europe and offered to both Germany and France assistance against mutual acts of aggression. While not abandoning France, a development in which the German government had put much hope, Great Britain did offer to Germany a hand of sincere friendship. France found in the Locarno Treaty a new pillar of national security accompanied as it was by a system of alliances with Poland and Czechoslovakia and of pacts with Yugoslavia and Rumania, a system which was seemingly not affected by the Locarno settlement with Germany. The League of Nations, another cornerstone of her policy, appeared to be only strengthened by the German participation.

A period of political stabilization set in, bringing high hopes for the preservation of peace in the years to come. These prospects were accompanied by economic prosperity, though in the case of Germany this was due to a considerable extent to the foreign loans which she was receiving in great sums.

When in April 1926 Germany signed a Treaty of Nonaggression with the Soviet Union, a tremor of hostile reaction occurred in some European capitals, which began to question Stresemann's sincerity; but he soon succeeded in alleviating British and French apprehensions and even developed with Aristide Briand a truly intimate friendship. The Pact of Paris, signed in August 1928, insignificant as its content was, seemed to epitomize this new climate of peace and good will. True, Stresemann had to struggle incessantly for support of his policy, for it was being subjected to vigorous attacks from German nationalists, Nazis, and communists. But he weathered all such parliamentary storms because the Social Democrats, aware of their leading role in German politics, came to his rescue in moments of crisis.

In 1928 Germany sought to reopen the question of reparations and continued to press for the evacuation of the Rhineland. After prolonged negotiations, the Young Plan, which brought to Germany new concessions in reparations, was adopted in August 1929 and by June 1930 the last Allied soldier had left the Rhineland. A new and significant step had been taken in her continuing struggle to do away with the hated Versailles Treaty.

However, at the beginning of 1929, clouds began to gather in Germany's bright skies. Economic depression first caused unemployment of two million workers; then, after the crash on the New York Stock Exchange, in October 1929, bankruptcy, closing of factories, lowering of wages, cutting off of foreign credits, and rapidly rising unemployment, all struck straight to the heart of the German democracy.

The new Chancellor, Heinrich Brüning, did little to arrest the plunge of the German economy into the abyss. Germany, now without Stresemann, had extracted from France all of the political concessions she could achieve by peaceful means.

Therefore, Brüning did not see any serious reason for a continuation of close relations with France. On the contrary, he wished to demonstrate that even with the concessions granted by the Young Plan, Germany was unable to pay reparations. And, indeed, after President Hoover, in June 1931, announced a one-year moratorium on all war debts, Germany never again met her reparations obligations.

Increasing economic chaos threw Germany into the maelstrom of political violence. Nazis and communists carried their struggle into the streets, fighting frequently side by side against the government. In the fateful elections in September 1930 the National Socialists, a previously insignificant group, elected 107 deputies—95 more than they had elected in 1928; the Communist Party of Germany gained, too, while Social Democrats and some center parties recorded losses. The government, harassed from the extreme Left and Right, ruled by decree. Democracy in Germany, never solidly entrenched, was about to die in its infancy. In July 1932 communists and Nazis achieved new election success. As governments quickly changed (from Brüning to Papen to Schleicher) and were weakened by intrigues (due both to the senility of President Hindenburg and the impotence of true democrats), the drama of German politics quickly and inexorably reached its catastrophic denouement: on June 30, 1933, Adolf Hitler became Chancellor of the German Reich.

As Germany passed through the short-lived period of peaceful construction from 1925 to 1928 and through the turmoil of abrupt changes in the period which followed, the Soviet Union underwent an equally dramatic process of reassessment of its policies. The Soviet efforts to break the ring of isolation which the Allies had thrown around Russia in the years following the October Revolution yielded only limited results. So, in 1925, the pendulum began to swing away from cooperation and back again to isolation. The Soviet-German political collaboration, which represented Moscow's principal avenue of contact with the rest of Europe, received a severe blow from Germany's adherence to the Locarno Pact and her entrance into the League. The Berlin Pact of April 1926 failed to alleviate Soviet mistrust of future German policy, even though trade continued to rise rapidly.

Relations with England deteriorated and in May 1927 were brought to a standstill after the British had discovered compromising materials at the Soviet Trade Mission and Trade Company in London. Tensions extended to vast areas of Turkey, Afghanistan, and Persia as the British regained their traditional position and Soviet influence simultaneously suffered. In China the strange combination of Kuomintang and communist cooperation, which had lasted for three years under Soviet auspices, was brought to an end and the Soviet representative, Michael Borodin, was expelled from the country.

Relations with Russia's Baltic neighbors, Latvia and Estonia, whom she tried to pull away from their self-appointed tutor, Poland, continued to be unsettled; and Poland herself continued to pursue a policy of defiance and hostility. Moreover, the prospect for communist revolutions was now nil, even though the Third International continued to appeal to working masses for violent uprisings. At its Sixth Congress in 1928 it did proclaim the end of capitalist stabilization and prophesied a new era of revolutions; but even the catastrophic depression failed to produce revolutionary zeal. On the contrary, it encouraged trends in the opposite direction—toward fascism.

It is highly questionable if Stalin really wished to see the communist parties of Europe and elsewhere lead the masses into revolutionary action. The strained relations with the outside world only occasioned a sort of self-imposed isolation. Political struggles with his opponents commanded his complete concentration on internal developments. The battle with Trotsky was reaching its climax and Stalin needed to master all elements of the Party leadership to bring about the successful liquidation of his most potent enemy. The Comintern's and Soviets' repeated proclamations that the capitalist powers were about to invade Russia were used by Stalin as a cover to eliminate opposition and as justification for asking from the Russian people supreme sacrifice as he embarked upon the long and strenuous road of industrialization and collectivization of land. For this the Soviet government needed foreign trade, credits, and technicians, not revolutions.

Completely immersed in the tasks of his first Five-Year Plan, Stalin failed to detect the significance of the Nazi movement in Germany. Acting according to the communist dictum, "the worse, the better," he expected that the decline of democracy in Germany would make her more dependent on Russia and neglected the real danger of an eventual Nazi victory. Hence, the Communist Party of Germany, acting upon Moscow's instructions, not only contributed, through acts of frequent violence, to the undermining of what remained of the Weimar Republic institutions but found in the Nazis eager accomplices. Although it was, curiously enough, through the parallel activities of these two extremes that the Weimar Republic crumbled, it was not the communists but the Nazis who emerged from the chaos and disorder as the victors.

It was not until in 1932, when Germany clearly became lost to Soviet political interests, that Stalin reconsidered the position of the Soviet Union in Europe. Since Poland and France were at that same time ready to review their own policy toward the Soviet Union, a mood of mutual understanding at last filled the air and led eventually to the signing of a French and Polish treaty of nonaggression with Russia. A shift in the balance of power resulted from these events, but it proved to be no match for the expansionist goals of Hitler's Germany.

CHAPTER 9

GERMANY ON THE MOVE

MENDING OF SOVIET-GERMAN FENCES

HAVING successfully opened at Locarno a new era in German-French relations, Stresemann now considered the situation propitious for mending fences with the Soviet Union. On October 2, 1925, the day he left for Locarno, he made it publicly known that Germany would soon sign a trade treaty with Russia. This was done October 12, 1925, while negotiations at Locarno were still in progress. Stresemann undoubtedly wished to soothe the wounds which he knew the Locarno negotiations would inflict upon Soviet-German relations; in addition, he probably also wished to demonstrate to Western negotiators not only his determination to resist any pressure to push Germany into an anti-Soviet front but also his determination to continue to cultivate good relations with Russia.

When Chicherin stopped in Berlin, toward the end of December 1925, on his way to Russia from France, Stresemann reassured him that neither Locarno nor the eventual entry of Germany into the League would change anything in Germany's relations with the Soviet Union. Moreover, he now agreed to open negotiations about a treaty of neutrality, which Russia had proposed a year before. Chicherin evidenced considerable satisfaction. While he termed it unrealistic to think about a war between Germany and Russia, "he considered a war between Russia and Poland or Rumania as altogether within the realm of possibilities" and was anxious to know Germany's stand if such a situation should develop. Stresemann did not hesitate to assure him that neither in theory nor in practice would it be possible to see Germany participating in such a war as a result of her adherence to the League.[1] This was a declaration that significantly affected Russian policy toward her two European neighbors; should Russia attack them, the League of Nations might react with economic and even military sanctions against the aggressor. These would be, however, of little practical value as Germany, the chief Soviet partner in trade and in a key strategical position toward the Soviet Union, would abstain from implementing the League's decision.

However, before a treaty of neutrality was signed, negotiations ran into several difficulties; Poland, strangely enough, was one of them. This time, instead of providing the usual stimulus for German-Russian solidarity, she became the cause of delay in the negotiations.

''EAST LOCARNO''

Poland had suffered a setback at the Locarno Conference and it was particularly painful for this proud nation to accept such a blow at the hands of her ally, France. Skrzyński, the Minister for Foreign Affairs, found the Polish *Sejm* near revolt when he presented the by-product of Locarno, the German-Polish Treaty of Arbitration, for ratification.[2] Also, very soon after the Locarno Conference, he developed plans to break the ring of isolation which Germany intended to throw around Poland. Skrzyński renewed with great intensity previous efforts to bring about a close cooperation of the Baltic States under Polish leadership; this time, however, he wished the Soviet Union to join this Baltic bloc. In addition, as the German Foreign Office "reliably established," Poland, by December of 1925, had attempted to persuade Sweden to join Finland, Poland, and Russia in a guarantee pact. These efforts were,

---

[1] *AA*, 1410/2860, 556507–16; December 22, 1925.
[2] Georges Bonnet, *De Washington au Quai d'Orsay* (Geneva: Les éditions du cheval ailé, 1946), p. 102.

however, unsuccessful, due to Swedish and Finnish opposition to the plan.[3] Poland then tried to negotiate an "East Locarno" with Russia, Latvia, and Estonia. Russia was, indeed, interested in reaching a political agreement with Poland, but she refused to enter into a regional Baltic treaty. Therefore, at the beginning of 1926 she renewed the proposal which Chicherin had advanced during his September 1925 visit in Warsaw, to sign with Poland a treaty of nonaggression and neutrality.

The Soviets, in renewing their proposal, had several goals in mind. They wanted to prevent the creation of an anti-Russian Baltic bloc, to paralyze what Moscow considered to be English anti-Soviet intrigues in Poland, to weaken the impact of Germany's joining of the anti-Soviet League of Nations, and finally, to establish peace on the Soviet-Polish border. The Soviet proposal included, in addition to the previous offer, an obligation that the signatories would not enter "into any combinations hostile to the other side." [4] This would prevent, at least legally, the Soviet Union from reaching any agreement with Germany, aimed against Poland, and at the same time, keep Poland from forming or joining an anti-Soviet bloc.

In an editorial, "Shall We Reach an Agreement with Poland?" *Izvestiia* commented on Poland's disillusionment with France since Locarno, noting that she was now left alone to face her powerful rival, Germany, and was presumably turning toward Moscow to seek an economic and even political agreement. It welcomed the alleged Polish overtures but at the same time warned against Polish attempts to establish a special position in the Baltic States.[5]

Litvinov, speaking before the Central Executive Committee of the Soviets, expressed publicly the wish for "a lasting agree-

[3] *AA*, 1426/2945, 572084.
[4] Potemkin, *op. cit.*, III, p. 358.
[5] March 5, 1926.

ment with [the] closest western neighbors, particularly with Poland. . . ." He reiterated at some length the communist notion that there would be no independent Poland had the October Revolution not succeeded in overthrowing the Czarist regime. Alluding to the grave economic situation in Poland, he tried to lure the Polish government into negotiations by pointing to the vast open Soviet market for Polish goods. But then he demonstrated the impossibility of reaching an agreement. "Unfortunately," he stated, "all our efforts to reach a lasting understanding with Poland have failed so far because of the Polish government's wish to play, so to say, the role of manager of foreign relations for all the Baltic States. . . . We do not, and are not ready to, recognize Poland's protectorate, open or hidden, over the Baltics. . . . We propose guarantee pacts with each of the Baltic States separately or with certain of them collectively." [6]

It was not only the Polish plan of creating a Baltic bloc which endangered prospects for an agreement with Russia. Poland, through a treaty of alliance signed in 1921, was an ally of Rumania, whose possession of Bessarabia so embittered Russia as to make any cooperative arrangements with the Soviet Union impossible. Just at the time the Soviet government was offering Poland a treaty of nonaggression, the Polish-Rumanian alliance came up for renewal. When the renewed treaty was published, on March 26, 1926, although its original openly anti-Soviet tone was slightly dulled, the possibility of a Polish-Soviet treaty all but disappeared.

Nor was Poland really interested in entering into a bilateral agreement with the Soviet Union. She rejected the Soviet proposal for a nonaggression treaty and, in addition, protested against the activities of the Third International. Skrzyński replying to Chicherin stated that, "if the Soviet government were free from an ideology which is followed by its leaders the

---

[6] *Tsentral'nyi ispolnitel'nyi komitet Soiuza SSR.* 3-vo sozyva zasedanie trinadtsatoe, April 24, 1926, pp. 1059, 1060, 1061.

question [of a treaty] could be discussed with a far greater success." [7] He was, of course, referring to the unabated subversive activities of the Third International. At the very time the Soviet proposal for a nonaggression treaty with Poland was being made, the Enlarged Executive Committee of the Third International had passed a resolution, pointing to the economic crisis and tense relations among nationalities in Poland as a situation ripe for revolution,[8] and Zinoviev had called upon the members of the Communist Party of Poland to prepare themselves for new responsible tasks. "If there is one land in which a direct revolutionary situation still might crystallize in a comparatively short time, that land is Poland . . . ," he exclaimed.[9]

Dmitrii Manuilsky, one of the leaders of the Third International, declared on the same occasion that, "the true function of Poland [was] to form a barrier preventing the spread of the communist idea westward. For that reason, the international proletariat must consider as its task the smashing of capitalist Poland and turning it into a Soviet Republic." [10] Little wonder that under the impact of such statements "capitalist" Poland was slow to negotiate an agreement with the Soviet Union.

GERMANY INTERVENES

Even though there was little or no chance to reconcile such Soviet-Polish differences, Germany was concerned lest their possible settlement strengthen Poland's position toward her. The German government, therefore, immediately intervened, making known to Moscow its views toward such a treaty and threatening not to sign the neutrality treaty with the Soviet Union.

After Rantzau returned to Moscow from Berlin, where he

[7] Potemkin, *op. cit.*, III, p. 358.
[8] Kun, *op. cit.*, p. 535.
[9] *Inprecorr*, Vol. 6, No. 17, March 4, 1926, p. 254.
[10] Umiastowski, *op. cit.*, p. 101.

had fought vigorously for several months against Germany's plan to join the League of Nations, he had a long conversation with Chicherin on February 3, 1926. When Chicherin told him about his experience in Paris the preceding December, Rantzau suddenly asked him if the question of Soviet guarantees of the Polish western boundary had been mentioned in the conversations. "Chicherin, who was obviously surprised by this question," reported Rantzau, "hesitatingly answered, 'No,' and after a short interval added, 'Not by France,' and after another interval, 'nor by Poland.'" This was, however, enough of an indication to alert such an ambassador as Rantzau to the fact that at least "feelers had been put out," and he reported that he would "keep this question keenly in mind." [11]

A few days later Rantzau warned Chicherin bluntly "that it [was] in the interest of German-Russian relations unconditionally necessary for Russia to abstain from guaranteeing the Polish west boundaries. . . ." [12] Chicherin assured him there was no possibility of such a guarantee. However, "less reassuring was another statement by the People's Commissar," reported Rantzau, "who stated that Russia could not avoid regularizing her relations with Poland and recognizing the Polish eastern boundary . . ." as she "wished to have peace on [her] border and wanted above anything else to prevent Poland from being used by Great Britain against the Soviet Union." [13]

In the middle of March Chicherin confided to Rantzau that Russia might negotiate with Poland a short-term treaty of nonaggression of three to five years' duration. Rantzau remarked, speaking "as a friend and without an official instruction," that it would be "extraordinarily suspicious" and reminded the Soviet Commissar of the December 1924 conversations which were based "on the common German-Russian

[11] *AA*, 1410/2860, 556691–2.
[12] *AA*, 1426/2945, 572051–2.
[13] *Ibid.*, 572108–9.

interest to push Poland back to her ethnographic boundaries."
Even a temporary arrangement would imply recognition of the
unnatural Polish boundaries by the Soviet Union, stated
Rantzau. When Chicherin remarked that no thought was given
to a guarantee of the eastern German border, which "after all
remains the main question" for Germany, Rantzau answered
that even so Germany's east border would be indirectly threatened. He could foresee that "Poland would be even more
arrogant toward Germany" if she does not need to worry for
three years about her relations with Russia, and "this will
finally lead to an untenable situation." He asked Chicherin to
proceed with extreme caution in the interest of the German-
Soviet relations. Chicherin, aware by that time of the small
chance of reaching an agreement with Poland, did not find it
difficult to assure the German Ambassador that "German-
Russian relations must in no way suffer injury," even if Russia
found it possible to gain "for a certain time the peace which
she absolutely needs toward her likeable (*sympathischen*) Polish neighbor." [14]

Stresemann now decided the time had come to take the
diplomatic offensive. On March 27 he instructed Rantzau to
convey to the Soviet government "that there could be no possible signing of a German-Russian treaty as long as [Germany]
had not an absolute certainty that Russia will not meet in any
way Poland's need for securing her eastern boundary—whether
this be through a guarantee pact, through a nonaggression
pact, or through an arbitration treaty." [15] Then he anticipated the possible Soviet argument that they were undertaking with Poland precisely what Germany had done at Locarno by signing the arbitration treaty. "Our arbitration treaty
with Poland," continued Stresemann, "is nothing else than an
inevitable consequence of the Rhine Pact. Politically speaking
the Locarno Pact does not *in toto* bring to Poland any security

[14] *AA*, 1426/2945, 572116–21 March 15, 1926.
[15] *Ibid.*, 572135.

or strengthening but rather the opposite." However, a Russian-Polish treaty would have an entirely different character. Nor was it possible for the Russians to speak about legitimate interests in attaining a temporary peace on the Polish border. The Soviet Union knew it need not worry about a surprise move from Poland in view of Germany's "well-known attitude toward Poland and Russia's armed strength." He wished to make it quite clear to the Soviet government that an agreement with Poland would be "incompatible with the basic thought of Article I" of the proposed treaty with Germany and "the whole treaty [would be] violated and treated as such." [16]

When the text of the Polish-Rumanian treaty was published, the German Foreign Office was relieved, for it saw in it an almost insurmountable obstacle to Soviet-Polish *rapprochement*. Undersecretary of State Schubert asked Rantzau to bring the "outspoken anti-Russian tendency" of the treaty to the attention of the Soviet leaders.[17] Dirksen, the head of the East European Division in the German Foreign Office, stated that "the renewal of the Polish-Rumanian alliance—even in a weakened form—[was] most useful to [Germany] as it [upheld] the old direction against Russia. As it prevented the Soviets from reaching an agreement with Poland, it also solved for Germany the dilemma of making the conclusion of [the German] treaty with Russia dependent upon the breakdown of the Russian-Polish negotiations." [18]

[16] *Ibid.*, 572136.

[17] *Ibid.*, 572141; March 31, 1926.

[18] Dirksen's letter to the Consul-General M. Schlessinger, *AA*, 2458/4829, 242242–3. The German diplomats appeared unworried about the meaning of the change in the treaty which de-emphasized its anti-Soviet implication but was this time extended to the common Polish-Rumanian defense against a German aggression as well. However, Lord D'Abernon, the alert British Ambassador in Berlin, noted the difference and wondered whether France or Italy was behind the move and what was the motive of the enlarged responsibilities which were implied in the treaty. As the German government appeared not to appreciate fully its significance, he brought it to their attention. However, he was satisfied that the Poles, having

The Soviet government expected some important gains from the treaty with Germany; after all, it was in Moscow that the idea had originated. The treaty was to redress to some extent the balance of power, which had swung in the West's favor as a result of Locarno; it was to re-establish close contacts with Berlin, which were endangered by the Locarno negotiations; it was to be a legal instrument in the hands of the People's Commissariat to exercise some influence on German foreign policy; it was to strengthen the Soviet position toward the increasingly hostile Great Britain; it still provided a basis for a mutually complementary diplomacy of pressure on Poland. With all these advantages at hand and with any Soviet-Polish treaty of nonaggression at this time made more impossible by Polish-Rumanian relations, Chicherin yielded to German demands and agreed not to recognize in any way the present Polish boundaries. Toward the end of April 1926, therefore, nothing stood in the way of a Soviet-German treaty.

Before such a treaty could be realized, however, the German Foreign Office had to do some explaining in London and Paris. The French and British governments were annoyed by the German negotiations with Russia, particularly as Germany was now at the final stage of entrance into the League of Nations; but they did not try to stop them. However, they insisted on knowing an exact interpretation of the text of the treaty and expressed displeasure with the haste with which it was to be signed. The German explanation was that postponement would have made it possible for the Russians to reach an agreement with the Poles at the expense of Germany. The possible willingness on the part of the Soviets to guarantee the Polish western boundary would make it impossible for Germany to seek a peaceful revision of that border, the

signed again an obligation to defend Rumanian Bessarabia, lost the opportunity to play the card of a Soviet-Polish agreement and thereby exercise pressure on Germany. "A Russo-Polish alliance no longer threatens," he wrote. D'Abernon, *op. cit.*, III, pp. 251, 252.

Germans argued. This argument had some weight, particularly with the British government.[19]

On April 24, 1926, Germany and the Soviet Union signed an Agreement on Neutrality and Nonaggression, the Berlin Treaty, as it became known.[20] Once again, German diplomacy could register a great success; once again, "the Polish card" had been used by both sides in the delicate negotiations leading to the treaty—by the Germans in a manifold diplomatic operation with considerable effect, by the Russians in vain. Nevertheless, the Berlin Treaty was greeted in the Soviet Union as a great success for Soviet foreign policy and a sign of the country's international strength; as a defeat of British anti-Soviet plans; as an effective move against Locarno; as a proof of close German-Soviet relations, reminiscent of the Reinsurance Treaty of 1887.[21]

In Germany, the Berlin Treaty was also greeted as a great success, as having established her balanced position between the West and the East, and as an unmistakable sign of growing German prestige. Her friendly relations with the West had not been endangered; the ties with the Soviet Union had now been solidified. Secret military cooperation with Russia received new stimulus and Poland's isolation from Russia was confirmed.

POLAND'S ECONOMIC ISOLATION

The isolation of Poland from the Soviet Union was not enough for Stresemann, however. To soften her resistance to German revisionist pressure, she was to be isolated in still other ways. Economic weapons were to serve this purpose.

---

[19] *AA*, 1411/2860, 557118, 557451–3; 1426/2945, 572149–50; 2316/4562, 157991–3.

[20] For the text, see *Soviet Treaty Series*, I, pp. 317–18.

[21] See Radek's article in *Inprecorr*, Vol. 6, No. 39, May 6, 1926, pp. 601–602; Zinoviev's speech in Moscow, published in *Inprecorr*, Vol. 6, No. 42, May 20, 1926, pp. 679–80; *Mirovoe Khoziaistvo i Mirovaia Politika*, No. 3, 1926, pp. 3–9.

German-Polish trade relations had remained unsettled since the war, despite the fact that Poland's agriculture and Germany's industrial strength were complementary and dependent to a considerable extent upon each other. In the summer of 1925 all trade contacts were suspended and the two countries engaged in a tariff war which lasted until 1934. The Polish economy was close to a breakdown. Polish finances were once again in a state of chaos; only substantial foreign loans could save the country from catastrophe. Stresemann worked energetically to prevent Poland's economic recovery. In the summer of 1925 German diplomats in London and Washington were busy counteracting Polish demands for loans by pointing out to American and British financial circles the great risks of helping a bankrupt country and by stressing that Poland's economic plight could be alleviated first of all only by Polish cooperation with Germany.[22]

The President of the *Reichsbank,* Hjalmar Schacht, had close contacts with the Western financial world. He told its representatives openly that German financial circles were ready to participate in the rehabilitation of Polish finances only if the Corridor and Upper Silesia were returned to Germany. When, on one occasion, Schacht discussed this question with Stresemann, the latter concluded his memorandum about the conversation with the remark, "He agrees fully with my slogan, 'A financial reconstruction without a political reconstruction is no reconstruction at all.' "[23]

Montagu Norman, the powerful Governor of the Bank of England, was most anxious to encourage the German policy of relating its territorial claims to the economic situation of Poland. At the beginning of April he advised the German Ambassador to Great Britain, Friedrich Sthamer, that so far he had been successful in his efforts to prevent various American and British banking houses from granting a loan to Po-

[22] *AA,* 1426/2945, 571957–8, 571959.
[23] *Ibid.,* 571973; January 5, 1926.

land. He preferred a restoration of Polish finances through the mechanism of the League of Nations, which would predicate help upon a Polish settlement of her economic and political differences with her neighbors, including the question of the Corridor and Upper Silesia.[24]

Encouraged by Norman's position, which he perhaps mistook for the attitude of the British government, Stresemann now postulated the extreme view that a peaceful solution of the boundary problem could be arrived at only after "the economic and financial catastrophe of Poland reached an extreme degree and the whole Polish organism was brought to a state of unconsciousness." Germany must, therefore, pursue the goal of delaying "Poland's financial recovery until that country becomes ripe for the settlement of the frontier question in accordance with our wishes and until our power position is adequately strengthened." [25]

Montagu Norman's power was not unlimited, however. The British government, though recognizing unofficially the German territorial claims and lending support to their peaceful pursuit, was not willing to utilize the Polish financial crisis for German political aims. The Foreign Office let it be known to Sthamer that Germany's participation in the restoration of the Polish economy would be desirable; that, however, Germany could not expect to connect this problem with a revision of the boundaries. She should not even ask for such a *junctim* and the question of frontier should be left to a later period.[26]

Even Norman now had to retreat from his previous radical position. When Schacht visited London, toward the end of May 1926, he was informed by Norman that Mr. Strong of the Federal Reserve Bank in New York was inclined to give a loan to Poland and that he himself was now in favor of separating financial problems from political problems. In spite of

[24] *Ibid.*, 572143–5; April 7, 1926.
[25] Gąsiorowski, "Stresemann and Poland after Locarno," p. 299, quoting from *AA*, 2339/4569, 168665–71.
[26] *AA*, 1426/2945, 572252. Sthamer's telegram of May 21, 1926.

Schacht's resolute defense of his position and veiled threats of Germany's continuous contacts with the Soviet Union, Norman maintained his newly adopted attitude.[27] However, the strike of coal miners in England provided the Polish government with an opportunity to escape this planned economic strangulation. Her coal found new markets, which had been served by the British, and her desperate economic situation was partly alleviated.

STRUGGLE IN THE LEAGUE OF NATIONS

Meanwhile, the League of Nations became the scene of a frantic battle between the German and Polish diplomats. In February 1926 Germany applied for membership in the League. Her permanent seat in the League's Council was assured by a previous consensus among the other permanent members. Poland, though she could not prevent this step, which inevitably would give Germany additional prestige and influence in European affairs, now worked to secure a permanent seat for herself. Germany worked as hard to prevent it. To Germany, the League of Nations and its chief organ, the Council, were to provide a platform for German attempts to secure the revision of the Versailles Treaty (most notably its discriminatory clauses on armament) and for presenting herself as the defender of German minorities in East and Central Europe, particularly in Poland. The League was swamped by ceaseless complaints from the German minority organizations in that country; and the German representatives in Geneva would now appear as legitimate advocates of their case. The League of Nations was to become a precious vehicle for exposing Poland's policy before world public opinion.

Even before the German government applied for admission to the League, its diplomatic representatives were instructed to work against Poland's attempt to receive a permanent seat

---

[27] *AA*, 1426/2945, 572263–7. Schacht's memorandum about the conversation, May 28, 1926. See also Höltje, *op. cit.*, pp. 180–84.

on the Council. As early as February 7, 1926, the German Ambassador in Paris reported that he had not been successful in his attempts to convince France not to support the Polish candidacy. France, he stated, was committed to support Poland, which had suffered a setback at Locarno. He recommended that other permanent and nonpermanent members of the Council be approached. The German Ambassador in London reported hopefully the same day that it should not be impossible to exercise influence over the opposition press. Other diplomats telegraphed to Berlin the results of their interventions.[28]

Austen Chamberlain appears to have been won over by Briand to support the Poles, but the British Ambassador to Berlin, Lord D'Abernon, was of a different view. He stated that "the argument that Germany and Poland [were] likely to compose their differences if they [were] colleagues or permanent members of the League Council [was] superficial in the extreme and [showed] little knowledge of human nature in general and Polish nature in particular." [29]

The Polish government, as anxious to receive a permanent seat as the German government was to prevent such an event, developed a campaign of its own. German diplomats reported repeated Polish hints in various capitals that a failure to obtain a permanent seat would lead to drastic changes in Poland which might result in closer cooperation between Poland and Russia.[30] Both Germany and Poland failed to achieve their objectives, however, and the matter was postponed until the fall session of the League.

Then, on September 10, 1926, Germany became a member of the League of Nations and received a permanent seat on its Council. Poland was partly compensated by a change of rules, which enabled the General Assembly to re-elect her without

---

[28] *AA*, 1426/2945, 572021–3, 572024.
[29] D'Abernon, *op. cit.*, III, p. 226.
[30] *AA*, 1426/2945, 572029ff.

interruption as a nonpermanent member of the Council. The scene was now set for Germany to pursue her major policy aim, the revision of the Versailles Treaty by way of cooperation with her Western signatories, Great Britain and France.

Stresemann used the platform of the League of Nations to turn the eyes of the international world to the delicate problem of the German minority in Poland. Minority complaints from Upper Silesia and the Corridor were pouring in to the League and the Court of International Justice in The Hague frequently had to pass judgments on their merit. There was hardly a session of the League's Council at which a complaint from the German minority in Poland was not on the agenda. These complaints found in Stresemann an ever more ardent spokesman.

The Polish government felt compelled to dissolve the German minority organization *Volksbund,* the upholder of an irredentist movement; Zaleski at the Council's session in December 1928 described the situation as intolerable and dangerous to peace. Stresemann, pounding his fist on the table, angrily called for the right of minorities to unhampered activities, to the point of expressing freely their love for Germany. This certainly bordered on open support of irredentist goals and was against the spirit and letter of the Covenant. It fitted well, however, Stresemann's policy of using such minority complaints as strategy in the achievement of a revision of the boundary.[31]

RE-ENTER PILSUDSKI

On May 12, 1926, an event of historical importance occurred in Poland. On that day, Marshal Pilsudski staged a military march on Warsaw, ousted the parliamentary regime and pressed for a new government. Living in retirement since 1923,

[31] Gąsiorowski, "Stresemann and Poland after Locarno," pp. 315–17. Stresemann, *Vermächtnis,* III, pp. 414, 425.

he had witnessed with increasing and unconcealed disgust the ineffective work of the parliamentary system and the ever-growing bankruptcy of the country's finances. On May 12, he struck. After two days of fighting—and it is reported he told his followers they were to fight Russians and not governmental troops [32]—he quickly established personal control, became first Minister of War and, from October 1926 until his death in 1935, Poland's virtual dictator. The strong man of Poland thus re-entered the scene of Polish and European politics. As one would expect, his personality and determined views were to exercise a profound influence on Polish policy. On the national scene he curtailed, step by step, the prerogatives of the parliament until, in 1930, he succeeded in establishing a one-party system, with only nominal opposition in existence. In the field of economics, he introduced some strict measures and Poland soon enjoyed a period, short as it was (only until 1930), of relative prosperity. In the international arena, Pilsudski set out to bring Poland into the circle of big powers, to make her independent from what he had always considered to be a humiliating French tutelage, to loosen her ties with the League of Nations and to establish her as the leading power in East European affairs, immune to German and Soviet pressures.

The unexpected coup not only produced lively reaction in the European chancelleries, particularly in Berlin and Moscow, but also created considerable confusion in the communist ranks. The Communist Party of Poland, or at least some of its factions, saw in the action of Pilsudski, who after all had once been a socialist, a move against the Rightists and a step toward the victory of the working class. Therefore, it gave to the coup "various degrees of critical support." [33]

A general strike led to a paralysis of transportation for all

[32] Jules Laroche, *La Pologne de Pilsudski* (Paris: Flammarion, 1953), p. 35.
[33] Ruth Fischer, *op. cit.*, p. 558.

but Pilsudski's troops, which were brought freely to the front.[34] It appears that some Polish communists even joined Pilsudski's fighting units. As Pilsudski said a few days later to the French Ambassador to Poland, Jules Laroche, they "wanted to profit from the row but he turned the machine guns against them." [35]

Stalin wasted no time in lashing out at his Polish comrades. In a speech at Tiflis, June 8, 1926, he condemned the Party's support of Pilsudski's *putsch* as a "very great error" because to him it was a struggle between two bourgeois groups in the midst of the complete disintegration in Poland.[36] Much later, toward the end of 1926, at a session of the Seventh Enlarged Plenum of the Executive Committee of the Third International, the Communist Party of Poland was accused of "the greatest mistakes of principle and opportunism . . . at the time of Pilsudski's *putsch*. As a result of these mistakes, the Party found itself temporarily in a position of submission to the petty *bourgeoisie*." [37]

Both Stalin and the Comintern were correct in their analysis of the developments in Poland. Pilsudski had been a socialist a long time ago (if indeed he had ever been a true one) and neither the Soviet Union nor Polish communists could expect from him a policy of leniency. He was primarily concerned with the practical effects of politics and, presiding over a disgruntled country and unruly population, he leaned increasingly toward a fascist pattern of government.

For the Soviet and German governments, the return of Pilsudski signified an event of major importance. Both the Soviet Union and Germany were well acquainted with his views from the time reaching back to prewar and wartime days. Though hostile to both of his major neighbors, he made a material dis-

---

[34] Dziewanowski, *op. cit.*, p. 118.
[35] Laroche, *op. cit.*, p. 41.
[36] *Inprecorr*, Vol. 6, No. 48, p. 786.
[37] Kun, *op. cit.*, p. 641. See also Dziewanowski, *op. cit.*, pp. 124–25.

tinction between them; for Russians he had nothing but contempt, for Germans he had respect.

The Soviet and German governments exchanged views on their attitudes toward the coup in Warsaw. Both governments decided, for different reasons, to keep aloof from the happenings in Poland. Germany did not expect any worsening of her relations with Poland; on the contrary, she had some reason to anticipate a trend in the opposite direction. Nevertheless, the German Foreign Office instructed its representatives abroad not to take sides but to state, on convenient occasions, that any government in Warsaw, due to the Polish mentality, would certainly remain basically anti-German.[38] In Russia the economic crisis and the fear of possible British plans against her forced the Soviets to follow a policy of nonintervention toward Poland. According to Aristide Briand, "Germany's and Russia's . . . attitude [was] peaceful. The idea prevails in Europe that Pilsudski, hostile and defiant as he is toward the Russians, will try to find an understanding with Berlin at least on economic questions and that he will meet there with a conciliatory disposition." [39]

When Rantzau met with Chicherin, they discussed the new situation in Poland at some length. Chicherin confirmed the Soviet policy of nonintervention and stressed that there was no concentration of Soviet troops on the Polish border. He stated further that Pilsudski was Great Britain's "man" and that he was basically anti-French; the influence of France in Poland was now reduced to a minimum. Pilsudski perhaps would seek a *rapprochement* with Germany, said Chicherin; however, this would not be motivated by any sympathies for Germany but by the desire to secure his rear so that he could turn against Russia.[40]

[38] *AA*, 1426/2945, 572212, 572272; 1411/2860, 557702.
[39] Laroche, *op. cit.*, p. 36, quoting Briand's telegram, May 16, 1926.
[40] *AA*, 1426/2945, 572253-4; May 16, 1926.

As subsequent events proved, Chicherin was close to the truth in his evaluation of Pilsudski's policy and plans. Before long, Pilsudski put out feelers in both directions, toward Moscow and Berlin. The two capitals reacted in different ways and without coordinating their moves. The Soviet government appeared eager to negotiate in spite of Pilsudski's notorious anti-Soviet stand; the German government, proceeding with extreme caution despite Pilsudski's feelers, indicated a desire for a settlement of German-Polish differences. As a result of these reactions, Poland became a bone of contention between the two powers, where once their mutual hatred of her had been a common tie. First unnoticed, the change signaled the beginning of a major shift in the intricate triangle relationship of the three countries.

SOVIET-POLISH MOVES AND THE GERMAN REACTION

On one occasion Pilsudski was reported to have said, "I do not wish to disquiet the Soviets; I want to live in peace with the whole world and be satisfied with the boundaries which are already too stretched and which I have to guard." [41]

At the beginning of August 1926 the Polish Minister of Foreign Affairs, Zaleski, suggested that he pay a visit to Moscow to return Chicherin's visit to Warsaw in September 1925. The Soviet government answered that Chicherin was ill and suggested instead that a treaty of nonaggression and neutrality should be negotiated and signed on the occasion of Zaleski's visit at a later date.[42] However, nothing came from this exchange of views since Warsaw continued to insist on a regional arrangement which would include the Baltic States and Moscow was still equally insistent on bilateral treaties. Poland wished to establish herself as the political leader of the area; Russia intended to deal with individual countries one by

---

[41] Laroche, *op. cit.*, p. 60.
[42] *Vneshniaia Politika,* III, p. 76.

one.[43] The basic attitudes remained, therefore, unreconciled.

Nevertheless, even such an attempt to negotiate with Poland provoked a critical reaction in Berlin; the Germans feared any improvement in the Soviet-Polish relations which might make Poland better able to resist German revisionist goals. The Soviet chargé d'affaires in Germany, Brodovski, disclosed gently to Schubert on August 24 that negotiations on a Polish-Soviet pact of nonaggression were underway. He stated that Russia did not expect the Poles to accept the Soviet proposal and that, at any rate, it would not affect in any way the Soviet intention to cooperate with Germany; "the Russian proposal to Poland has a pronounced propaganda character," added Brodovski.[44]

Schubert's reaction was at first mildly critical. But four days later, when he met Brodovski again, he was "astonished that the Russians had not made contact with [Germany] before they made the proposal to Poland." While not raising an official complaint or a protest, Schubert, however, considered the proposal to go against the Berlin Treaty. He added that it would stiffen Poland's back and that, in fact, this had already happened through the very act of the Soviet's expression of readiness to sign such a treaty. Brodovski was immediately thrown on the defensive and only repeated that "the Russian proposal [had] all through a character of a provocation and that [was] . . . its only purpose." [45] Such indignation by the German Foreign Ministry over the Soviet move was, however, only pretense. Dirksen telegraphed to the German Embassy in London August 30, "For your confidential information I add that we do not believe in the success of Polish-Russian negotiations; Poland takes a stand which is unacceptable to Russia on the question of the Baltic States." [46]

The following day the German Minister to Warsaw,

[43] L. Fischer, *op. cit.*, ii, pp. 720–21.
[44] *AA*, 2317/4562, 157810–4.
[45] *Ibid.*, 157818–22; August 28, 1926.
[46] *AA*, 1426/2945, 572382.

Rauscher, confirmed the correctness of Berlin's analysis of the situation. He had seen the Polish Undersecretary of State, Knoll, who had told him that Poland was not interested in the Soviet offer. Ridiculing it, he said that Poland knew "the Russians well enough to be aware of how they waged only 'defensive' wars. The whole thing is a bluff and a proof of Russian double-crossing." [47]

Nevertheless, there is evidence that both the Soviet Union and Poland did have some serious interest in exploring further the possibilities of settling their political relations. Zaleski, at the beginning of January 1927, spoke on two occasions about Polish-Soviet relations and indicated Polish desire for their improvement.[48] The newly appointed Polish Minister to the Soviet Union, S. Patek, made a similar statement to the Soviet press and created among the members of the Moscow diplomatic corps the impression that he had been entrusted with the mission of bringing about an understanding with Russia. The Soviet press responded positively; yet it also stressed that improvement in economic and cultural relations must be preceded by the establishment of a sound political foundation.[49]

On the Soviet side, Zinoviev explained in a memorandum, which was "most secret, in three copies only," the Soviet need for negotiations with Poland "in the light of the deterioration of the international position of the USSR." Suspecting that Great Britain was organizing a united action against the Soviet Union, he pleaded for the traditional communist policy of exploiting the contradictions that could always be found in the capitalist world. In this case, he asked for an agreement with France as well as a new agreement with Germany. In com-

---

[47] *AA,* 3036/6698, 111787.

[48] See his statement before the Foreign Affairs Committee of the *Sejm,* January 4, 1927 and before the Research Institute of International Affairs, January 9, 1927. August Zaleski, *Przemowy i deklaracje* (2 vols.; Warsaw: 1929, 1931), I, pp. 50–1, 63.

[49] *Izvestiia,* March 1, April 3, 1927.

plete contradiction to the official views as represented by Chicherin, he stated, "We must support the trend toward a French-German understanding, minimizing thereby the danger of Polish aggression. We must pursue a systematic struggle for a settlement with the Polish *bourgeoisie*. We must pass over from buying seasonal goods from Poland to a systematic support of economic relations with Poland."

Pointing again to the gravity of the Soviet international situation, Zinoviev asked the Central Committee of the Party to take such appropriate measures as: "(1) Along the *Narkomindel* line: It is indispensable to adopt a series of steps in Japan, France, Germany, Poland and in the Balkans. (2) Along the Comintern line: Immediate preparation of conspiratorial work of communist parties and awareness of the seriousness of the situation." [50] As an old Bolshevik leader, Zinoviev felt perfectly justified in recommending such a policy: official cooperation with Poland and, at the same time, a conspiracy against her government.

However, basic disagreement persisted, as can be seen in a speech delivered by Rykov, the Chairman of the Council of People's Commissars, on April 18, 1927, before the Soviet Congress. He acknowledged the Polish gestures of signing a treaty with the Soviet Union but rejected, as had been done several times before, Poland's plan of posing as "the guardian of all the Baltic States and of trying to erect from Rumania to Finland an unbroken chain of states" which would negotiate with Russia through Poland only.[51]

In spite of the futility of the Soviet-Polish negotiations,

[50] *Trotsky Archives, Nabrosok o zadachakh nashei vneshnei politiki pered litsom ukhudsheniia mezhdunarodnogo polozheniia SSSR;* written probably at the beginning of 1927.

[51] Soiuz Sovetskikh Sotsialisticheskikh Respublik. *4 S'ezd Sovetov SSR.* Stenograficheskii otchet (Moscow: Izdanie TsIK Soiuza SSR, 1927), p. 26. In the 1938 trials Rykov, among others, was accused of cooperating secretly with Polish reactionaries and receiving orders from the Polish Intelligence Service. See *Report of Court Proceedings in the Case of the Anti-Soviet "Bloc of Rights and Trotskyites,"* March 2–13, 1938 (Moscow: People's Commissariat of Justice of the U.S.S.R., 1938), pp. 68ff, 193ff.

Berlin nevertheless continued to watch any sign of *rapprochement* with misgivings. When *Pravda* indicated at the beginning of January 1927 the possibility of an understanding with Poland, Stresemann immediately pointed out to the Soviet Ambassador, Krestinski, that this was in contradiction to Chicherin's assurances. Krestinski answered in the now familiar manner that *Pravda* had no official character.[52] In Moscow Ambassador Rantzau watched with keen interest and concern the moves of the new Polish Envoy, Patek. He was confidentially informed that at Patek's request, submitted immediately after his arrival, the Soviet press was given instructions to discontinue attacks on Poland. When he met Patek at the first formal acquaintance visit, he did not fail to indicate to him his contemptuous attitude and later told Litvinov about this first contact with malicious satisfaction.[53]

When in the spring of 1927 contacts were resumed between Warsaw and Moscow to investigate again the possibility of signing a nonaggression pact, Rantzau nervously pressed Litvinov for information about it. He was assured that not only had no progress been made but that neither side viewed the negotiations in earnest and that these were only tactical maneuvers.[54]

---

[52] *AA*, 1427/2945, 572506–7; Stresemann's memorandum, January 5, 1927.

[53] *Ibid.*, 572558–60; January 31, 1927. When, a few weeks later in February 1927, the inexperienced Patek committed a grave sin against basic rules of diplomatic protocol by not inviting Rantzau, the *doyen* of the diplomatic corps, to one of the formal dinners, the German Ambassador raged and insisted that the Polish Minister must apologize. He refused to accept an apology made through Patek's secretary and went so far as to make him rewrite a personal letter before he considered the incident closed. When someone said to Rantzau that after all Patek was a "good guy," he snapped back that it was possibly so but in any case, as a *junker*, he knew that he must "like the horses and *dogs* [underlined in the text] with which one had to grow." *AA*, 2318/4562, 158728–34; Rantzau's telegram, February 25, 1927.

[54] *AA*, 3036/6698, 111822.

GERMAN-POLISH MOVES AND THE
SOVIET REACTION

While the German government was attempting to deter the
Soviet government from negotiating with Poland, it did not
itself shut the door to the possibility of establishing some
closer contacts with her. The initiative came from Pilsudski.
According to one source of information, Pilsudski originally
wished Prince Janusz Radziwill to become the foreign minister
in the new Polish government as he was considered to have
pro-German sympathies.[55] But even though Zaleski was appointed, there were nevertheless some indications of Pilsudski's
designs for a Polish-German *rapprochement*.

Toward the end of July 1926 Dr. H. Diamand, a member
of the *Sejm* for the Polish Socialist Party, visited Germany in
the capacity of an official emissary of Pilsudski. On July 28
he was received by Stresemann to discuss the Polish claim for
permanent representation on the Council of the League of
Nations. In return, "Poland would be ready to offer Germany compensation," he stated, according to Stresemann's
record of the conversation. "Herr Pilsudski puts extraordinary
importance on reaching friendly relations with Germany, his
whole attitude is anti-Russian and he would greatly welcome
an improvement in relations with Germany," stated Diamand.
He went on to quote Pilsudski as having once said that "in
general it was correct that the more land one possessed the
more power one has. Poland, however, has far too many aliens
among her population and under the circumstances it would
be better to give up land in order to strengthen national
unity." Stresemann reacted to this amazing statement with obvious caution, expressing in general terms only Germany's wish
for an understanding between the two countries.[56]

Stresemann probably doubted the correctness of such state-

[55] Laroche, *op. cit.*, pp. 47–8.
[56] Stresemann, *Vermächtnis*, II, p. 551.

ments. He was not interested in reaching an agreement with Poland on matters of minor importance and realized that Pilsudski, no less than other Polish statesmen, was opposed to a new settlement of the paramount problem—the boundary. This, he was convinced, could be achieved only through concerted international pressure and in cooperation with France.

As early as June 1926, the Polish Envoy to Berlin had observed that Germany's tactics to revise her east boundary had changed. He stated that the road to this goal would now be paved by French-German cooperation, which was already being developed in the field of trade and accompanied by cultural exchange. The question of revision would be raised at an appropriate moment when Germany was assured of French support.[57]

When Stresemann met secretly with Briand on September 17, 1926, at the famous conference at Thoiry, many uninformed reporters concluded that the two statesmen had reached an agreement on a Polish-German settlement. However, Stresemann wrote in his diary, "I declined to open up either the Eastern or the colonial question at Thoiry. These matters can take place only step by step. However, when the time comes to debate the Eastern question, then people in Germany must fully realize that this question can be settled only in concert with France and that therefore the first step to take is to reach an understanding with France. . . ."[58] On a later occasion he mentioned privately, "I never thought more about the East than during the time I was looking for an understanding in the West."[59] It appears that Briand gave some encouragement to Stresemann in developing this particular line of action. Though he does not mention the date of the conversation, a close associate of Stresemann noted that Briand

---

[57] *Ciechanowski Deposit*, No. 1106/T, June 8, 1926.

[58] Stresemann, *Vermächtnis*, III, p. 38; see also the German Foreign Office's telegram to the Embassy in Moscow about the Thoiry meeting, *AA*, 1412/2860, 558128-9.

[59] Freund, *op. cit.*, p. 245, quoting from *Nachlass*, 3167/163659.

told the German statesman, "Once France and Germany reach an understanding on general policy, then we don't need to worry about Poland." [60]

Even if the revision of the German-Polish boundary was considered premature by Stresemann, the Soviet government harbored suspicions about its possibilities. During November 1926, Chicherin and Litvinov in Moscow, and Krestinski in Berlin raised this question on several occasions.[61] One evening Chicherin and Rantzau held a long and intimate conversation which lasted until 2 o'clock in the morning. Chicherin was very tired and looked gravely ill, reported Rantzau. At this time he confided to Rantzau the otherwise strictly kept secret, his serious diabetic condition. When they spoke about Poland, Chicherin said, "We will be happy, of course, if Germany succeeds in changing the boundaries which were imposed upon her by the Versailles dictate. However, we wish that this not be done at the expense of Russia." Rantzau assured him that "there was no question of a political understanding" with Poland.[62]

However, the Russian fears were not alleviated and when Chicherin visited Berlin, he had two long meetings with Stresemann on December 2 and 3. They first discussed the question of Lithuania, which was going through one of her periodical crises in her relations with Poland. Then Chicherin mentioned the Thoiry meeting and indirectly inquired about the concessions Germany had supposedly made to France and the concessions which she had received. Stresemann told him that concessions were neither asked for nor received. The main problem for Germany was the evacuation of the Rhineland and for its accomplishment Germany would not give any compensation. As to the German-Polish boundary, continued Stresemann, there existed two nonofficial groups in France.

[60] Henry Bernard, *Finis Germaniae* (Stuttgart: Kurt Haslsteiner, 1947), p. 59.
[61] *AA*, 1426/2945, 572433-4; 1412/2860, 558155-8.
[62] *Ibid.*, 572466; November 25, 1926.

One would want Germany to guarantee the Polish boundaries; but even the *Quai d'Orsay* understood that this was an absurdity. The other group, one of whose members was the French journalist, Jules Sauerwein (who, however, at times was a nonofficial spokesman for the *Quai d'Orsay*), was exploring the idea of Germany's gaining Danzig and the Corridor but not Upper Silesia. This group also suggested that Poland be compensated at the expense of Lithuania. "About such a solution —quite regardless of the idea of compensation—there can naturally never be a question," stated Stresemann and added that the Poles would have to be satisfied with permission to use the Danzig port. Under no circumstances would he renounce German claims to Upper Silesia. Chicherin then confirmed the principle that it was "very good to keep Poland constantly under pressure, not only from the West but also from the East," and Stresemann gladly assured him that such was also his wish.[63]

After the visit with Stresemann, Chicherin gave a lengthy interview to the press in which he reaffirmed the closeness of Soviet-German ties. He restated Soviet opposition to the Polish idea of signing a collective treaty in East Europe which would establish a Polish protectorate over the Baltic States. He expressed the conviction that sooner or later these states would sign bilateral treaties with Russia.[64]

As time went by, Germany and the Soviet Union continued to reassert officially their common interest in exercising pressure on Poland and keeping her restrained. However, their mutual relations became increasingly complex and their policies toward other European powers were frequently at cross-purposes; consequently, their policies toward Poland lacked coordination.

Germany was now a permanent member of the Council of

---

[63] *AA*, 1412/2860, 558166–78. The memorandum about the conversation was written by Schubert, who had been present at the meeting.

[64] *Vneshniaia Politika*, III, pp. 89–91.

the League of Nations and Stresemann was therefore able to establish intimate contacts with two leading statesmen of the West, Briand and Chamberlain. Her relations with France were friendly and though she was suspicious of some aspects of British policy in East Europe, she was eminently interested in maintaining good relations with London. Russia, on the other hand, continued to be dependent on Germany in all major European problems. She would not join the League of Nations, which she considered an assembly of imperialist nations, committed to an anti-Soviet policy. Her relations with France were unsettled and Chicherin's or Litvinov's occasional hints, addressed to Germany, that she might reach an agreement with Paris left Stresemann unimpressed. The British-Soviet relations had been strained since 1924.

Germany was unquestionably the stronger partner in Soviet-German relations; whenever Moscow or Berlin had occasion to exchange views in regard to Poland, Germany consistently exercised more influence over Soviet policy than Moscow did over Berlin. Stresemann simply was in the position of pursuing some diplomatic avenues which were not open to Chicherin. At the League meetings in Geneva, Stresemann was often able to reinforce his policies toward Poland. For example, when Zaleski met the German Foreign Minister there on December 10, 1926, he inquired about the possibility of resuming trade negotiations. The German statesman bluntly retorted that there could be no normalization of the relations of the two countries "without a solution of the frontier problem," making it clear that such included "Danzig, the Corridor and Upper Silesia." [65] Such experience in Geneva confirmed, however, Stresemann's belief that frequent international conferences and contacts with foreign representatives could provide a precious opportunity to push German territorial claims and gain new supporters.

[65] Gąsiorowski, "Stresemann and Poland after Locarno," p. 305, quoting from *AA*, 2339/4569, 168905-9.

The critical British attitude toward the German-Polish boundary was not a secret and Briand and some French diplomats in private conversations would often indicate their understanding of the German position. At the 1927 fall session of the General Assembly of the League of Nations, Stresemann received another expression of support of his policy toward Poland from the big powers. The Polish delegation presented a proposal which called upon the member nations to conclude nonaggression treaties. If accepted, this would have meant for Germany an indirect recognition of the Polish boundary and a renunciation of force—a commitment which Stresemann, while pleading adherence to peaceful methods, had repeatedly rejected during the pre-Locarno negotiations. To him it was the "East Locarno" idea revived in a new Geneva-clad form. He fought against the Polish proposal successfully and gained British and French support. When Chicherin expressed concern about the Geneva proceedings, Stresemann assured him, through Rantzau, that nothing was being done against Russia and conveyed to him his satisfaction that the Polish plans had met with complete failure.[66]

It would appear that Poland now occupied a key position in the Soviet-German wrangle. As both capitals feared a weakening of their own positions should Poland settle her differences with one of them, she had some freedom for political maneuvering. However, because her basic attitude toward the Soviet Union remained unaltered and she resolutely refused to consider any change in her boundaries with Germany, a move in either direction (toward Berlin or Moscow) was really nothing more than temporizing, leaving her highly vulnerable to the possibility of another concerted action against her. It is this fundamental idea which Pilsudski, enamored with artificial Polish power and prestige, conveniently and shortsightedly overlooked. It is difficult to see much sense in the direction he took; in weakening Polish ties with France and minimizing the

[66] *AA,* 1427/2945, 573028–9, 573045–7, 573058–61.

importance of the League of Nations, he did not seem to realize the eventuality that Poland, isolated from friends, might some-day again face a powerful squeeze from Germany and the Soviet Union.

A WAR SCARE

For a few months in 1927 German and Soviet diplomatic maneuvers in regard to Poland were overshadowed by two events which reverberated throughout Europe and caused a war scare in Russia. In May 1927 Great Britain suspended diplomatic relations with the Soviet Union. The Soviet govern-ment saw in this move only one part of a preconceived plan to isolate Russia, to provoke incidents, and to draw her finally into a war. Poland, according to this plan, was assigned the important role of a spearhead for British aggression.

Germany was always worried about her own "middle posi-tion" between Russia and England. She was now gravely alarmed at the prospect of being compelled to choose sides in any diplomatic conflict between Moscow and London. France, on the other hand, showing from time to time her displeasure at the growing influence of England in Europe, contemplated using the conflict to strengthen her own position by a possible closer understanding with Russia. The Soviets, in turn, saw in such an understanding a welcome opportunity to under-mine the central position of her friend, Germany, in European politics. All these variations led to a series of diplomatic en-tanglements in the summer of 1927.

Then, one month after the suspension of the British-Soviet relations, a shot was fired in Warsaw which echoed alarmingly in all European capitals. On June 7, 1927 the Soviet Minister to Poland, Voikov, was assassinated by a Russian *émigré*. The Soviet government immediately lodged a strong protest, con-necting the outrageous "unprecedented and criminal act" with anti-Soviet demonstrations in Peking and Shanghai, with the police search of the Soviet Trade Mission in London, and with "the provocative suspension of diplomatic relations by England." It held the Polish government responsible for the murderous attack by tolerating on its territory counterrevolutionary White Russian organizations.[67]

The Polish President, the Foreign Minister, and Envoy Patek immediately expressed deepest regret over the incident. Patek, however, stated on behalf of his government that, while it gave asylum to political refugees, it never allowed them to organize any action against foreign governments; nor could it be held responsible, Patek's note continued, for an act committed by a madman.[68]

Litvinov answered in a strongly worded note. Presenting a long list of terrorist acts perpetrated from Polish territory against the Soviet Union, he repeated the accusation that Poland not only did not give enough attention to such terrorist organizations but in a number of cases even supported them.[69]

The anger of the Soviet government was reflected in the Soviet press.[70] Stalin later stated that "the murder of Voikov, organized by agents of the conservative [Polish] party, had been intended by its originators to play the role of the Sarajevo murder and embroil the USSR in a military conflict with Poland." [71] As could be expected, the assassination of Voikov had repercussions not only in Soviet-Polish relations, which were once again at their worst, but also in the relations of the Soviet Union with other countries. On the day of the murder Chicherin was at the German resort, Baden-Baden, taking one of his periodic medical cures. Stresemann personally informed him about the event. According to Stresemann's record of the conversation, Chicherin gave the impression of being worried about his own life, for he remarked that it might be better for

[67] Kliuchnikov and Sabanin, *op. cit.*, III, I, pp. 385–86.
[68] *Ibid.*, p. 386; note of June 9, 1927.
[69] *Ibid.*, pp. 387–89; note of June 12, 1927.
[70] See *Izvestiia*, June 8, 23, 30, 1927.
[71] *Pravda*, July 28, 1928, as quoted by Ross, *op. cit.*, p. 281.

him in the future to travel by car rather than by train to avoid
the formalities of going to and from a station. Turning then
to British-Soviet relations and Poland, Chicherin declared
that the principal danger was Pilsudski, who was "a romantic
and an adventurer at the same time." His only political idea
was to tie Belorussia, the Ukraine, and Lithuania to Poland.
"Then, East Prussia will be fully encircled," Chicherin significantly remarked. Poland was under strong British influence,
he continued, and even if Chamberlain did not support a
policy of expansion, the English die-hards would. Therein lay
the real danger of a new world war in which Germany would
be involved. France would join Poland under a pretext of
some border incident, "provoked" by Russia, and the question of passage of her troops through Germany would come
up.

Stresemann did not share Chicherin's bleak outlook. According to his information, the Poles did not plan any offensive action against Russia. But above all, he could not share
Chicherin's views about France: "What in the world could
move the French nation to fight for Poland and lead a hopeless march against Russia?" [72]

One week later, June 14, European statesmen met in Geneva
to attend a Council session. The Foreign Ministers of Great
Britain, France, Germany, Italy, Japan, and Belgium were
closeted in a secret meeting to discuss the tense situation
created by the British-Soviet and Polish-Soviet conflict. Communist agitation was at its peak, they maintained, and Briand
expressed the fear that Russia might send an ultimatum to
Poland. He suggested that a way be found to bring their concern to Moscow's attention. Chamberlain then proposed that
Stresemann, in view of friendly Soviet-German relations and
particularly in view of his good personal relations with Chicherin, contact the Soviet government. Stresemann was non-

[72] *AA,* 1413/2860, 558813–27; June 7, 1927.

committal and only promised to inquire with Rantzau about the usefulness of such a step.[73]

Before Stresemann could undertake any concrete action, the Soviet government learned what had transpired in Geneva. According to its information, "Stresemann [had] accepted the task of emphatically warning the Soviet government" against the danger of war. Chicherin, relating the report to Rantzau, considered this a direct threat to Russia. He again reminded the German Ambassador of their negotiations, which had opened toward the end of 1924, aimed at "pushing Poland back within her ethnographic boundary." To him, this was an axiom of Soviet policy and a real link between Germany and Russia. However, now the Soviet-Polish conflict threw a long shadow over Soviet-German relations and, Chicherin stated, it was becoming increasingly difficult to defend his policy before his own government.[74] Stresemann was obviously not impressed by Chicherin's veiled threat; rather, turning the tables, he began to threaten Chicherin.

GERMANY THREATENS—RUSSIA RETREATS

On September 17, 1927, the French telegraphic agency, *Havas,* surprised European capitals with an official communiqué of the French government, which reported that the Soviet Union had proposed a pact of nonaggression with France. The announcement indicated French willingness to enter into such negotiations but also expressed France's desire to keep in mind the security interests of her allies, Poland and Rumania.[75] The statement was based upon a confidential exchange of views between Briand and Litvinov, who had been in Geneva in connection with the work of the Preparatory Commission for the Disarmament Conference. Briand had told the Soviet Deputy Foreign Commissar that the disarmament

[73] *AA,* 1427/2945, 572919, June 15, 1927. Stresemann, *Vermächtnis,* III, p. 152.
[74] *AA,* 2318/4562, 159104–9; August 27, 1927.
[75] *AA,* 1413/2860, 558994.

problem hinged to a considerable extent upon the security of the states bordering Russia, which was not a member of the League of Nations. Then, he brought up the question of a Polish-Soviet nonaggression pact.

Informed by Briand about the conversation with Litvinov, Stresemann immediately asked Rantzau to inquire about the prospects of a Soviet-Polish *rapprochement*.[76] Following Stresemann's instructions, Rantzau had a heated discussion with Chicherin. He told Chicherin that he could not free himself in the last few weeks from the impression that there was a change in the Soviet policy toward France and that such a change had been made at the expense of Germany. Chicherin answered, somewhat provocatively, that the question of choice between Germany and France did not exist as yet. "I answered sharply," reported Rantzau relating the conversation, "that there can be no question of Russia turning away from Germany, but rather that Germany may find it necessary to turn away from Russia." Chicherin retreated quickly. While it seemed that France had entertained the idea of a nonaggression pact as a diplomatic weapon against Germany, the Soviet government would not sign any pact with France which could be damaging to German interests, Chicherin stated. Paraphrasing the famous sentence of Bismarck, he declared, "In order to prevent any misunderstanding it is for Moscow unconditionally desirable to see to it that the wires with Berlin which permit a frank exchange of views not be cut off." As to the possibility of signing a Russian-Polish nonaggression pact, Chicherin characterized the Polish proposals "as simply ridiculous." [77]

Chicherin's explanation was, however, far from reassuring to the German government. Stresemann wished Rantzau to continue in his conversations but to keep in mind as a back-

[76] *Ibid.*, 559005.
[77] *AA*, 1427/2945, 573100–3; September 21, 1927; *Ibid.*, 573105; September 22, 1927.

ground the following points: (1) that French-Russian alliance was hardly possible though (2) a French-Russian pact of non-aggression expressing only in general terms a friendly attitude would be on the whole welcomed by Germany; (3) a guarantee pact with Poland, though improbable, would go against the foundation of the German-Soviet relations, the Rapallo Treaty and the Berlin Treaty, although (4) Germany could not formally object to a nonaggression pact with Poland, since such opposition would expose her to the accusation of being a disturber of peace; nevertheless, it would be disadvantageous to Germany because it would stiffen Poland's back. Finally, a collective nonaggression pact of Russia with France and her satellites, Poland and Rumania, would be of far-reaching significance and would, therefore, exercise a strong influence on Russian-German relations.[78]

Rantzau questioned Chicherin sharply and was reassured that the proposal of a nonaggression pact with Poland was nothing else than a maneuver, just as it was a maneuver on the part of Poland.[79] Thus ended another round of diplomatic exchanges between Berlin and Moscow with Poland, as usual, in the middle. Once again, the Soviet government's weak international position was exposed while Germany's influence and potential power in European politics grew.

[78] *AA*, 1427/2945, 573109–12; September 24, 1927.
[79] *Ibid.*, 573139–42; October 7, 1927.

CHAPTER 10

BETTING ON THE
"LITHUANIAN HORSE"

T H E R E was another pawn on the chessboard of East European politics which both Germany and the Soviet Union thought of manipulating in their moves against Poland. This was Lithuania. Lithuania's hatred of Poland matched that of the Soviet Union and Germany. Unreconciled to the Polish possession of Vilna and afraid that Poland might attempt to force a union upon her, Lithuania refused even to open diplomatic relations with Poland. As a matter of fact, since 1920 Poland and Lithuania had continued to be officially in a state of war. Moreover, she vigorously opposed Polish plans for establishing a Baltic bloc under Polish leadership. Obviously, for all these reasons her attitude toward Poland was similar to Russia's and Germany's and they, conversely, were anxious to encourage Lithuania's hostility toward the common foe.

As early as 1920, Victor Kopp, the Soviet representative in Berlin, speaking with German Foreign Minister Simons about unsettled Soviet relations with Poland, stated that at the moment when "Poland's turn" would come "Russia [would] rely on Lithuania" as she "could bet on the Lithuanian horse." Dr. Simons could "confirm a parallel view of the German government" on the possibilities offered by Lithuania.[1]

The betting, however, was not quite safe. As in other areas of Soviet-German relations, Berlin and Moscow viewed the

[1] *AA,* 1424/2945, 570264; November 24, 1920.

position of Lithuania toward Poland in different lights. The Soviet government on several occasions expressed its solidarity with Lithuania on the question of Vilna; in 1926 it signed a treaty of neutrality with Lithuania to strengthen her position toward Poland, and, in turn, to weaken Poland's position in the Baltic area. The German government, however, though not opposed to this policy, did not offer any public support for it; in spite of its efforts to undergird Lithuania's hostility to Poland, it had its own claim on the Lithuanian territory of Memel. Russia, on the other hand, was equally cautious about openly supporting Germany on the Memel question; she did not wish to estrange Lithuania, nor was she interested in increased German strength on the Baltic Sea, an inevitable result of the acquisition of Memel by Germany.

The Locarno Conference generated a rumor which proved unfounded but one which, nevertheless, set the chancelleries in Berlin and Moscow in motion. It was said that the French government had begun to explore the possibility of solving the problem of the Polish-German boundary by ceding to Germany the Corridor and Danzig. In turn, Poland would be compensated with Lithuanian territory, including perhaps Memel, and again in turn, Lithuania would be satisfied by the return of Vilna. Stresemann was questioned about this proposal on several occasions but he denied it emphatically.[2] He stated that this alleged idea ignored Upper Silesia and that he would not renounce Germany's right to Memel. He was particularly anxious that the Soviet Union not give Lithuania any support in keeping this territory. When Lithuania asked for such support, Rantzau warned Litvinov of the gravest damage to the Soviet-German relations should Moscow comply. Litvinov promised that the Soviet Union would refuse the Lithuanian request as soon as the treaty of neutrality, which was being negotiated at that time with Germany, was signed. He further

[2] *AA,* 2314/4562, 156018–20; November 5, 1925; 1412/2860, 558166–78; December 2, 1926.

explained that Russia's policy in the Baltic area was directed against Poland.[3]

After the Soviet-German neutrality treaty had been signed, Stresemann wanted the Soviet government to know that although he expected constantly to exchange confidential views and to reach an understanding on Lithuania and Poland, he also wanted something beyond this. "I would be pleased if you . . . would come back to this question," he wrote to Rantzau, "and if we could receive an assurance from the Soviet government that in the future, too, it would not guarantee the possession by other nations of any territories which belonged to Germany." [4]

Rantzau immediately answered that the Soviet government was in accord insofar as Poland was concerned; that in regard to Lithuania, it had conveyed the suggestion to the Lithuanians—according to a report Litvinov had given to Rantzau —to seek an agreement on Memel in Berlin.[5]

Meanwhile, the Lithuanian government exploited what appeared to be a particularly propitious anti-Polish atmosphere in Berlin. On one occasion the Lithuanian Minister to Germany expressed to Schubert the wish for a strengthening of Lithuanian-German relations, although he understood that Memel was a serious obstacle. However, he stated, the main principle of the Lithuanian foreign policy was to establish the best possible relations with Germany and Russia. The Lithuanian and German policies toward Poland, he continued, could be coordinated; there could be an exchange of information on Poland, a common approach toward minorities in Poland, a concerted action in the League of Nations on Poland—and then, later, on the basis of this new relationship, even Memel could be discussed. Schubert mainly listened;

[3] *AA,* 1410/2860, 55890; March 13, 1926; 1411/2860, 557353-4; April 23, 1926.
[4] *AA,* 1426/2945, 572166; April 29, 1926.
[5] *Ibid.,* 572169-70; 1411/2860, 557617-8, 557647-8.

then, having nothing to lose, agreed in principle but expected some concrete suggestions.[6]

When Pilsudski seized power in May 1926, there was anxious speculation that the new dictator of Poland might attempt to force a solution of the unsettled relations with Lithuania. He had never become reconciled to the existence of an independent Lithuania, which centuries before had been united with the Kingdom of Poland. If, by force of circumstances, he had abandoned his plan of reunification in the early 1920's, perhaps now, in 1926, the dream might be realized.

Soon after this event, messages began to reach Moscow and Berlin about an impending settlement of the Lithuanian-Polish dispute. According to some reports, Pilsudski was determined to subdue Lithuania by military action or by enforced negotiations through which he would offer to her far-reaching concessions, including the cession of Vilna. However, at the same time, he would insist on a Polish-Lithuanian Union. Other reports stated that Lithuania had concentrated troops on the border, ready, if possible, to exploit the shock and uncertainty produced by Pilsudski's *putsch*. Still other sources maintained that now the question of the Corridor would be related to the problem of the Lithuanian-Polish tension; that Germany would receive the Corridor and Poland would be compensated at the expense of Lithuania.[7]

Moscow asked Berlin to comment on these reports, particularly those which were indicative of a possible German-Polish settlement. Answering the inquiry, Schubert told Krestinski that he doubted that Poland would attempt to take Lithuania by force; as to the rumors about a German understanding with Poland, he declared them senseless.[8]

All such rumors appeared to ignore the realities of the

---

[6] *AA*, 2316/4562, 157325–31. The memorandum, dated April 28, 1926, is unsigned but was probably written by Schubert.

[7] *AA*, 1426/2945, 572260–61, 572268–70, 572275–7.

[8] *Ibid.*, 572287–8, 572296–9; see also Rantzau's conversation with Chicherin, July 30, 1926, *AA*, 2317/4562, 157719–22.

situation: Poland would not consider making boundary concessions to Germany even if she were given a free hand against
Lithuania. Germany would not be satisfied with gaining only
the Corridor and Danzig and would insist on having Polish
Upper Silesia, too; moreover, she would not renounce her
claim to Memel. The Soviet Union would not look passively
at the growth of Polish power on the Baltic Sea and would
regard a German-Polish settlement as a direct Polish threat to
Soviet security. Hence, after all pros and cons were taken into
account, all involved powers, except Poland, were at least
temporarily interested in maintaining Lithuania's *status quo*.

On August 5, 1926, Schubert met with Litvinov, who was
passing through Berlin on his way from France. The Soviet
Deputy Commissar for Foreign Affairs spoke at some length
about his fear of a possible Polish attack against Lithuania.
Then, in spite of previous denials, he inquired again about
the rumors concerning a secret German agreement with Poland. Even Briand had "told him that he had not considered
the rumor unfounded." Schubert expressed his astonishment
and stated again that it was absolute nonsense. Litvinov then
declared categorically that Russia would not sit idly by in the
case of a Polish attack on Lithuania and asked whether Germany would remain passive. Schubert answered that a course
of inaction would not be possible for Germany, but added
that he did not believe the attack would occur. When Litvinov
further discussed the Soviet-Lithuanian negotiations concerning a forthcoming treaty of neutrality, he stated, according to
Schubert's memorandum, "again quite cynically that the purpose of the treaty [was] to keep Lithuania from an understanding with Poland." [9]

Germany's lack of concern about the Polish-Lithuanian tension undoubtedly created suspicion in Moscow and Schubert's
attitude did not help to alleviate it. The Central Committee
of the Communist Party of Poland and of Lithuania issued an

[9] *AA,* 2317/4562, 157791–802.

appeal to workers to prevent Pilsudski from annexing Lithuania; the Soviet publicist, A. Rosenberg, published an article in which he stated that Zaleski was negotiating "a deal" with Stresemann. The terms of this "deal" were that Germany would give Poland a free hand against Lithuania for the return of the Corridor.[10]

On September 28, 1926, the Soviet Union and Lithuania signed a treaty of neutrality. Chicherin, in a letter which accompanied the treaty, referred to the "violation of the Lithuanian frontiers" in 1920 by Poland and confirmed the previous attitude of the Soviet government of not recognizing such a change.[11] The Polish government protested against the treaty, which in its opinion was referring to Vilna, "unquestionably an integral part of the Polish Republic's territory." [12] This touched upon the old controversy as to whether the Soviet Union by signing the Riga Treaty in March 1921 had recognized Vilna as a part of Poland. The Soviet government retorted, on November 19, that the Riga Treaty left the question of the Polish boundaries with Lithuania open to an agreement between the two countries but that such an agreement had not been reached.[13] The Soviet press, of course, vehemently supported the position of its government. *Izvestiia*, in a series of articles, reviewed Polish attempts to create a Baltic bloc. It warned the Baltic States against being dragged into a war with Russia and invited them to sign separate neutrality treaties, similar to those which the Soviet Union had signed with Germany and Lithuania.[14]

Moscow's suspicions about the possibility of a German-Polish "deal" at the expense of Lithuania persisted. Chicherin went to Berlin at the beginning of December 1926, determined to get an answer to this question. In a conversation with

---

[10] *Imprecorr*, Vol. 6, No. 62, pp. 1052–1053; No. 64, pp. 1081–1082.
[11] *Soviet Treaty Series*, I, p. 234.
[12] *Vneshniaia Politika*, III, p. 86.
[13] Kliuchnikov and Sabanin, *op. cit.*, III, pp. 356–57.
[14] *Izvestiia*, October 2, 3, 22, 28; November 2, 20; December 3, 1926.

Stresemann he referred to a series of incidents which, taken together, indicated that Germany was prepared to negotiate with Poland an exchange of Lithuanian territory for the Polish Corridor. In addition, Chicherin felt compelled to state that Germany had given the Soviet government no support in its policy toward Lithuania. All this was to Moscow most disagreeable.

Stresemann, in answer, assured Chicherin that in the discussions he had had with the Western powers the question of exchange of territory had never been mentioned, although he admitted that the Corridor itself had been. However, it was quite clear to him that Poland was not ready as yet to reach an understanding with Germany. At any rate, Germany could never allow Memel to be turned into a Polish port. Chicherin, not fully satisfied with Stresemann's explanation, pursued his attack. "One has to keep in mind," he stated, "that once Lithuania was swallowed by Poland, Poland would become a big power, and that, of course, must be prevented under any circumstances." Also, he declared that on various occasions he had encouraged Lithuania to seek closer contacts with Germany but, in return, Lithuania expected Germany's support in her relations with Poland. Stresemann expressed his readiness to cooperate with Lithuania but, he admitted, her policy in regard to Memel made this difficult.[15]

On December 17, 1926, the Lithuanian government was overthrown in a coup led by A. Voldemaras, who established himself as dictator. Polish-Lithuanian relations immediately reached the boiling point. All major capitals of Europe became gravely worried about the danger of a war which might well spread over all of East Europe. Each country, however, followed the crisis with different interests in mind. Britain used the opportunity to try to bring about an understanding between Lithuania and Poland which, as Russia suspected, would strengthen her own position toward the Soviet Union.

[15] *AA*, 1412/2860, 558166–78.

France was mainly interested in avoiding further strain on Polish-German relations. Germany and the Soviet Union continued to share an interest in preventing any growth of Polish political power, whether by way of an understanding with Lithuania or through a victorious war with her.

These varied interests in the Lithuanian-Polish conflict produced some sensitive maneuvering in European capitals. In a lengthy telegram to the German Ambassador in England Stresemann carefully explained the German position as well as his concern over possible developments in the conflict. Alluding to the British attitude, he stated that there were forces at work in Europe which were seeking to bring about an understanding between Poland and Lithuania and trying to detach the latter from cooperation with Russia and Germany. He expressed fear of the possibility that events might turn against German interests, which were, "of course, to prevent cooperation between Poland and Lithuania." [16]

In a similar message to the German Ambassador in Paris, Stresemann added that Pilsudski had no desire for an open war against Lithuania but would rather attempt to force her into friendly relations. To counteract this danger, Germany was willing to consider the Soviet suggestion of assuring Lithuania that she could count on German and Soviet support. However, this posed a dilemma for the German government, reasoned Stresemann. How could they, on the one hand, strengthen the position of Lithuania against Poland, while on the other, keep her in a position of weakness in respect to German claims on Memel? Yet, "any kind of political union of Lithuania and Poland [is] unbearable" for Germany, stated Stresemann, and instructed the Ambassador (as he did in the message to London) to seek a clarification of the precarious situation.[17]

He was pleased to hear that Paris and London had both

[16] *AA*, 1427/2945, 572513–15; January 12, 1927.
[17] *Ibid.*, 572561–8; February 3, 1927.

addressed notes to the governments of Poland and Lithuania advising caution and a peaceful policy. However, he continued to be suspicious of Britain, where "the mood, as of the moment, [ran] against German interests." [18]

As had been the case in the past when other problems were of direct interest to Germany and Poland, no views were exchanged between Warsaw and Berlin on the Lithuanian-Polish conflict. However, the contacts between Berlin and Moscow were frequent and intimate. Litvinov remarked to Rantzau "that he considered it unconditionally [necessary] in the Russian as well as in the German interest to prevent a Lithuanian-Polish understanding." He asked the German government to intervene in Kaunas "to keep Lithuania at her post." However, Rantzau reported that he had detected "in [Litvinov's] statement a sense of a faint Russian worry about [a German] understanding with Poland." [19] The German Foreign Office answered the Soviet query immediately. Germany had undertaken several steps to make Lithuania "stick to her post," the answer said. She had informed the Western powers of her interest in the Lithuanian-Polish *status quo;* she had offered Lithuania a trade agreement; she had overlooked for the moment the controversy about Memel; she had expressed readiness, together with the Soviet Union, to give to Lithuania political support. The Foreign Office could not "understand the worry of Mr. Litvinov concerning a German-Polish understanding in view of the notorious character of German-Polish relations. Even should there be a renewal of trade negotiations, the basic character of [German] relations with Poland will not be touched," the German message concluded reassuringly. [20]

Less than twenty-four hours after the first message had been dispatched, Berlin sent another message to Moscow. It was

[18] *Ibid.*, 572575–80, 572587, 572817–9.
[19] *Ibid.*, 572655–6; March 1, 1927.
[20] *Ibid.*, 572657–9; March 3, 1927.

distinctly different in tone from the preceding telegram. Moscow, the note protested, had approached Warsaw without previously informing Berlin, proposing a conference of Eastern powers to settle the Polish-Lithuanian conflict. The German government objected to Litvinov's undertaking this "double-faced" step, while at the same time advocating common German-Soviet procedures. Though such a conference might be envisaged as a move against Poland, its proceedings might also become very uncomfortable for Germany, stated the German Foreign Office.[21] Rantzau answered the telegram on behalf, so to say, of the Soviet government. He emphatically rejected the accusation of "a double-faced" Soviet policy and was bluntly critical of the German Foreign Ministry.[22]

Stresemann concluded the exchange of views on the Lithuanian-Polish conflict by conveying to the major German embassies his basic stand on all principal East European problems. He stated that in general Germany welcomed any attempt to pacify the area. She recognized, however, two types of states. One type, such as Finland, Estonia, and Latvia, had the boundaries which were considered stable; the other type, such as Poland and Lithuania, had unstable boundaries. It was not in the German interest to develop a positive attitude toward any kind of a so-called "East Locarno." Moreover, it was not in Germany's interest to have the Western powers participate as arbitrators and guarantors in the settlement of East European questions, which, as far as big powers were concerned, interested only Russia and Germany. As long as the climate was not favorable for opening the German boundary question, it was not in Germany's interest to have an "East Locarno" conference, concluded Stresemann.[23] Once again, Stresemann proved to have a more realistic grasp of the situation than other statesmen in Europe; however, he also introduced a new trend of thought which, though unexpressed,

---

[21] *AA*, 1427/2945, 572662–3; March 4, 1927.
[22] *Ibid.*, 572689; March 8, 1927.
[23] *Ibid.*, 572771–4; March 21, 1927.

must have been on his mind for several years—the idea of eliminating the Western powers' active interest in East European affairs. In his mind this area belonged solely within the German and Soviet sphere of influence.

The last quarter of 1927 saw a new flare-up in Lithuanian-Polish relations. This time the Soviet and German governments took concerted diplomatic action, though again with a different emphasis. Scores of telegrams were exchanged between Moscow and Berlin on the subject. This diplomatic struggle began when the Lithuanian government made it known that it would present the controversy with Poland to the next session of the League of Nations. The Polish press replied with a violent propaganda campaign. Reports reached Moscow and Berlin that Polish troops were being concentrated on the Lithuanian border. On several occasions Chicherin expressed grave concern to Rantzau about the developments, which he expected would lead either to war or to a Polish-Lithuanian union.

Stresemann was less alarmed than Chicherin, but he was, nevertheless, disturbed about the developments. He was worried that Germany might be bypassed while steps were being taken behind the scenes in London and Paris. He stated in one of his instructions to the embassy in Paris, "It is clear that a final solution of the Vilna question in favor of Poland would be in the highest degree against our interests. It is impossible to pursue a solution in favor of Lithuania under present circumstances. Therefore, a further suspension of its solution is still in our best interest." [24]

He asked Rantzau to explain the German position to Chicherin and try to convince him that it was in Russia's interest, too, to seek a postponement of the solution of the Vilna problem. He emphasized the need for close cooperation between the two countries.[25] The Soviet government agreed and suggested that Germany, concurrently with Russia, advise Lith-

[24] *Ibid.*, 573181–4; November 3, 1927.
[25] *Ibid.*, 573195–7.

uania to proclaim the end of a state of war with Poland. It further expressed hope that Germany would use her veto power in the League's Council against any proposal which would be unfavorable to Lithuania.[26] Germany supported the Soviet recommendation to intervene in a friendly manner in Kaunas, though she could not see in a declaration ending the state of war any distinct advantage to Lithuania.[27]

The Soviet government now decided to take a more resolute step. On November 21, 1927, according to a report of the French Ambassador in Moscow, Chicherin stated to Patek, "that if Poland acted against Lithuania, Russia would act against Poland." [28] Three days later the Soviet government sent a sharp note to Poland stressing that "the maintenance of peace depends to a much larger extent on Poland than Lithuania." Russia wished to bring "with greatest emphasis to the attention of the Polish government the immeasurable dangers of an attack by Poland on the independence of Lithuania whatever form it might take. . . ." [29] The note, which was not published for a few days, was accompanied by warnings from the Soviet press.[30] The Polish government answered in a rather conciliatory tone. It pointed to the forthcoming discussion of the Polish-Lithuanian relations before the League of Nations and declared that it had "no intentions directed against the political independence and territorial integrity of Lithuania." It further complained that Lithuania was prolonging the state of war with Poland and expressed the hope that other governments would use their influence to bring this situation to an end.[31]

On November 25 Litvinov, in a two-hour visit with Strese-

[26] *AA*, 1427/2945, 573248–50; November 17, 1927.

[27] *Ibid.*, 573275–80.

[28] Laroche, *op. cit.*, p. 61.

[29] *Vneshniaia Politika*, III, p. 161. The German government was informed about the content of the note; see *AA*, 1413/2860, 559188.

[30] *Izvestiia*, November 25, 30, 1927.

[31] *Vneshniaia Politika*, III, p. 162.

mann, urged him to recognize the gravity of the situation. Stresemann, though not complacent, did not consider war to be imminent. When asked what the Russian attitude would be in case of war, Litvinov answered that the Soviet Union would under no circumstances look at such developments passively. Unfortunately, he added, Germany had not even suggested her own position concerning the conflict. Stresemann retorted that Germany had made her views known in London, Paris, and Geneva. However, he added, Germany was in no position to wage a war. Litvinov then urged Stresemann to intervene in Warsaw; Stresemann indicated his willingness to consider this possibility and suggested that he would speak with the Polish Envoy in Berlin and mention to him the as yet confidential Soviet note. Thus the Polish government would see and appreciate the cooperation between Moscow and Berlin on the Lithuanian problem. Also, at Litvinov's insistence, Stresemann agreed to issue a communiqué which would indicate that the two statesmen had discussed the Lithuanian-Polish conflict.

When at the end of the visit Stresemann asked Litvinov about Soviet-Polish negotiations on a nonaggression pact, the Soviet statesman said that nothing had happened in the recent past and that Russia was not in a hurry to sign. Krestinski, who was present, added, with a smile, "Unfortunately, the Poles are not in a hurry either." [32]

With the session of the Council of the League of Nations in December 1927, the Polish-Lithuanian conflict was transferred to Geneva. Litvinov met Stresemann on the eve of the meeting and discussed at length the mutual differences in their approach to the conflict. The two men agreed that these were of tactical rather than substantial nature and that their conversation had now cleared up all misunderstanding. At the end of the meeting Litvinov told Stresemann, "Be aware that in

[32] *AA*, 1413/2860, 559200–12; the memorandum about the conversation was written by Schubert, November 25, 1927.

this important question you represent [in the League] three countries. Protect German interests, Russian interests, and protect Lithuania from herself." [33]

There was certainly no need to urge the German Foreign Minister to protect his own country's interests; he did so on every occasion with vigor, intelligence, and effectiveness. As to the other two countries, however, their interests would be advanced by Stresemann only to the extent to which they were in harmony with the aims of German policy. Inasmuch as the Geneva meeting offered an opportunity for numerous confidential conversations, in which all manner of possibilities could be explored, the idea of exchanging the Corridor for Memel was again mentioned. Coupled with reports that the paramilitary organization in East Prussia, the *Stahlhelm,* was mobilized, the rumor of such a secret exchange of views in Geneva immediately produced a wave of protests from the Soviet government. Berlin was forced to deny all these reports to calm Moscow's misgivings.[34]

On December 9, 1927, Pilsudski surprised the political world by a hurried visit to Geneva. The following day he made an equally theatrical appearance at the secret session of the Council and, turning to the Lithuanian Prime Minister, addressed him dramatically: "Monsieur Voldemaras, do you want peace or war?" After some strenuous negotiations, Lithuania agreed to end the state of war with Poland; in turn, Poland reaffirmed respect for Lithuanian independence. The Council then recommended that the two parties in dispute open direct negotiations toward a normalization of their relations.[35]

The Communist International was even more vocal than the Soviet government about the danger of a Polish-Lithua-

[33] *AA,* 1428/2945, 573378–40; December 4, 1927.
[34] *Ciechanowski Deposit.* A report of the Polish Consul General in Königsberg, November 16, 1927, 1207-T-27. *AA,* 1413/2860, 559310–12; *AA,* 1428/2945, 573414–6, 573449; *AA,* 1414/2860, 559383. See also Bernhard, *op. cit.,* pp. 59, 278–79.
[35] *AA,* 1428/2945, 573417–9. Joseph Beck, *Dernier rapport* (Neuchâtel: Editions de la Bacounière, 1951), p. 4n.

nian war. The year of 1928, it declared in numerous statements, was another year that portended war by the imperialist
world against the Soviet Union. The forthcoming Polish war
on Lithuania would be its prelude. On January 27, 1928, the
Executive Committee of the Communist International passed
a resolution which condemned the "hypocritical" policy of the
League toward the Lithuanian-Polish conflict and accused
Pilsudski of making preparations for the annexation of Lithuania. "If up to now he has not realized his plans, it is only
due to the fact that the Soviet Union, which always takes its
stand against all annexations and the enslavement of small nations, and Germany, whose interests lie in the maintenance of
Lithuania's independence, have energetically opposed them,"
stated the resolution.[36]

When the Sixth Congress of the Communist International
convened in Moscow in the summer of 1928, the international
situation was characterized as one of "increasing imperialist
aggression," led by an American expansionist policy. In this
program Poland played a prominent role and indeed even
Germany was now preparing for war against the Soviet Union.[37] Some Polish delegates at the Congress acknowledged
that Poland was being turned into a springboard for attack
and that "the occupation of Lithuania was imminent. The
whole internal and external situation of Poland is such that
more than in any other country one has to expect in the near
future events which could set on fire the whole world," declared the Polish communist leader, Wera Kostrezewa.[38]

Bukharin pointed to the growing influence of capitalist
Germany in international relations, relations in which she
still was taking every advantage of her intermediary position
between the West and the USSR. But, he felt, the fundamental
tendency now was that Germany would "willingly allow itself

[36] *Inprecorr*, Vol. 8, No. 8, February 16, 1928; p. 177.
[37] Kun, *op. cit.*, pp. 771–74.
[38] *VIe Congrès de l'Internationale Communiste*. Compte rendu sténographique (Paris, 1928), p. 903.

to be 'violated' and [would] march side by side with its colleagues against the USSR." [39] In this connection, the position of the Communist Party of Poland was of particular importance. "In the present situation," stated Bukharin, "our Polish Party occupies a very responsible post. Everyone realizes what an important role our brother Party in Poland is destined to play in the event of war. The Party will become one of the principal forces at the disposal of the Communist International." [40] Bukharin's statement was echoed by the Polish delegate, Królikowski, who promised that Polish communists, in case of war against the Soviet Union, would fulfill their proletarian duty. They would defend the USSR as their fatherland because "only in the struggle under the banners of the Social Revolution and of Communism, only by the defense of the USSR against Poland, only by an armed uprising to transform Fascist Poland into a Soviet Poland, can the country be freed from the shackles of slavery," meaning, of course, Pilsudski.[41]

When Bukharin's speech reached Warsaw, there were decidedly different repercussions. The Polish Minister to Moscow, Patek, was instructed to lodge a protest against Bukharin's speech as an interference in Polish internal affairs and a violation of the Riga Treaty. Soviet Deputy Foreign Commissar Karakhan refused the protest, voicing the by now threadbare and transparent argument that the Third International was a "private organization" which had nothing in common with the Soviet government. Moreover, he declared that Poland herself had interfered in Soviet internal affairs by giving assistance to Russian *émigreés*.[42] The main theme of Bukharin's speech about the danger of war and Polish complicity was then developed at length in Soviet newspapers.[43]

[39] *Inprecorr*, Vol. 8, No. 41, July 30, 1928; p. 730.
[40] *Ibid.*, p. 739.
[41] *Ibid.*, No. 61, p. 1063.
[42] *Izvestiia*, July 31, 1928.
[43] *Inprecorr*, Vol. 8, No. 40, pp. 719–20; No. 47, pp. 824–25; No. 51, pp. 906–907; No. 58, pp. 1014–1016; *Izvestiia*, August 16, 1926.

It is now generally believed that Stalin and his associates in the Soviet Party and in the Comintern raised the war cry as a pretext for appealing to Soviet people for sacrificial efforts when Stalin launched his drive for industrialization and also as an argument for eliminating opposition to his struggle for one-man exclusive power. The Comintern's evaluation of the revolutionary potential of the Communist Party of Poland in this war-infested atmosphere was either another smoke screen to give cover to the Soviet retreat from revolutionary plans in Europe or another cardinal mistake in Soviet analysis of the real situation in Poland. By 1928 the Polish Party, subjected to Pilsudski's repressive measures, as a political factor was all but dead.

CHAPTER 11

INDEPENDENT POLICIES

THE December 1927 meeting of the League in Geneva gave leading European statesmen a precious opportunity to acquire a direct impression of the man who was the architect of Polish policy and who led Poland along the proud but perilous path of defying both her powerful neighbors. The impression they gained of Joseph Pilsudski was as encouraging as it was perplexing.

When Austen Chamberlain suggested that Polish-Lithuanian tension be eased by posting the League's neutral officers along the border, Pilsudski burst out that "he was sick of the League controls, that they had so many in Poland that the mere name stank in the nostrils of the people . . . and that the proposal was offensive to him." Nevertheless, the following day, December 9, at breakfast with the British, French, Italian, and German Foreign Ministers, he confided "that his real ambition was to be Chief of Staff for the League" and elaborated his concept of collective security and action.[1] The man who always despised the League and ultimately contributed to its impotence now wished to lead its armed forces for which, at any rate, there was no provision in the Covenant. The incongruity of the situation was so obvious that his proposal could have been understood only as a joke in poor taste. The conversation that morning zigzagged from one subject to another as the Marshal spoke at length about the past, World War I, peppering his monologue with laughter and anecdotes. "I have seldom assisted at a more amusing gather-

[1] Sir Charles A. Petrie, *The Life and Letters of the Right Hon. Sir Austen Chamberlain* (2 vols.; London: Cassel and Comp., 1940), II, pp. 319, 320.

ing," recorded Austen Chamberlain.[2] However, it must have been less amusing to the representatives of Great Britain, France, and Italy, to whom Poland owed her resurrection after the war, when in their presence—and undoubtedly to Stresemann's satisfaction—Pilsudski, who never concealed his respect for the German army and German efficiency, seized upon this inopportune occasion to extol the German army's "heroic achievements."[3]

IMPROVEMENT IN POLISH-GERMAN RELATIONS

After the breakfast, Pilsudski and Stresemann met privately. Pilsudski assured Stresemann of his sincere desire to establish good relations with Germany and rejected emphatically the allegation that he harbored a secret desire to seize East Prussia. "When you go to Königsberg [the ancient capital of East Prussia] you can tell everybody on my behalf that there are not half a dozen people in Poland who would have such thoughts," stated Pilsudski. He continued, "What should we do with East Prussia? We do not need it." When Stresemann mentioned a few questions of a practical economic nature which divided the two countries, Pilsudski answered with a sweeping gesture and indicated that he wanted to settle all questions with Germany. "We can settle the whole thing in six months," he stated.[4] Stresemann was obviously impressed by Pilsudski's sincerity; but, aware of the complexity and the emotional intensity of the Polish-German relations, he reacted rather cautiously to Pilsudski's exuberant offer.

Two days after the conversation, Briand asked Stresemann if he had mentioned to Pilsudski the question of the Polish boundary. Stresemann answered in the negative and explained that he had seen the Polish statesman for the first time in his

[2] *Ibid.*, p. 320.
[3] *AA*, 1428/2945, 573408.
[4] *Ibid.*, 573408–10; Stresemann's note about the meeting, December 9, 1927.

life and therefore could not raise immediately the question of frontiers. Briand expressed regret, for he was convinced that Stresemann "would have found him [Pilsudski] on all questions which [existed] between Germany and Poland more open-minded than [he] perhaps [thought] himself." Briand and Stresemann then discussed a possible compensation for Poland, and according to Stresemann, "Herr Briand was quite enthusiastic about the idea" of giving Poland a free port in Danzig and eventually a free port in Memel. Stresemann recorded with particular satisfaction that Briand "did not utter a single word of criticism against the thought of a change of boundaries." [5]

If Briand's official position prevented him from giving more affirmative support to Stresemann's repeated statements on Polish boundary revision, some of his subordinates were less inhibited and on a number of occasions disclosed the real feelings of the *Quai d'Orsay*. The French legal expert, Henri Fromageot, remarked to his German colleague, Gaus, that "the boundary between Germany and Poland must be settled." [6] Phillippe Berthelot, the Secretary-General of the French Ministry for Foreign Affairs, expressed similar sentiments to the German Ambassador, Leopold von Hoesch.[7] The French military attaché in Berlin reported with approval German military views about the untenability of the German-Polish boundary.[8] It is quite probable that at least some of these confidential statements reached the Polish government. It is hardly surprising that Poland's sentiments toward her ally, France, suffered and a nagging thought began to work in Pilsudski's mind that France might not stand behind Poland in a moment of crisis. A few years later, he did not hesitate to express his worries to French officials.

[5] *AA*, 1428/2945, 573425–7.
[6] *Ibid.*, 573426; Stresemann's note of December 11, 1927.
[7] *Ibid.*, 573481–2; February 5, 1928.
[8] George Castellan, *Le réarmament clandestin du Reich, 1930–1935* (Paris: Librairie Plon, 1954), pp. 468–70.

On December 16, 1927, at a closed meeting in Königsberg, Stresemann reported his conversation with Pilsudski. He assured the eager but somewhat hostile listeners, who were impatient at his cautious policy of peaceful change of their Polish borders, that the idea of a boundary change was being increasingly understood in the West. At the same time, he warned that Germany could not think of taking the Corridor by way of war because she "had no power." He was confident, however, that she could achieve her goal by negotiations, particularly with France.[9]

Chamberlain went even further than Briand in his support of Stresemann's policy. He expressed full agreement with Germany's refusal to sign a German-Polish guarantee pact before the change of boundary. He then continued, "There exists only one man who can do it [solve the German-Polish question]: Pilsudski." [10] Subsequent events proved that both Briand and Chamberlain were mistaken about Pilsudski; there is no evidence other than the somewhat suspicious statement made by Dr. Diamand in July 1926 which would indicate any willingness to give up any territory to Germany.

The Polish government had followed with dismay the French policy toward Germany since the time of the pre-Locarno negotiations in 1925. Though outwardly relations remained cordial, it now began to question the sincerity and faithfulness of France's alliance with Poland. When General Kutrzeba visited Paris in 1928 he bluntly asked the French Chief of Staff, General Debeney, what France would do in case of a German attack on Poland. "General Debeney answered evasively that in such a situation the decision would depend on political factors." [11] The answer really was not as

[9] Stresemann, *Vermächtnis,* III, pp. 247–48. Gąsiorowski, "Stresemann and Poland after Locarno," pp. 312–13.

[10] *AA,* 1428/2945, 573431–5; Stresemann's note, December 12, 1927.

[11] J. Lipski, "Przyczynki do polsko-niemieckiej deklaracji o nieagresji," *Bellona,* Nos. I and II, 1951, p. 25. Still later, in the summer of 1929, the French attempted to give to the French-Polish alliance treaty a restrictive interpretation. *Ibid.,* pp. 27–9.

evasive as Kutrzeba thought, for an alliance which is dependent on political developments may prove not to be an alliance at all.

Such signs of the weakening Polish-French friendship augured well for Stresemann's patient but determined policy of wresting boundary regions from Poland through diplomacy rather than violence. Skillful diplomacy had freed Germany from the hateful Allied Military Control prior to the originally fixed date and the negotiations on the evacuation of the Rhineland were about to reach an equally successful conclusion. Perhaps the time had now come to force the issue of the Polish boundary—by way of negotiations.

Stresemann decided to tackle the problem by making a few gestures of friendship toward Poland. Near the end of January 1928 he instructed the Envoy to Warsaw to thank Zaleski for keeping him informed about the Polish-Lithuanian negotiations and to assure him that the forthcoming visit to Berlin of the Lithuanian Prime Minister, Voldemaras, should in no way be interpreted as an anti-Polish move.[12] A few days later, on January 30, speaking about Polish-German relations, he stated, "We need to live in peace and good understanding with our neighbors to the west and east." He then reviewed the past efforts of the government to reach a trade agreement with Poland.[13] When in March 1928 he met privately with an emissary of Pilsudski, Prince Michael Radziwill, he spoke in a benevolent manner about German-Polish relations and suggested that "now was the last and best moment to reach an integral agreement with Poland." He also spoke about Germany's eventual financial aid to Poland.[14]

During the year, some agreements and conventions were signed by Berlin and Warsaw concerning such matters as

---

[12] *AA*, 1428/2945, 573471-4; January 24, 1928.

[13] *Documents on International Affairs*, 1928, ed. John W. Wheeler-Bennett (London: Oxford University Press, 1929), pp. 93-4.

[14] Gąsiorowski, "Stresemann and Poland after Locarno," pp. 314-15, quoting from *Nachlass*, 3149/7348, 165204-5.

inheritance rights, frontier regulations, customs formalities, passports, emigration, and export of timber—all signifying at least some improvement in the atmosphere. In September 1928 trade negotiations were even resumed, although they soon broke down after President Hindenburg made a tactless statement in German Upper Silesia, asking for the restoration of Polish Upper Silesia to Germany. On this question the Poles were as adamant as the Germans were persistent.

Poland at first reciprocated Germany's public gestures of good will. On January 9, 1928, speaking before the Research Institute of International Affairs, Zaleski acknowledged some signs favorable to a German-Polish understanding.[15] Then, on May 18, 1928, before the Foreign Affairs Committee of the *Sejm*, he emphasized the importance and usefulness of the Geneva meeting with Stresemann. However, he also indicated that Poland would like to receive some additional guarantees against growing German strength, an inevitable result of the contemplated withdrawal of Allied units from the Rhineland.[16]

The German reaction to Zaleski's statement was quick and forceful and overnight the patina of good will disappeared. Schubert instructed the Ambassador in Paris to query the French government as to whether it stood behind this "new campaign" of Zaleski or whether there was a change in its policy. Then, to cast suspicion on the reliability of the Polish foreign policy, the French government was to be told that Zaleski, according to very secret information, had recently explored a new idea. This was the possibility that Poland might be willing to cooperate closely with Italy, Hungary, and Rumania; such cooperation would be achieved at the expense of France's two allies, Czechoslovakia and Yugoslavia, and at the same time would jeopardize Polish-French relations.[17] As the

---

[15] Zaleski, *op. cit.*, pp. 96–7.
[16] *Ibid.*, pp. 135–38.
[17] *AA*, 1428/2945, 573629–33; June 16, 1928.

French and European system of security was based on France's alliances with Poland and the countries of the Little Entente, and as Hungary received in her revisionist policy increasing support from fascist Italy, any mention of the possibility of Poland's close cooperation with these two powers was bound to reverberate negatively in the chancelleries of Paris and those of her allies.

All these happenings were eloquent evidence of growing German prestige and power and of Stresemann's confidence in the effectiveness of his policy. They were also indicative of a distinctly new trend in German foreign policy. No longer did Stresemann need the cooperation of the Soviet Union to pursue his goal of boundary revision. To be sure, he continued to cherish Soviet friendship and to use it as a counterbalance against possible Western pressures; he encouraged continuing, secret Soviet-German military cooperation and was anxious to develop lucrative trade relations with Russia. However, he no longer exchanged confidential views with her on Poland and any mutual plan "to push Poland back to her ethnographic boundary" was no longer mentioned. In fact, he was undoubtedly aware that any common Soviet-German policy on Poland would only strengthen Russia's international position and might indeed prove fatal to plans for boundary revision, which he now felt could be best accomplished through cooperation with the West.

By 1928 Rantzau was the sole advocate of exclusive, anti-French, German cooperation with the Soviet Union. In a letter to his friend, Count Bernstorff, Rantzau complained bitterly about a "thousand difficulties" which beset him as he tried to uphold his policy of the East against the West.[18]

Rantzau, however, was soon to disappear from his Moscow outpost of German-Soviet friendship. He had been seriously ill for several years and in September 1928 he died. His last

[18] Graf Johann H. Bernstorff, *Erinnerungen und Briefe* (Zurich: Polygraphischer Verlag, 1936), p. 192.

thoughts were occupied with his six-year mission in Moscow; his brother, Count Ernst Rantzau, sent Chicherin the following message at his request: "My twin brother, Ambassador Count Brockdorff-Rantzau, had me called to his bedside this afternoon and requested me to convey the following to you, People's Commissar, and Mr. Litvinov: That, after the verdict of his physician, he was aware that he had to reckon with his sudden death any hour. That he was, in his hour of death, requesting me to tell both gentlemen that he had regarded it as his life's task to carry the policies pursued by him in the last years to the desired aim.

"He further asked me to tell you that he thanks both Commissars, especially you, for the faith in collaboration that he has always found with you in the difficult years. His last and firm hope, he said, was that the German and Russian people may in common work attain the end they desire." [19]

IMPROVEMENT IN POLISH-SOVIET RELATIONS

Simultaneously with the improvement in German-Polish relations, the Soviet government renewed its efforts to sign a nonaggression treaty with Poland. In 1928 the Soviet Union was passing through perhaps the weakest period of its ten-year existence. The struggle against Trotskyists and other anti-Stalinists was far from ended; the first Five-Year Plan, which was designed to launch Russia on the road to becoming an industrial and military power, was still only a blueprint; the prospect of collectivization of the land provoked violent reactions all over the country. British-Soviet relations remained suspended and the resulting tensions found expression in violent attacks on each other over the future of China. Germany was obviously lost as a reliable partner for any anti-Western plans, lost indeed as any bulwark of defense against the constant threat of alleged Western designs against Russia. Poland and some Baltic States were viewed as pawns of an

[19] Hilger, *op. cit.*, p. 95.

aggressive British policy. Moreover, the "unpredictable" Pilsudski represented still another danger, for the Soviet government was convinced that he had not given up his hope that Belorussia and the Ukraine might be detached from the Soviet Union and brought into a federation, which would extend from the Baltic to the Black Sea, under Polish leadership.

Therefore, the Soviet Union sought some guarantees of peace on her Polish borders. A treaty of nonaggression would not only alleviate some of her fears and worries, but it would accomplish also a much needed strengthening of Russia's hand in regard to Germany. Furthermore, such a treaty would facilitate a *rapprochement* with France and blunt the Polish drive to become the leader of an anti-Soviet coalition of the Baltic States. Moscow, of course, would no more put its trust in Pilsudski's commitment to nonaggression than it would seriously reject for all time the possibility of an aggressive act against Poland; but for the time being, a pact of nonaggression would serve its limited purpose.

There were, as well, some signs that Poland desired to reach an understanding with Moscow. Zaleski stated on two occasions that Soviet-Polish relations had improved but that Poland could not accept the Soviet proposal on nonaggression because of Russia's hostile attitude toward the League of Nations and because she refused to include in the proposal an arbitration clause.[20] This was the first time that this argument had been heard in the year-long exchange of views over the possibility of a Soviet-Polish treaty of nonaggression. Until 1928, the Polish government had insisted upon the inclusion of the Baltic States in any such treaty. The absence of such a counterproposal on this occasion was perhaps indicative of the sincere Polish desire to negotiate a bilateral treaty. On one occasion, Stomoniakov, a prominent member of the *Narkomindel,* remarked to Rantzau sarcastically that the Poles wanted "to present themselves as the most faithful force of the

[20] Zaleski, *op. cit.,* pp. 96–7, 138–40. *Vneshniaia Politika,* III, p. 254.

League of Nations." Chicherin was convinced that they had no serious desire to sign either a trade convention or a nonaggression treaty.[21]

Then, toward the end of 1928, an unexpected opportunity to renew the offer, though in a modified form, presented itself. Since spring, the big powers, including this time the United States, had been negotiating what that summer became known as the Kellogg-Briand Pact. Poland, however, was not invited to participate in the preliminary negotiations and openly resented the fact that she seemed neither to be recognized nor treated as one of the big powers.[22] In her attempts to become known as a major power her prestige frequently had been hurt—at Geneva, at Locarno, and now again. The sting was partially removed when on August 27, 1928, her name appeared on the Pact as one of the original signatories, but nevertheless, she still held a grudge against her Western friends. Also, she rightly saw the basic ineffectualness of the document, which called, without sanctions, for "the renunciation of war as an instrument of national policy." All this perhaps prepared Poland psychologically and politically for a reconsideration of the repeated Soviet proposals on a nonaggression treaty.

On December 10, 1928, Litvinov recounted in a public speech all efforts which his government had pursued in normalizing Soviet relations with Poland. He dealt in some detail with the past proposals on a nonaggression pact and offered new assurances of Soviet desires to live with Poland in peace and friendship.[23] Then, on December 29, confirming Russia's "unchangeable readiness to sign a nonaggression treaty," Litvinov invited Poland to sign a protocol, according to which

[21] *AA*, 1414/2860, 559564-7; June 13, 1928; 559419-20; January 30, 1928; also 3036/6698, 111880.

[22] *Foreign Relations Papers*, 1928, I, p. 4.

[23] M. M. Litvinov, *Vneshniaia Politika SSSR. Rechi i zaiavleniia, 1927-1935* (Moscow: Gosudarstvennoe Sotsialno-ekonomicheskoie izdatel'stvo, 1935), pp. 11-12.

the Kellogg-Briand Pact would become valid between the two countries without waiting for its ratification by "fourteen designated states" as prescribed by the Pact. Litvinov's note further stated that the Soviet government had addressed a similar invitation to Lithuania but not to the other Baltic States because they as yet did not adhere to the Pact of Paris.[24] It was not difficult to see the motive behind this discriminatory approach. Lithuania was openly hostile toward Poland and to bring her into direct negotiations with both Russia and Poland would strengthen her position toward the latter. Furthermore, to leave the other Baltic States out of the picture, at least temporarily, would block Poland's continuing attempts to conduct collective negotiations with Russia.

The Polish government, on January 10, 1929, expressed its willingness to accept the Soviet proposal but insisted upon the participation of the Baltic States as well as Rumania, with which the Soviet government did not even maintain diplomatic relations. It also was indignant about the proposed participation of Lithuania, with which Russia had no common boundary. The Soviet government immediately met these Polish demands and pressed for a speedy conclusion of a treaty.[25]

DETERIORATION IN GERMAN-SOVIET RELATIONS

German reaction to these negotiations was immediate and direct. In the series of conversations and messages which followed, the German Foreign Office objected to the fact that the Soviet government had not informed them in advance of this important offer to Poland; it expressed fear that the proposal would create the impression that Poland did indeed play a leading role in East European affairs. Furthermore, should the Kellogg-Briand Pact not be ratified, the proposed regional

---

[24] Litvinov, *Vneshniaia Politika SSSR*, pp. 341–42.
[25] *Ibid.*, pp. 342–47.

pact would put Germany into an "impossible," "disagreeable," and "most uncomfortable" position, as Poland would now be free of Soviet pressure. However, Germany would not join the pact, continued Berlin's arguments, because it would then have the quality of an "East Locarno" and, by implication, would mean German acceptance of the present German-Polish boundary.

The Soviet government first tried to soothe the German Foreign Office by expressing its belief that the Poles would decline the Soviet proposal; that it had actually been offered to compel Poland to show her true color; that in any case such a protocol did not imply recognition by Russia of the present Polish boundary.[26]

The newly appointed German Ambassador to the Soviet Union, Herbert von Dirksen, had the rather unpleasant task of opening his new diplomatic assignment by making Stresemann's terse attitude known to the Soviet government. Dirksen lacked the forcefulness of his predecessor, Rantzau, and though completely devoted to Rantzau's old policy of close Soviet-German cooperation, he did not enjoy in any sense his predecessor's prestige and authority in German political circles. He was, in fact, only an unimaginative bureaucrat, who executed his government's instructions. However, it must be said that when Dirksen came to Moscow at the beginning of 1929, Soviet-German relations had lost much of their glamor; "the Rapallo spirit" had vanished, the period of bold and sometimes adventurous designs had passed. Moreover, Dirksen failed to find in Moscow Rantzau's counterpart, Chicherin, who had always been willing to listen to Rantzau's anti-French outbursts. Now Chicherin was gravely ill and Litvinov appeared to be more skillful in handling German diplomatic interventions.

Litvinov assured Dirksen that the Soviet proposal had no

[26] *AA*, 2319/4562, 159815–8, 159839–46; 1428/2945, 573824–5; 3042/6698, 115652, 115660–1.

other aim than to impale Poland on the horns of a disagreeable dilemma: either to sign an unpleasant pact or to appear
to be a disturber of peace. Nor did he see the danger of bringing the Baltic States under Polish influence—a strange novelty
in the Soviet arsenal of argumentation. Of course, he admitted,
should Poland accept the offer, the Soviet government could
hardly retreat from its position.[27] Yet, the Poles did accept
and the Soviet government did not back down.

On February 9, 1929, the Litvinov Protocol was signed in
Moscow; the signatories were the Soviet Union, Rumania,
Latvia, Estonia, and Poland. Lithuania delayed its accession
until April 1. Litvinov called the occasion "without precedent
in history." [28] This was undoubtedly an overstatement, but
the Russians had reason to be satisfied for they had succeeded
in reversing Poland's negative attitude. The Poles were happy
for they had managed to maneuver Russia into a situation in
which she signed a collective treaty with the Baltic States—a
move she had opposed for years. Germany was the loser, but
her fears were assuaged when the Kellogg-Briand Pact was
ratified and the Litvinov Protocol thereby lost much of its
original significance, as interpreted by Berlin.

The political harvest which Russia gathered from the
Litvinov Protocol proved to be meager. Only three months
after it had been signed, the Chairman of the Council of Commissars, Rykov, complained before the Fifth Congress of the
Soviets of the USSR that "Poland was abandoning the spirit"
of the Protocol. He re-emphasized "the serious anxiety" of the
Soviet government about reaching "lasting friendly relations
with Poland." Enumerating various measures, including the
offer of a nonaggression pact, which were meant to prove the
Soviet government's peaceful intentions, Rykov stressed, however, that these had not been "made from cowardice, as every-

---

[27] *AA*, 1414/2860, 560110–2, Dirksen's report January 7, 1929; 560118–20,
January 20, 1929.
[28] Litvinov, *op. cit.*, p. 292.

one [knew] that [the Soviet Union] can and will fight back in the right manner." [29]

The last remark provoked a sharp reaction from the Polish Minister in Moscow, Patek, who during the delegates' applause following this declaration, "ostentatiously left the hall." According to Patek's report, the Soviet government must have subsequently realized the "absolute inappropriateness" of Rykov's statement for the press reported the speech with the words, "if [it] is attacked and compelled to fight," which were not in the speech itself.[30]

The Litvinov Protocol could not possibly remove the deep-rooted mistrust and the hostility between Russia and Poland, regardless of the outward manifestations of friendship. Tensions mounted and incidents continued to take place. When, for example, the Russian *émigrés* in Warsaw celebrated the tenth anniversary of Georgia's independence (which had lasted only for two years), the Soviet Minister to Poland, Bogomolov, protested vigorously that Polish officials had participated at the celebration.[31] A few days later, June 8, 1929, retaliatory demonstrations were staged at Tiflis in front of the Polish consulate. These were followed four days later by larger and more violent crowds, and, of course, by a Polish protest. The Soviet government expressed regret; but there is no evidence of a Polish apology.[32]

There was an ostensibly anti-Polish overtone in the prominence given by the Soviet government to economic delegations from East Prussia, which came to Moscow, and to the reception in the Soviet capital in honor of the President of the free city of Danzig.[33]

[29] Soiuz Sovetskikh Sotsialisticheskikh Respublik. *5 S'ezd Sovetov SSSR.* Stenograficheskii otchet [n.p., n.d.]. Rykov's speech, May 20, 1929; biulleten No. 1, p. 28.

[30] *Ciechanowski Deposit.* Reports of the Polish Legation in Moscow, 1929–1931, 543-T-29, May 22, 1929.

[31] *Izvestiia,* June 2, 1929.

[32] *Ibid.,* June 19, 1929.

[33] *Ciechanowski Deposit.* Reports of the Polish Legation in Moscow,

If the Polish-Soviet relations were again tense, the pattern of the past seemed changed. In 1929 the tension no longer encouraged Russian cooperation with Germany. In fact, by 1929 Soviet-German relations, too, had become so strained that both Germany and the Soviet Union appeared content to follow separate policies toward Poland. The Soviet Union bitterly resented German involvement with the West and was particularly offended at the neglectful manner in which Germany defended Soviet interests in China, with which the Soviet government had no diplomatic relations. Germany, on the other hand, repeatedly protested against the subversive activities of the Communist International, which with the first signs of the economic depression became once again increasingly aggressive. The Polish legation in Moscow did not fail to observe this process of steady deterioration in Soviet-German relations and reported it to Warsaw with understandable satisfaction.[34]

Ambassador Dirksen, who had always been devoted to the idea of an intimate German-Soviet relationship, was seriously concerned with this development. When he was on vacation in Berlin in October 1929, he wrote a lengthy memorandum which set forth some basic principles in respect to Soviet-German relations. He stated that there was no longer any need for a justification of friendly Russian-German relations as the two nations now clearly had common interests in East European politics, particularly in regard to Lithuania and Poland. They also had common interests in such international questions as disarmament. He recognized that the old-fashioned, romantic concept of "the partnership of fate" (*Schicksalsgemeinschaft*) had given way to a realistic policy of common interests. This policy was based on the Rapallo and Berlin treaties and although there was no question of enlarg-

1929–1931, P. III, 10976/29, May 15, 1929. Report by Polish Consul General in Danzig, June 29, 1931, 817/31. See also Litvinov's speech December 4, 1929, Litvinov, *op. cit.*, p. 47.
[34] *Ciechanowski Deposit*, P. III, 11871/29; September 12, 1929.

ing them into an alliance, they must not be permitted to "become a dead letter." [35]

When, toward the end of 1929, Dirksen reviewed the developments of the past year, he characterized Soviet-German relations as economically and politically stagnant and overshadowed by the German ties with the West. He mentioned numerous points of friction but was convinced that German national interests still called for friendly Soviet-German cooperation. As to the future, he recommended continuation of this policy because "the assumptions for political friendship which had led to Rapallo and to the Berlin Treaty have remained the same." [36]

Dirksen's recommendation sounded almost like an appeal to revive the ghost of an all but forgotten past. In 1929 the international situation in Europe, and particularly the position of Germany, was fundamentally different from the Rapallo era. At that time Germany was tenaciously fighting for a place in the international arena and needed the support of Russia; by 1929 she was recognized as an equal by the big powers.

CHANGE OF GUARD

However, by the end of 1929 German foreign policy was no longer in the hands of that skillful and relentless statesman, Gustav Stresemann. He had died on October 2, 1929, and with him Germany lost not only the chief architect of her foreign policy but also the great manipulator of the manifold forces of European power politics. He had followed systematically the goal of undoing the Versailles *diktat* and in this respect had identified himself with the German leaders of all other political denominations. However, his uniqueness lay in his vision and in his skillful maneuvering to achieve his goal through cooperation with rather than opposition to the West, while at the same time insisting on friendly and—in the mili-

[35] *AA*, 1415/2860, 560829–34; October 31, 1929.
[36] *Ibid.*, 561042–8; December 27, 1929.

tary and economic fields—even close relations with Russia. As numerous German documents have somewhat belatedly revealed, his avenues were intricate, his sincerity frequently questionable, the integrity of his policy not beyond reproach. When he was glorified by many publicists and even awarded the Nobel Peace Prize as a great European and a man dedicated to the cause of peace, few people understood the ulterior motives of his policy. Nevertheless, Stresemann is remembered today as a brilliant political strategist and as an outstanding Foreign Minister of his country—but not as a great conciliator of Europe.

His successor, Julius Curtius, lacked many of Stresemann's qualities. Under his guidance German foreign policy drifted back and forth between the West and Russia in a state of indecision and increasing confusion. However, it must be added that with the advent of the world economic depression, Curtius and Heinrich Brüning, the Chancellor, lost the relatively stable and solid political conditions which Stresemann had enjoyed and put to full use. In 1930 there were 3 million unemployed in Germany. Gloom and despondency over economic conditions made the people responsive to Nazism and in the autumn election the Nazi Party rose from its 800,000 votes of 1928 to 6½ million. By 1932 the number of idle men rose to 6 million and in the July elections nearly 14 million persons had succumbed to the chauvinistic appeals of Nazism. Not only many German political leaders, but other statesmen as well failed to read properly the handwriting on the wall, the significance of the whirlwind proportions of Nazism. In Eastern European politics "business as usual" prevailed; the powers, unmindful of the coming storm, continued to maneuver for positions of strength which were unrelated to farsighted, constructive policies.

Stresemann had left the scene, the voice of the influential Ambassador Rantzau was no longer heard, and the third key figure in the area of Soviet-German relations, Chicherin, was declining in both political and physical strength. As early as May 1929, Dirksen reported that Chicherin's health was failing, that his grave diabetic condition had now been complicated by polyneuritis. He reported that Chicherin suffered from unbearable pain—such as had driven Ioffe to suicide. A struggle for succession between Litvinov and Karakhan was going on behind the scenes.[37]

When in January 1930 Chicherin returned to Moscow from a long rest in Germany, he wished for reasons of health not to be welcomed by anyone at the station and shortly thereafter went to the Caucasus. Litvinov was considered most likely to become his successor, though Dirksen reported that very pronounced anti-Semitism on the part of a group of Georgians (led by Stalin) in Moscow impaired his chances.[38] Despite this opposition from the Georgians, Litvinov was appointed the Commissar for Foreign Affairs on July 21, 1930. Although his first statement to foreign correspondents in Moscow was not indicative of any change,[39] nevertheless, from that moment on Soviet foreign policy gradually began to turn away from Germany and draw closer to France. It is, however, open to serious doubt whether the change was due so much to Litvinov's personal convictions and influence as it was to Stalin's own decision and to political changes in Germany.

Litvinov, who served as Chicherin's deputy in the People's Commissariat for Foreign Affairs for twelve years, was politically more influential than his superior. An old Bolshevik, he was close to Soviet leaders and clashed from time to time with Chicherin in matters of basic Soviet orientation. He refused to see in Soviet relations with Germany any foundation for Soviet policy in Europe and advocated the utmost flexibility in the conduct of Soviet affairs. If anything in Soviet foreign policy could be characterized as definitely leaning toward one

[37] *AA,* 1415/2860, 560311; May 18, 1929.
[38] *Ibid.,* 561049; January 6, 1930.
[39] Litvinov, *op. cit.,* pp. 51-4.

power, it was the fact that Litvinov, in opposition to Chicherin, was both anti-German and pro-French. It was his idea to participate in the Geneva disarmament negotiations and even to join at a later date (1934) the League of Nations. In personal qualities he also differed sharply from Chicherin. He was ruthless, unsentimental, friendless; his work was systematic, well organized, and not burdened by details.[40] Stalin appeared to appreciate fully his skills for he entrusted him with the execution of Soviet foreign affairs during the perilous years between 1930 and 1939. However, in 1939 a radical reversal in Soviet policy, the close cooperation with the Nazi Germany, necessitated the removal of this protagonist of Western orientation and the man of Jewish origin.

Still another powerful supporter of a close Soviet-German cooperation, General von Seeckt, was no longer on the scene. He had been dismissed from his position as Chief of Staff in 1926. He continued, however, to speak and write on his favorite theme and even debased himself to become a candidate of the German People's Party for parliament, an institution which he had always profoundly despised.

In 1930 General von Seeckt had prepared a long memorandum in which he urged an Eastern oriented policy for his country. In the west, he maintained, the German nationality (*Deutschtum*) was not threatened in terms of its biological existence, but in the east it was in danger of losing even more than it had already lost.[41] To him the struggle for the German boundary in the west was not national (*völkisch*) but rather of a political, military and economic nature. In the east it was "a purely racial struggle"; [42] there, it was not a struggle for boundaries—they had been shifted frequently—but a struggle for nationhood, for "the spread of the German cultural mission, civilization and colonizing mastery over the Slav

---

[40] See L. Fischer, *The Soviets in World Affairs*, I, pp. xiii–xiv; L. Fischer, *Men and Politics*, pp. 127–28.
[41] *Seeckt Papers*, reel 25, *stück* 237, pp. 20–1.
[42] *Ibid.*, p. 21.

masses. . . ." The alternative was, he stated, one of the German nation "being washed away by the Slav sandwave. . . ." [43] In his position, of course, there was an appropriate link between the past Prussian *Kulturträger* and the emerging Nazi racist.

After World War I, Seeckt's memorandum continued, Poland's mission had been to guard Germany; but while treaties may be signed, "the life and death struggle between the Polish (*Polentum*) and German nationality continues." Poland was no longer a *"Saisonstaat"* but was "growing in strength through a firm national will." [44] He thought it was an illusion to hope for a lasting and honorable understanding with Poland.

To Seeckt, Germany's cooperation with the West would inevitably make her its vassal; he wanted "to be spared seeing the *Reichswehr* under the command of General Weygand or Marshal Pilsudski." However, between Russia and Germany there was no direct conflict, though he would not wish to march against the West in the service of Russia. On the contrary, Russia was interested in strengthening Germany in view of their common hostility toward Poland.[45] One can easily see that Seeckt's views had not changed since the period immediately following World War I; however, in 1930, his voice had lost the official authority of a military leader. And when, nine years later, Hitler did execute Seeckt's dangerous suggestion, the temporary cooperation with Russia proved to serve primarily Soviet needs and facilitated, in the final analysis, the march of communism into Central Europe.

Meanwhile, Soviet-German relations continued to shift back and forth between crises and attempts at cooperation. Scores

---

[43] *Ibid.*, pp. 22, 32.

[44] *Ibid.*, pp. 34-5.

[45] *Ibid.*, pp. 44, 46, 47. Seeckt developed similar ideas on two other occasions, in a lecture and in a booklet: *Wege deutschen Aussenpolitik* (Leipzig: Verlag von Quelle & Meyer, 1931); *Deutschland zwischen West und Ost* (Hamburg: Hanseatische Verlagsanstalt, 1933).

of telegrams were exchanged between the two capitals on such critical issues as the German attitude toward the serious situation in Manchuria; the Third International's continuing activities in Germany; and Stalin's brutal policy of collectivization of land and religious persecution, a policy which created widespread public indignation in Germany.

On February 9, 1930, reported Dirksen, Litvinov, with whom he was having supper, was deeply depressed about the state of Soviet-German relations. "This is the end of Rapallo," exclaimed Litvinov.[46] A few days later Dirksen acknowledged that relations had indeed reached a critical point. The Soviets were convinced that German policy was swinging increasingly toward the West, making inevitable a growing anti-Soviet attitude. Germany, it was felt, had completely joined the capitalist countries, going so far as to attempt to reach an agreement with Poland on all political and economic questions. Though Dirksen considered these complaints unjustified, in his opinion the German government did nothing to repair the growing breach. Assuming that Rapallo still remained the basis of Soviet-German relations, he suggested that the German Foreign Minister discuss the situation in the parliament at an early occasion and that economic and financial negotiations be resumed.[47]

After prolonged preparations, the two governments began negotiations in June and brought them to a successful conclusion on July 9, 1930. As a result, the political atmosphere improved so rapidly that after months of silence the governments were able to resume the exchange of confidential views on such matters as the protracted Lithuanian-Polish controversy and to a limited extent even on the problem of Poland.[48] However, "the spirit of Rapallo" was gone and Soviet and German policies toward Poland now took independent roads.

---

[46] *AA*, 1416/2860, 561159–62.
[47] *Ibid.*, 561196–205; February 14, 1930.
[48] *Ibid.*, 561818ff.

RENEWED POLISH-GERMAN TENSIONS

Curtius pursued much the same policy toward Poland as had Stresemann, though without his authority and his systematic, methodical approach. As with Stresemann, Curtius' main goal was to achieve the revision of the boundary, but he, too, knew that Germany had no military strength to force the change and that for the time being negotiations offered small promise. He appears to have thought that Pilsudski was in favor of ceding the Corridor to Germany if Poland could be compensated at the expense of Lithuania; but there is no evidence to support his views.[49] At any rate, he further felt that even such a deal was "not negotiable" because of Lithuania's anticipated opposition. So he pursued the only course he thought open to Germany,—the establishment of closer economic relations with Poland—and worked toward conclusion of a trade agreement and the elimination of the tariff war with her.

Indeed, a trade agreement was signed on March 17, 1930, and was greeted in Europe as an important step on the strenuous road toward pacification and reconciliation between the two traditional adversaries. However, these hopes did not last for long. The ratification was postponed while both parliaments debated the text of the treaty in an atmosphere of mutual recrimination. As a result, the tariff war was intensified.

At the beginning of June 1930 a shooting incident on the Polish-German border brought a strong German protest and created a new crisis between the two countries. Curtius spoke about the incident with the British Ambassador and "rather went out of his way to affirm in particularly energetic terms that Germany could not rest content with her present frontier in the east."[50] To make things even worse, a member of the

---

[49] Julius Curtius, *Sechs Jahre Minister der deutschen Republik* (Heidelberg: Carl Winter, 1948), pp. 98–9, 244.
[50] *D.B.F.P.* Second Series, I, p. 490.

German government, Gottfried Treviranus, on August 10 delivered a provocative speech urging in strong language the revision of the boundaries. This, in turn, brought a vehement protest from the Polish government.[51]

To add fuel to an already inflamed situation, Pilsudski's political bloc won the elections of November 1930—by highly irregular methods—in which the national minorities registered heavy losses. This brought an immediate German complaint to the League of Nations. However, the sincerity of this indignation was highly questionable. Though it was not known at that time, the German Foreign Office was giving regular but, of course, clandestine financial support to the election campaigns of not only the German but also the Belorussian minorities of Poland.[52]

By now, the virulent Nazi agitations had reached a peak, compelling other German parties to compete in manifestations of patriotism. Various cities close to the Polish border were the best location to prove such national feelings. Aggressive charges were hurled at Poland at mass meetings, and the Polish government and various national organizations repaid these in kind. In turn, charges of violence and repressive measures found their familiar way to the councils of the League of Nations and the International Court of Justice. As an inevitable corollary to the growth of Nazism in Germany, the Nazis in Danzig became increasingly arrogant and the free city's relations with Poland deteriorated, too.

Furthermore, in September 1931 the Polish press published some documents which showed that the German military circles were in close cooperation with Ukrainian terrorist organizations in East Poland.[53] The British military attaché in

---

[51] *AA*, 1430/2945, 575234-6. *D.B.F.P.* Second Series, I, pp. 491–92, 499.
[52] A German Foreign Ministry document reveals the sums given to various minority groups in 1928 and the figures proposed for the fall campaign in 1930. *AA*, 2390/4624, 203099–100.
[53] Though the accusation was officially denied, Bülow, the recently ap-

Berlin, Colonel Marshall-Cornwall confirmed in his annual report that "Poland [remained] the *bête noire* of the German military mind. The feeling of animosity is a product of the claim to moral and cultural superiority coupled with a sense of the military and political disadvantages imposed by the treaty [of Versailles]." [54]

On the other hand, the German government seemed to be genuinely worried that the Polish government might exploit the internal difficulties in Germany; they feared an invasion of Upper Silesia or East Prussia should a combined Nazi-communist uprising render Germany defenseless. Heinrich Brüning, the Chancellor, was in possession of "a new Polish mobilization plan about which [he was] told the same year [1931] through a foreign power. . . . The Polish mobilization plan was set up in such a way as to point beyond any question to their determined intention to take by a surprise attack the whole of Silesia at any offered opportunity." [55] Toward the end of October 1931, the Polish Minister to Washington, Tytus Filipowicz, reportedly stated to President Hoover on behalf of Pilsudski that he must counteract "a threatening attack by German irregular troops . . . by marching into Germany to settle the thing once and for all." [56]

pointed Undersecretary of State, admitted such contacts until 1928. *AA*, 1430/2945, 575703, 575694. See also *Foreign Relations Papers*, 1931, I, pp. 595–604.

[54] *D.B.F.P.* Second Series, II, p. 521.

[55] Heinrich Brüning, "Ein Brief," *Deutsche Rundschau*, Vol. 70, No. 7, July 1947, p. 2. He adds, not quite convincingly, that he succeeded, until he left the office in June 1932, in preventing this danger by working toward an improvement in the Polish-German relations. See also Ross, *op. cit.*, pp. 37–8. General Groener, the Minister of Defense, had prepared in November 1928 a secret memorandum for the German government in which he had based his request for building a new type of armored cruiser upon expectation of a Polish attack on East Prussia. *Nauticus*, "New Germany's New Navy," *The Review of Reviews*, LXXVIII, No. 468, January 15, 1929, pp. 17–21. See also Höltje, *op. cit.*, pp. 193–98.

[56] Ross, *op. cit.*, p. 38. Indeed, the Polish Minister himself reported that in a conversation with Colonel House, who asked him on December 31, 1931, about the Corridor, he "answered with the usual turn of speech, 'There is

In this pressing situation the international position of Poland suffered some serious setbacks. The evacuation of the Rhineland by the Allied armies in June 1930 occasioned serious forebodings in Warsaw that Germany, released from pressure in the west, would now turn with additional energy to the east. Moreover, when the Council of the League of Nations decided at its January 1931 session to convene a disarmament conference in February 1932, Germany again made it clear that she would insist on recognition of the principle of equality in armament. France's opposition to this demand appeared, under British pressure, to be already weakening—the development which Poland feared most.

France officially still stood behind the policy of the territorial integrity of Poland, but in secret diplomatic conversations she showed an increasing distaste for the Polish position. The British attitude toward the question of boundary revision was widely known. Even the United States, though not actively interested in East European affairs, did not hesitate to show where her sympathies lay on the question of the Polish-German boundary. The Secretary of State, Henry L. Stimson, told the Polish Minister on January 9, 1931, that "one thing [was] sure, that the Germans had succeeded in establishing in public opinion a just case for the revision of the Corridor. . . ." [57] Senator William E. Borah, the Chairman of the Senate Foreign Relations Committee, stated on October 23, 1931, that peace treaties must be revised and that it would be most necessary to revise particularly those parts which were related to

no problem of a Corridor. There is only the problem of East Prussia.' " *Ciechanowski Deposit.*

[57] *Ciechanowski Deposit.* Previous to that, the American Ambassador to Germany, after a visit to East Prussia in August 1930, stated to Carl Budding, the Prime Minister of West Prussia, that he realized now the gravity of the situation, though he had known for long, as had the rest of the world, about the untenability of the existing boundary. He recommended that change could be brought about only through a unified and determined effort by Germany and by some dramatization before the whole world of the untenability of the situation. *AA*, 1430/2945, 575230–2.

the Polish Corridor, Silesia, and Hungary.[58] In such a situation Poland might have rightly felt that she "could handle her enemies if God would only guard her against her friends."

[58] Arnold J. Toynbee, *Survey of International Affairs* (London: Oxford University Press, 1932), pp. 126–27.

CHAPTER 12

AN EQUILIBRIUM

THE POLISH-SOVIET PACT
OF NONAGGRESSION

◪ WITH Poland exposed to Germany's attacks and deprived
of the West's active support, and with the Soviet-German
relations at a low ebb, the situation at last appeared propitious
for negotiation of a Soviet-Polish treaty of nonaggression. On
December 4, 1929, Litvinov, in a speech before the Central
Committee of the Congress of the Soviet Union, expressed regret that Polish-Soviet relations did not show signs of improvement as a result of the Litvinov Protocol. However, his statement was remarkably restrained and he noted with satisfaction
a "more favorable development in trade relations with Poland." [1]

A few months later, *Izvestiia,* while attacking the Polish anti-
Soviet policy, extended anew to the Polish government the
hand of friendship and reaffirmed the Soviet government's
desire to sign a treaty of nonaggression.[2]

These promising signs were suddenly overshadowed, at least
temporarily—as had been the case so many times before—by
an act of violence. On April 26, 1930, a bomb was found in the
Soviet Legation in Warsaw and once more the prospect of improved relations was clouded by acrimonious and recriminatory correspondence between the two governments.[3]

However, the political exigencies of the moment carried
more weight than did such a local incident. Zaleski, in a

[1] Litvinov, *op. cit.,* p. 47.
[2] March 18, 1930.
[3] *Vneshniaia Politika,* III, pp. 418–21.

speech before the Senate Foreign Relations Committee at the beginning of January 1931, indicated that views were being exchanged between Warsaw and Moscow.[4] Then, on August 23, 1931, Patek handed to Litvinov a confidential note in which he summed up the negotiations based on the Soviet draft proposal of 1926 for a nonaggression pact. The note appeared to imply Polish readiness to resume the negotiations. It would have probably remained secret for some time had not circumstances compelled Moscow to react to the note publicly.

The French agency, *Havas,* on August 26 published an official communiqué which made several revelations. It stated that as early as October 1930 the Soviet government had proposed to the Polish government a resumption of negotiations, which would lead to the conclusion of a nonaggression pact. In December the Polish government expressed readiness to consider the Soviet proposal in principle. The Soviet government now had no choice but to acknowledge these previous contacts with the Polish government. On August 27 it made its position publicly known through the TASS agency but stressed that even this time Patek had not proposed formally any resumption of negotiations.[5] This was obviously an escape clause to answer persistent inquiries from Berlin.

When Litvinov met Curtius in Berlin at the beginning of November 1930, he expressed grave worry about the situation in Poland and, then, quite contrary to facts, stated that "the Poles had recently approached the Soviet Union once again to sign a nonaggression pact; Russia, however, declined." Curtius was astonished, but Litvinov repeated the statement and added that "the Soviet Union [would] not abandon its present course" of friendship with Germany.[6] On other occasions the Soviet representatives in Moscow and Berlin, exposed to repeated German prodding, found refuge in the niceties of the

[4] Zaleski, *op. cit.,* II, pp. 158–73.
[5] *Vneshniaia Politika,* III, pp. 501—502.
[6] *AA,* 1416/2860, 561876–82.

diplomatic vocabulary and admitted that "discussions" but not "negotiations" with Poland were taking place.[7]

German suspicions were doubled when messages began to reach Berlin that the Soviets were also engaged in political negotiations with France; the Foreign Office was convinced that they were parallel and complementary to the negotiations with Poland. Litvinov admitted to Dirksen in May 1931 that during the previous month the French Foreign Office had suggested on several occasions the idea of signing a nonaggression pact with Russia. However, he and other Soviet diplomats stressed that the initiative came from Paris, that great difficulties were expected, and that there were no negotiations with Poland paralleling those with France.[8] However, on August 12, 1931, Litvinov informed Dirksen that against all expectations the negotiations with France had led to positive results and that a nonaggression pact had just been initialed. Though it was to remain secret for the time being, Litvinov read some of its passages to Dirksen and attempted to satisfy his anxiety by stressing that the pact would weaken the Polish-French alliance.[9] The Soviet explanations, or rather excuses, were further pursued by Litvinov when he met Curtius toward the end of August in Berlin and again a few days later in Geneva. In an interview with the press he stated that Russia was ready to sign a nonaggression pact with Poland if the traditional Polish conditions for such a pact were omitted.[10]

Further surprises were to follow in quick succession. The Polish-Soviet negotiations were now being carried on in earnest. At first, both sides maintained their original position; the Poles reiterated their wish for a collective nonaggression treaty (which would include the Baltic States), for tying the treaty

---

[7] *AA*, 1417/2860, 561967, 561974, 561979, 561988–9, 561990–1, 562035–7.
[8] *Ibid.*, 562104–5, 562119–22, 562129, 562134–5.
[9] *Ibid.*, 562168–70.
[10] *AA*, 1430/2945, 5756675–83; 1417/2860, 562205–7, Curtius' memorandum about the conversation with Litvinov. For the latter's statement to the press see *Vneshniaia Politika*, III, pp. 503–504.

text to the League of Nations, and for the inclusion of an arbitration clause. The Soviets insisted on their proposal of a simple bilateral treaty. Finally, the Poles acquiesced and agreed to open negotiations on the basis of the Soviet draft.[11]

At this moment the German government, unable to stop the negotiations, developed intensive diplomatic pressure to seek at least an adjustment of some terms of the draft. Dirksen "was summoned to Berlin several times in order to explain the intentions of the Soviet government and to be exhorted to bring the utmost pressure to bear on the *Narkomindiel* [*sic*]." [12]

Litvinov kept assuring the German Ambassador of the Soviet determination to maintain close and friendly relations with Germany regardless of the envisaged pact with Poland. These assurances were based on a momentous secret decision which Stalin had reached in the summer of 1931. In August 1931 a special commission of the Soviet government, the Communist Party of the Soviet Union, and the Presidium of the Executive Committee of the Communist International held a series of secret sessions "to study the possibilities of a revolution in Germany" and to take measures for a decisive struggle in Germany, now torn by severe political and economic crises. The commission's deliberations were based on a detailed report about conditions in Germany, prepared for the Comintern by the Soviet Consul General in Hamburg, Krumin. The report stated that the Communist Party of Germany supported the Nazis for tactical reasons, but, on the other hand, was in urgent need of money to organize the masses and take over power at a decisive moment. The Presidium of the Comintern considered Krumin's report of such importance that it was submitted to the Politburo of the Soviet Party. The Politburo held a session on August 17, and after estimating that the Communist Party of Germany would need 60 million gold marks, it asked for a

[11] TASS's statement, November 22, 1931.
[12] Dirksen, *op. cit.*, p. 105.

meeting of the Politburo, the Comintern's Presidium, and the financial organs of the Soviet government to consider the matter.[13] A report on these activities found its way to the German Foreign Office,[14] a fact that would have undoubtedly brought German-Soviet relations to a most serious crisis had not Stalin reversed the trend.

There were in Moscow's leading political circles several groups with varied opinions about Soviet policy toward Germany. The Comintern representatives believed that the situation was ripe for revolution in Central Europe, but the Soviet Foreign Affairs Commissariat was convinced that the interests of the USSR were inseparably linked with official Germany. As it was not convinced of the favorable revolutionary situation, it opposed the Comintern's plan, which, if unsuccessful, could lead to the weakening of all European communist parties. A *putsch* in Germany would threaten further the German economic situation and thereby threaten also Soviet economic interests. It further maintained that the Comintern's plan would lead to full isolation of the Soviet Union and that, on the contrary, the Soviet Union must seek cooperation with France without losing the cooperation of Germany.

The Politburo met on September 5 to consider these two conflicting policies. Stalin first listened without taking sides, but at the end of the session he made the final decision. The Foreign Commissariat was instructed to take the course of cooperation with France and the United States and to seek, next, the participation of French and American capital in the economic construction of the Soviet Union. The Comintern was to be asked to give up for the time being the idea of a *putsch* in Germany, because a civil war in Germany would only sharpen the relations between the Soviet Union and Western Europe and would hinder the Five-Year Plan. "The chances

[13] *AA*, 1417/2860, 562241–6.

[14] Brüning saw it on October 20, 1931, and marked it in his own handwriting: "Please, strictly confidential. In no case to name the source of the secret report."

for a world revolution will be better through the success of
the construction of the Soviet Union and not through street
actions which are condemned to failure," ended the Politburo
resolution.[15]

Nevertheless, the German government pressed its point in
Moscow to dull the anti-German edge of the Soviet negotiations with Poland. Dirksen saw Litvinov several times a week
in this period of significant change in East Europe. Germany's
principal concern was that the nonaggression treaty should
not imply a guarantee of the Polish boundaries and that the
Soviet Union should have an entirely free hand in case of Poland's attack against a third power, namely Germany. Litvinov
tried to assure Dirksen on both points and stressed that the
Soviet Union would have the right to denounce the treaty
with Poland immediately in case she should launch an attack
on Germany.

Dirksen repeated on several occasions that in the absence
of adequate assurances from the Soviet government, the treaty
with Poland would have "grave consequences for Soviet-German relations" and that its text must be brought into con-
sonance with the Berlin Treaty. He saw behind these negotiations with Poland the fine hand of France, which intended to
isolate Germany before the opening of the disarmament conference and to disrupt German-Soviet relations. Litvinov was
anxious to dispel doubts about Soviet friendship for Germany
and stated that the interview which Stalin had just given to
Emil Ludwig was meant to assure the German people.[16]

Stalin's interview, on December 13, 1931, went far indeed

---

[15] *AA*, 1417/2860, 562233–6. The report, undated, was seen and initialed
by the German Foreign Minister on October 19, 1931.

[16] *Ibid.*, 562261–5, 562266–8, 562273–5. The Soviet chargé d'affaires in
Paris, Rosenberg, went so far as to indicate to the German Ambassador
there that in case of a German attack on Poland, the Soviet Union would
be freed from the obligations of remaining neutral. It would be up to the
Soviet government "to decide about the existence of an attack and it would
itself interpret the meaning of this highly dubious and unclear term."
Ibid., 562283–5, Ambassador Hoesch's report, January 5, 1932.

to alleviate German apprehensions. Ludwig mentioned the concern of some German politicians about the possible negative consequences which the negotiations with Poland might have upon traditionally friendly Soviet-German relations. The whole German nation would be gravely disappointed, he stated, should the negotiations lead to recognition of the Polish boundaries.

Stalin stated, ". . . if we are to speak of [our] sympathies toward any particular nation. . . , then, of course, [we] must speak of our sympathy for the Germans. Our feelings for the Americans cannot be compared with our sympathies for the Germans. . . ." He then assured his visitor that a treaty with Poland would not imply the Soviet Union's sanction or guarantee of Polish possessions and frontiers. The Soviet government wished seriously to sign a treaty of nonaggression with Poland, Stalin declared, and added that this simply meant what it said—not to resort to war; it did not mean a recognition of the Versailles system or a guarantee of Polish boundaries.[17] This statement, as disconcerting as it must have been to the Poles, did not divert them from the course which by now they had definitely adopted: to bring about a fundamental change in Poland's international position.

Polish foreign policy was now in the hands of Colonel Joseph Beck. Since his appointment as Deputy Foreign Minister in 1930, his influence had grown in proportion to the diminishing role of Foreign Minister Zaleski. While Zaleski was a tacit and ineffective opponent of Pilsudski's policy, Beck executed it with fidelity and recklessness. It became his goal to conduct a policy that was independent of France (upon which he thought he could no longer rely), yet still would maintain the appearance of alliance. Poland, in his and Pilsudski's opinion, was a big power and deserved to be treated with respect as one of the decisive political forces in Europe. If her long-time policy of defying both her powerful neighbors

[17] Degras, *Soviet Documents on Foreign Policy*, ii, pp. 517-18.

had not achieved this recognition, then perhaps a formal agreement with them would command the respect of all European powers. Perhaps she could thus better secure the nation and even hold the balance of power in European politics —a difficult task in view of her own lack of power.

Nevertheless, Poland now moved vigorously in this direction. First she brought the negotiations with the Soviet Union to a speedy conclusion; then, she approached Germany. The Treaty of Nonaggression between Poland and the USSR was initialed on January 25, 1932. Poland had withdrawn its frequently repeated request to have the Baltic States included and the Soviet Union, in turn, signed bilateral treaties of nonaggression with them at about the same time the Polish treaty was initialed.[18] Russia further recognized Polish obligations toward the League of Nations and her allies, France and Rumania. Poland, on the other hand, dropped the request of including an arbitration clause in the treaty.

Beck revealed to one of his confidants, Boguslaw Miedziński, that "in connection with the happenings in Germany [Poland] must foresee grave troubles with her. An indispensable preparation for this is a relaxation of tensions with Russia. The West is of the opinion that we are caught between the pincers of two enemies. . . . We must prove that we can tear the pincers apart." Beck then instructed Miedziński to establish cordial relations with the Soviet Minister to Warsaw to convince him "not only about [Poland's] complete desire to maintain the agreement but also about [her] readiness to pass over from a state of *sui generis* cold war to truly loyal and good neighborly relations." [19]

Beck himself explained the Polish attitude toward the pact

[18] With Finland on January 21, 1932, with Latvia on February 5, 1932, with Estonia on May 4, 1932. Lithuania had been covered by a pact of December 22, 1926, which was prolonged on May 6, 1931.

[19] Boguslaw Miedziński, "Polska polityka zagraniczna w okresie przedwojennym," *Wiadomości* (London), October 26, 1952. One cannot abstain from raising doubt about Beck's using the words, "cold war," an expression which became familiar only after World War II.

as an effort to improve permanently Soviet-Polish relations and to maintain an equilibrium of the Polish position toward both the Soviet Union and Germany.[20] The Treaty of Non-aggression was at last signed on July 25, 1932. Its preamble confirmed "that the Treaty of Peace of March 18, 1921 [the Riga Treaty] [constituted] now as in the past, the basis of [the contracting parties'] reciprocal relations and undertakings." If the Soviet government had any mental reservations that the treaty did not imply a recognition of the Polish boundary, it certainly did not let them be known, for in the Riga Treaty the Soviet government had accepted that boundary and was committed to respect it. Now, in addition, the two countries undertook reciprocally, according to Article 1, "to refrain from taking any aggressive action against or invading the territory of the other Party. . . ." [21]

In November the two countries signed a Conciliation Convention [22] and both documents were ratified on December 23, 1932. The treaties were concluded for three years and renewed May 5, 1934, for a period to last at least till December 31, 1945. A Soviet-Polish peace was thus supposedly assured. The Soviet organs hailed the agreements as a major victory of Soviet policy and of the world proletariat.[23] Beck, who since November 1932 had been in complete charge of the Polish foreign policy, accompanied the conclusion of the agreements with a somewhat obscure statement, viewing the treaties as a step "which [was] very realistic and also very characteristic both for Poland and the Soviet Union." [24]

Beck now turned impatiently toward Germany.

[20] Beck, *Dernier rapport,* pp. 37–8. See also Grigore Gafencu, *Last Days in Europe* (New Haven: Yale University Press), pp. 31–2.

[21] For the text see Shapiro, *op. cit.,* II, pp. 55–6.

[22] *Ibid.,* pp. 59–60.

[23] *Izvestiia,* November 28, 1932; *Communist International,* IX, No. 20, December 1, 1932, pp. 701–707.

[24] Józef Beck, *Beiträge zur Europäischen Politik,* Reden, Erklärungen, Interviews, 1932–1939 (Essen: Essener Verlagsanstalt, 1939), pp. 15–16. After World War II, a Polish communist writer condemned the Pact as an "act of perfidy" meant to deceive Polish public opinion and to throw a cover

THE POLISH-GERMAN PACT
OF NONAGGRESSION

Developments in Germany now moved inexorably toward an explosion. The government was unable to rule, even with exceptional powers bestowed upon it by the controversial Article 48 of the constitution. On May 30, 1932, Brüning resigned and Franz von Papen became Chancellor; General von Schleicher was the new Minister of Defense. The revision of the boundaries with Poland became a matter of daily agitation. The Poles answered with counterattacks.

Whether it was justified or not, German governmental circles were again concerned about the danger that Pilsudski would invade East Prussia or Upper Silesia to weaken Germany, which he expected to fall under Hitler's command before long.[25] The Third International gave additional strength to the rumors of an impending Polish attack. On May 4, 1932, the Communist Party of Poland issued a declaration on the imminent danger of seizure of Danzig by Pilsudski and appealed to workers to develop "a decisive struggle against all the attempts of Polish imperialism. . . ."[26] The Executive Committee of the Third International passed a resolution in September 1932, which appealed to the Polish Party to "mobilize the broad masses of town and country against the criminal policy of anti-Soviet war. . . ."[27]

In an atmosphere of increasing pressures, fantastic ideas

over the Polish government's cooperation with German imperialists. B. Jawornicki, "Polskoradziecki pakt o nieagresji r. 1932," *Sprawy Miedzynarodowe* (Warsaw), v, No. 5, 1952, pp. 70–82.

[25] Richard Breyer, *Das Deutsche Reich und Polen, 1932–1937* (Würzburg: Holzner Verlag, 1955), pp. 33–6. Ross, *op. cit.*, p. 42. *Ciechanowski Deposit.* Report of the Polish Minister in Berlin, May 13, 1932.

[26] *Inprecorr*, Vol. 12, No. 21, p. 408.

[27] *Theses and Resolutions. XII Plenum of the Executive Committee of the Communist International (September 1932)* (Moscow: Cooperative Publish. Society of Foreign Workers in the USSR, 1933), p. 15. See also Kun, *op. cit.*, p. 980; *The Communist International*, IX, No. 13, July 15, 1932, pp. 457–61; No. 14, August 1, 1932, pp. 471–77.

followed each other in quick succession, sometimes supporting, but more often contradicting each other. Papen was considered an advocate of French-German cooperation (including a possible understanding with Poland); his Minister of Defense, Schleicher, envisaged a German-Soviet cooperation which would crush Poland between them.

Little credence was given to a report that the German communist paper, *Berliner Volkszeitung,* had published what was purported to be a protocol of a meeting, on February 27, 1932, of the *Deutscher Herrenklub.* According to this report, Papen spoke before this conservative, aristocratic and nationalistic club and declared there was the distinct possibility of reaching an agreement on all questions between France and Germany. This would be possible if the two countries, together with Poland, reached an *"accord à trois"* and signed a Franco-German-Polish alliance against the Soviet Union.[28] Only later, after the war, did German documents confirm the authenticity of this information, adding that Papen did however expect a revision of the German-Polish boundary.[29] Nevertheless, at the same time Papen was voicing this hastily conceived plan, General Schleicher was trying to re-establish contacts with Moscow.

In September 1932 the German army held large-scale maneuvers in the area of Frankfort on the Oder. Marshal Tukhachevsky, the Soviet Chief of Staff, was present as were many military attachés, with one notable exception—the Polish military attaché, who had not been invited.[30] Schleicher accentuated his anti-Polish policy when he became Chancellor on December 4, 1932 and reportedly found a sympathetic ear among Soviet military circles, particularly with Marshal Yegorov. "It seems possible that at the time of the nomination of Schleicher's government, a German-Soviet military agree-

[28] *Inprecorr,* Vol. 12, No. 26, June 9, 1932.

[29] *AA,* 1417/2860, 562329, Memorandum of June 23, 1932, about a report of a Dr. Reuter, who was present at Papen's lecture. See also F. von Papen, *Memoirs* (New York: Dutton, 1952), pp. 175–77.

[30] Ross, *op. cit.,* p. 51.

ment concerning Poland was reached and that the general staffs had prepared a common operational plan." [31] According to Polish sources, Hitler and Goering at a later date confirmed to Polish diplomats that Schleicher had recommended to Hitler that he reach an understanding with the Soviet Union "for the suppression of Poland." [32]

The German official sources do not record Schleicher's alleged plans; they become significantly scanty in the latter half of 1932. One may be allowed to conjecture that the German diplomats, usually so productive in submitting detailed reports, elaborate memoranda, and daring ideas, had become by that time extremely cautious in expressing their views, waiting for the outcome of the internal struggle between the forces of Nazism and the remnants of German democracy.

At any rate, when Litvinov met the new Foreign Minister, Baron von Neurath, in Berlin on December 19, 1932, the two statesmen did not mention the idea at all. The conversation probably was rather restrained as Litvinov was obviously reserved and Neurath quite noncommunicative. In response to Neurath's question, however, Litvinov assured him that the Soviet Union considered its good relations with Germany the basic factor in its foreign policy.[33] One may surmise, however, that Germany had no such equal regard for Soviet friendship. Her political ambitions at that moment were concentrated on Geneva, on the disarmament conference.

In the middle of September 1932 the German government had withdrawn from the disarmament conference because her plea for the recognition of equal rights in armament had been declined. Three months later, December 14, its representatives were back—the big powers, including France, had recognized the principle of equality. This was a historic victory, but the inevitable repercussion followed: Poland, who for years had

[31] *Ibid.*, p. 57.
[32] République de Pologne, *Les relations polono-allemandes et polono-soviétiques* (Paris: Flammarion, 1940), pp. 45, 47.
[33] *AA*, 1417/2860, 562400-2.

fought against the idea of German armament, resented deeply the French change in attitude and found in this decision only a new impetus for pursuing an independent policy.

On November 18, 1932, the State Undersecretary, Jan Szembek, and the Polish Minister to Germany, Alfred Wysocki, suggested to Neurath the idea of settling all disputes by negotiation.[34] This was merely a preliminary move which was meant to lead to the establishment of a position of Polish balance between her two giant neighbors. Before long, this was consummated though under the entirely different circumstances which prevailed in Germany.

As the year 1932 was coming to an end, so too was an era of orderly negotiation. What France had persistently denied to Germany under a democratic rule, she felt compelled to concede to Hitler's precursors, Papen and Schleicher. England failed to understand the nature of the European crisis and particularly the events in Germany. The Soviet Union perpetually disrupted the constructive efforts of the League of Nations and, in fact, gave support to the nationalistic forces in Germany. The United States lived in complacent isolation. Germany herself was in the grip of the vulgar agitation of the Nazi Party. The Nazi threat was obviously a threat to the peace of Europe and of the world, for Hitler had made clear in his *Mein Kampf* every detail of the policy he intended to follow. Few statesmen seemed to understand this, however, and only a few of them read his book. In this situation Poland played for high stakes, hoping to reach an expedient agreement with Germany and Russia that would divert their expansionist and subversive efforts against her. She contributed to the weakening of a constructive system of peace within the framework of the League of Nations and to undermining the French network of alliances with herself, Czechoslovakia, Yugoslavia, and Rumania. Before the first month of 1933 came to a close, Adolf Hitler was appointed Chancellor of Germany.

[34] Ross, *op. cit.*, p. 56.

An entirely new situation, a new balance of power, emerged in Europe.

There was a touch of tragicomedy in a document called *Duchemin Protocol,* which was submitted to Bernhard von Bülow, the Undersecretary in the German Foreign Office on January 30, 1933, the day Hitler came to power. According to the document, a tripartite meeting was held on January 29 and 30, 1933. *Herr Geheimrat* Bosch and *Herr Geheimrat* Bücher represented Germany; MM. Duchemin, W. d'Ormesson, and Parmentier represented France, and representing Belgium-Luxemburg were MM. Barbanson, Guth, and A. Meyer. Though the participants were private individuals, one can assume that they acted with the knowledge of their respective governments. According to a résumé of their conversation, they "reached an agreement" on a number of important political points. The German participants stated that Germany would participate "without an ulterior thought" in establishing a stable peace in Europe, including complete cooperation with France and Poland, if certain conditions were met. They asked for the elimination of the Corridor, the return of Danzig to Germany, and the rectification of the Upper Silesian border, without substantial loss to Poland. By way of compensation, the German members proposed that Poland be indemnified by access to the sea through Memel and by receiving commercial privileges in Danzig. Above all, however, Germany would guarantee, together with France, Poland's new boundary with Germany as well as her other frontiers. Germany would then pursue a friendly policy toward Poland. Once the Polish problem was solved, the problem of armament and security would be also solved; Germany, Belgium, France, and Poland "would mutually guarantee their security." [35] When he submitted the Protocol, Duchemin asked Dr. Bücher to let him know if the new German government agreed with the text of the declarations made by the German

[35] *AA,* 2390/4622, 203066–70.

participants so that it could be presented to the French Minister of Foreign Affairs.

It is difficult to determine the exact nature of this significant document. From a memorandum which Bülow attached to it, one can see that the negotiations were instigated by Papen. However, Papen was no longer the Chancellor of Germany and in a few days Foreign Minister Neurath put an end to the whole episode. In a letter of February 9, addressed to Papen, he stated that the "negotiations were steered on a wrong course," that German negotiators' demands were "far short of . . . actual demands," and that the idea of a German-French guarantee of Poland's eastern frontier "can never be considered." [36]

The change of the political regime in Germany brought the German-Polish tensions to a boiling point. The newspapers in both countries were inundated by mutual invectives; daily demonstrations were organized in numerous cities; national organizations competed in "proofs" of patriotism and in mutual threats. A real crisis developed over Danzig in February when Poland sent reinforcements to Westerplatte, the harbor of the free city, to enforce her rights, which were being endangered by its administration, now under full Nazi control. Some chancelleries spoke about Pilsudski's intentions to provoke a general preventive war against Germany.[37]

However, all these appearances were misleading. Under the surface of violent outbursts, the leaders of Germany were contemplating an entirely different course. It was probably at the beginning of April that Hitler "remarked dreamily" to Ambassador Dirksen, "If only we could come to an agreement with Poland! But Pilsudski is the only man with whom that would be possible." [38]

---

[36] *D.G.F.P.* Series C, I, p. 40. There was a touch of irony in the abortive idea in Duchemin's message to Berlin that the French government had approved the protocol. *Ibid.*, p. 41.

[37] *D.G.F.P.* Series C, I. See also André François-Poncet, *Souvenirs d'une Ambassade à Berlin* (Paris: Flammarion, 1946), p. 165.

[38] Dirksen, *op. cit.*, p. 110.

Then, on April 19, the German Minister to Poland, Hans von Moltke, had a long conversation with Beck. Though they exchanged mutual recriminations about agitation in their respective countries, Beck significantly stated that certain politicians found satisfaction in the Polish-German tensions; that, for example, "in Geneva it would be a disappointment to many if the conflict between German and Polish representatives did not occur at every session of the Council." The German Envoy did not fail to detect in this remark an indication of Beck's willingness to open direct negotiations with Germany.[39]

Indeed, the next day the Polish Minister to Germany appeared in the Foreign Office and asked to be received by Adolf Hitler as soon as possible, placing great emphasis upon the urgency of his request. He indicated that he did not know what the subject for discussion would be, saying that he would receive instructions only after the date of the audience had been fixed.[40] The meeting took place on May 2 and lasted 40 minutes. The Polish diplomat, speaking in a determined tone, raised with Hitler the question of Danzig, which was producing increasing uneasiness in Poland. He was instructed by his government "to obtain from the Reichschancellor an assurance that Germany did not intend to change anything in the present situation in Danzig." He also stated that access to the sea was of vital interest to Poland, an interest which she was ready to defend to the last breath.

Hitler replied that Germany had more reason for uneasiness than Poland. He pointed to the untenability of the Corridor, though he, a nationalist himself, fully understood Polish nationalism. "A forceful expropriation of Polish territory was far from [Germany's] thoughts," he declared. Then, according to the Polish record of the conversation, Hitler pointed significantly to "the birth statistics in Russia. The extraordinary fecundity of her people led him to a serious thought

[39] *D.G.F.P.* Series C, 1, p. 306.
[40] *Ibid.*, p. 311.

about the danger which could result from this fact for Europe and consequently for Poland." [41]

At the request of the Polish Minister, a communiqué was issued about the visit, according to which Hitler "stressed the firm intention of the German government to keep its attitude and its conduct strictly within the limits of the treaties." Furthermore, he "expressed the wish that both countries might review and deal with their common interests dispassionately." [42]

In an equally conciliatory vein, Hitler stated on May 17 before the *Reichstag* that Germany wished to respect the rights of other nations and that no German government would violate the Versailles Treaty, a treaty which could not be suppressed without being replaced by a better one. "Germany is prepared to join every solemn pact of nonaggression because Germany does not think of an attack but solely of her security," [43] stated Hitler.

Beck was now quick to express to the German Minister in Warsaw his satisfaction with Hitler's speech and with the improved relations between the countries. He informed him further that measures were being taken to prevent anti-German agitation in the Polish press, particularly in case of the Reichschancellor.[44]

In return, the Polish Minister in Berlin was received on July 13 by Hitler, who spoke again in a friendly manner about Poland and assured him that war was not the right means of solving differences. He even expressed conviction "that the authors of the Treaty of Versailles established the so-called Corridor in order to open an abyss between Germany and Poland. . . ." [45] This was a new argument in the German diplomatic armory.

[41] *D.G.F.P.* Series C, I, pp. 365–67. *Les relations polono-allemandes* . . . , pp. 31–3.
[42] *D.G.F.P.* Series C, I, p. 367.
[43] *Les relations polono-allemandes* . . . , pp. 34–5.
[44] *D.G.F.P.* Series C, Vol. I, pp. 470–71.
[45] *Les relations polono-allemandes* . . . , p. 36.

When Beck and Neurath met in Geneva in September, Beck demonstrated particular friendliness toward him and expressed his pleasure over the considerable relaxation of tensions during recent months. "The Polish government was tired of always letting itself be played off against Germany," he stated.[46] He then met with Goebbels at lunch and pursued with him further the idea of direct negotiations.[47] Indeed, direct negotiations were now well under way. Agreements on such matters as social insurance, the Mixed Arbitral Tribunal, the Upper Silesian mines, and frontier traffic, all of which had been awaiting final approval since 1931, were now, in the period between August and November 1933, ratified. The Westerplatte incident was forgotten and negotiations were even opened to end the seven-year-old tariff war. In still another conversation, Neurath stressed to the newly appointed Polish Minister, Joseph Lipski, the necessity of liquidating all misunderstandings between the two countries.[48]

The grounds were now carefully established for the final step. Poland seized the initiative by proposing a concrete measure to regulate her relations with Germany. Lipski was received by Hitler on November 15 and, speaking on behalf of Pilsudski, stated that the security of Poland was based on two factors: the direct bilateral relations of Poland with other countries and the cooperation of states within the League of Nations, which was a sort of reinsurance. The Polish diplomat explained forcefully that with Germany's withdrawal from the League in October, Poland had been deprived of this second factor of security. Marshal Pilsudski wished, therefore, to ask Hitler "if he did not see a possibility to offset, in direct Polish-German relations, the loss of this security factor."

The idea of direct negotiations was the first indication of a development which finally led to a complete breakdown of the

[46] *D.G.F.P.* Series C, I, p. 840.
[47] Beck, *Dernier rapport*, pp. 30–1.
[48] *Les relations polono-allemandes* . . . , p. 37; the Minister's report of October 17, 1933.

system of collective security and to a policy of accommodation with Nazi Germany. Pilsudski had never believed in the League of Nations; now he delivered a powerful blow to its already feeble prestige. Other similar blows from such small countries as Belgium, whose national defense depended to a large extent on the idea of collective security, were soon to follow, encouraged as they were by Poland's example. Nor did Pilsudski trust France, an attitude not without justification. As to his neighbor to the south, Czechoslovakia, he could not care less about the consequences for her of his bilateral approach to Hitler or her complete exposure to German pressure. He sincerely hated the Czechoslovakian democracy and had never given up the thought of acquiring the territory Poland had failed to gain from Czechoslovakia after World War I. Certainly, he had never believed in her viability and therefore would never admit that his own country's independence was fatally linked to the independent existence of Czechoslovakia. Moreover, direct negotiations with the feared Germany would give Poland the prestige which he was seeking and had been claiming for years.

Poland's decision to open bilateral negotiations with Germany was to Hitler a most welcome opportunity. The intent of his policy was to destroy the League by negotiating bilateral treaties with the neighboring countries, thus preventing their concerted action. The Polish Minister's proposal had, therefore, a sweet sound to Hitler's ears.

Hitler first answered the idea of direct relations with the old arguments about Versailles but also repeated "with firm resolution that he did not intend at all any change whatsoever by way of war" in German-Polish relations. He stated that war would only bring communism to Europe and that "Poland [was] a bastion toward Asia. Destruction of Poland would be a misfortune for the states which would then become neighbors of Asia." Then, having suggested to the Polish Envoy that in the relations between the two countries "the idea itself of a possibility of a war should be excluded," and having recognized in Pilsudski "a great personality," he accepted the proposal of making his "peaceful inclinations" publicly known.[49]

The official communiqué issued the same day was indicative of things to come. It spoke about a plan for direct negotiations between the two countries with the aim of renouncing, in their mutual relations, any use of force.[50] Further developments followed at an accelerated speed. A few days later, on November 28, Moltke presented to Pilsudski a draft of an agreement which was to have a special form and special formulation, making it distinctly different from the outworn treaties which were no longer held in very high esteem. Pilsudski welcomed the new approach as he disliked the old "detested articles" of these treaties; he also repeatedly expressed "sympathetic recognition of the personality of the Reich Chancellor." [51] However, there was something more serious behind the German proposal than Hitler's disrespect for traditional diplomatic forms. The German Foreign Office did not wish to speak about a nonaggression pact because such might imply that Germany was giving up her territorial claims against Poland. A "no force agreement" was therefore preferable.[52]

In redrafting the German proposal, Poland asked for German acquiescence to Polish membership in the League of Nations and to her alliance with France and Rumania. The negotiations were kept in strict secrecy; Berlin instructed its ambassadors in Moscow, Rome, London, and Paris to inform the respective governments about the forthcoming event less than 48 hours before the agreement was signed. They were to stress the far-reaching importance of the agreement for European

[49] *Les relations polono-allemandes* . . . , pp. 37–40.
[50] *Ibid.*, p. 40.
[51] *D.G.F.P.* Series C, ii, pp. 145–46, 148–49, 156–57.
[52] *Ibid.*, pp. 139–41.

peace and that it should be viewed as a conclusive evidence of the German will for peace.[53]

On January 26, 1934, the Declaration of Non-Aggression and Understanding between Germany and Poland was signed and published. It declared that the relations between the two countries would be based "on the principles contained in the Pact of Paris"—a pact which was then already recognized to be totally ineffective. It mentioned only obliquely Poland's commitments to other countries but stressed both German and Polish intent to reach direct understanding on all questions concerning their mutual relations. Any dispute would be solved by peaceful means; "in no circumstances, however, will [the signatories] proceed to use force in order to settle such disputes." The Declaration was to be ratified and valid for ten years.[54]

The Declaration carried the imprint of Hitler's and Pilsudski's disregard for the usual form of international agreements in that it omitted all articles and was not called a pact or a treaty. Legally, however, it was a treaty because it provided for ratification, and ratification instruments were subsequently exchanged in February. One epoch in German-Polish relations had come to an end; a new epoch was beginning. The same was true of the relations between Poland and the Soviet Union.

[53] *Ibid.,* p. 420. It seems that Poland, however, did not inform her own allies. At least, the French Ambassador, François-Poncet, relates that on the eve of the signature of the treaty, Lipski answered his query about the negotiations by saying they were concerned with economic questions. When the pact was signed on the following day, Lipski stated that he had had to obey instructions as "Colonel Beck had told him to guard the negotiations with absolute secrecy." François-Poncet, *op. cit.,* p. 163.

[54] For the text see *D.G.F.P.,* Series C, II, pp. 421–22.

POSTSCRIPT

THE FULL CIRCLE

❧ DURING fifteen years of turbulent developments in East Europe, Poland was harassed by her two unruly neighbors. First, they plotted against her militarily and politically. Then, when their own mutual interests began to clash, the Soviet Union tried to lure Poland into a bilateral agreement to weaken her position in East Europe and Germany planned to force a revision of her boundaries through cooperation with the West. Poland boldly defied both.

By 1932 the relationship of forces in Europe was undergoing a change which was to affect Poland deeply. Hitler's victory in Germany appeared inevitable, the disarmament conference was about to collapse, the influence of France, the chief continental power and still the principal ally of Poland, was in decline. A crushing economic crisis gripped Europe; the somber forces of fascism, which corroded the foundations of democracy in almost all countries of Europe, were on the march. Stalin's Russia was flexing her industrial muscles; her goal was the establishment of a strong socialist state—a precondition of world expansion.

In this situation Poland decided to act. She signed a treaty of nonaggression with the Soviet Union in the hope of receiving new assurance about the boundary with her eastern neighbor. She signed a treaty of nonaggression with her western neighbor who, in the time of the Weimar Republic, had refused to subscribe to such a commitment. She cut the bonds which once had linked Germany and Russia; she was able, in Beck's words, "to tear the pincers apart." Her ambition was fulfilled—she was recognized as a big power. Her peace appeared assured for at least one decade. However, in half of that time all these dreams were shattered by one terrible blow. What followed after a few years of calm was the most tragic period of development East Europe, and particularly Poland, had ever experienced.

The first few years which followed the German-Polish pact seemed to support the correctness of Polish policy. Soviet-German relations grew more hostile as official and press attacks on communism and Nazism became a daily feature of politics in the two countries. Poland enjoyed, on the other hand, a honeymoon period with her erstwhile enemies. Beck traveled to Berlin, to Moscow, and to almost every other capital in Europe; he was received everywhere with respect but seldom with cordiality.

Hitler embarked upon a policy of violent revision of peace treaties. In quick succession he declared general conscription, occupied the Rhineland, annexed Austria, mutilated and then completely dismembered Czechoslovakia and swallowed Memel.

The policy of the West lost all sense of direction. After an unsuccessful attempt to pacify East Europe by a pact of mutual assistance (an attempt which was foiled by the common efforts of Germany and Poland), France and Britain embarked upon a policy of appeasement of Germany and isolation of the Soviet Union. Hitler's violations of international obligations were met with only feeble, ineffective protests. The League of Nations was all but forgotten. Czechoslovakia's western allies not only did not oppose but even negotiated with Germany Hitler's grab of her territory; Poland, too, joined in this act. They wished to preserve peace—at another country's expense.

The Soviet Union, on the other hand, posed as the defender of democracy in Europe, as the principal protagonist of the *status quo*—after fifteen years of violent agitation for a revision of these same peace treaties. She entered the League of Nations—after fifteen years of equally violent denunciations of this instrument of imperialism—to become the most eloquent spokesman of the principle of collective security. Russia offered close cooperation to Britain and France but was rejected.

It was a period of hectic regrouping of forces, of utterly selfish maneuvering to assuage momentarily the Nazi frenzy. It was a period of political madness. In this whirlwind, Poland appeared to bask in security behind the wall of nonaggression treaties with Germany and the Soviet Union. Marshal Pilsudski had been dead since 1935, but the heirs of his political concept, the colonels who had gathered around his radiating personality during their youthful adventures of World War I and whom he later called his children, faithfully executed his bequest.

In the spring of 1939 Britain and France, seemingly awakened from the lethargy administered at the Munich Conference, opened negotiations with Moscow on a pact of mutual assistance against German aggression. Their halfhearted efforts were met by an equally elusive response from Stalin. Poland refused to participate in this hastily and belatedly conceived scheme, preferring to maintain a balanced position in the explosive situation. Hitler's and Stalin's unscrupulous minds quickly put an end to all these combinations. On August 23, 1939, to the stupefaction of the world, they signed a treaty of friendship and nonaggression.

The following week the lightning struck. In violation of all the solemn commitments of the treaties of nonaggression, Germany invaded Poland and in less than three weeks the Soviet Union joined in the crime, according to a preconceived secret plan with Hitler. For the fourth time in her modern history Poland was divided between her neighbors, Germany and Russia.

BIBLIOGRAPHY

DOCUMENTS ON SOVIET FOREIGN POLICY

Akademiia nauk SSSR. Institut prava. *S'ezdy Sovetov SSSR v postanovleniiakh i rezoliutsiiakh.* Pod obshchei redaktsiei akademika A. I. Vyshinskogo. Moscow: Izdatel'stvo Vedomostei verkhovnogo Soveta RSFSR, 1939.

Bunyan, J., and Fisher, H. H. *The Bolshevik Revolution, 1917–1918; Documents and Materials.* Stanford: Stanford University Press, 1934.

Degras, Jane (ed.). *The Communist International, 1919–43.* Documents. 2 vols. London: Oxford University Press, 1956, 1960.

———. *Soviet Documents on Foreign Policy.* 3 vols. London: Oxford University Press, 1951, 1952, 1953.

The Essentials of Lenin. 2 vols. London: Lawrence & Wishart, 1947.

Eudin, X. J., and Fisher, H. H. *Soviet Russia and the West, 1920–1927.* A Documentary Survey. Stanford: Stanford University Press, 1957.

Eudin, X. J., and North, R. C. *Soviet Russia and the East, 1920–1927.* A Documentary Survey. Stanford: Stanford University Press, 1957.

Exécutif Elargi de l'Internationale Communiste. *Compte rendu analytique de la session du 21 Mars au 6 Avril 1925.* Paris: Librairie de l'Humanité, 1925.

Gankin, O. H., and Fisher, H. H. *The Bolsheviks and the World War: The Origins of the Third International.* Stanford: Stanford University Press, 1940.

Institut Marksa-Engelsa-Lenina pri TsK VKP (b). *Kommu-*

nisticheskii Internatsional v Dokumentakh. Resheniia, tezisy i vozzvaniia Kongressov Kominterna i Plenumov IKKI. 1919–1932. Ed. Bela Kun. Moscow: Partiinoe izdatel'stvo, 1933.

Kommunisticheskaia Akademiia. *S'ezdy Sovetov vserossiiskie(kh) i Soiuza SSR v postanovleniiakh i rezoliutsiiakh.* Moscow: "Vlast' Sovetov," 1935.

Kommunisticheskaia Partiia Sovetskogo Soiuza v resoliutsiakh i resheniiakh s'ezdov, konferentsii i plenumov TsK. Moscow: Gosudarstvennoe Izdatel'stvo politicheskoi litratury, 1953.

Lenin, V. I. *Sochineniia.* 35 vols., 4th edition. Moscow: Ogiz, 1941.

Molotov, V. *The Struggle for Socialism and the Struggle for Peace. Government's Report to Sixth Congress of Soviets of USSR.* Moscow: "Moscow Worker," 1931.

Narodnyi Komissariat po inostrannym delam. *Conférence de Moscou pour la limitation des armaments.* Moscow: Édition du Commissariat du Peuple aux Affaires Etrangères, 1923.

———. *Dogovory o neitralitete, nenapadenii i o soglasitel'noi protsedure, zakliuchennye mezhdu Soiuzom SSR i inostrannymi gosudarstvami.* Moscow, 1934.

———. *Godovoi otchet Narodnogo Komissariata po inostrannym delam za 1923 god k II s'ezdu Sovetov.* Moscow, 1924.

———. *Godovoi otchet Narodnogo Komissariata po inostrannym delam za 1924 god k III s'ezdu Sovetov SSSR.* Moscow, 1925.

———. *Krasnaia Kniga. Sbornik diplomaticheskikh dokumentov o russko-pol'skikh otnosheniiakh 1918–1920.* Moscow, 1920.

———. *Materialy Genuezskoi Konferentsii.* Moscow, 1922.

———. *Mezhdunarodnaia Politika:* Dogovory, deklaratsii i diplomaticheskaia perepiska. Ed. A. V. Sabanin. 3 vols. 1928, 1929, 1930. Moscow, 1930–1932.

———. *Mezhdunarodnaia politika noveishego vremeni v dogovorakh, notakh i deklaratsiakh.* Ed. I. V. Kliuchnikov and A. Sabanin. 3 vols. Moscow, 1925–1928.

———. *Mezhdunarodnaia politika R.S.F.S.R. v 1922 g.* Moscow, 1923.

———. *Sbornik deistvuiushchikh dogovorov, soglashenii i konventsii zakliuchennykh R.S.F.S.R. s inostrannymi gosudarstvami.* Moscow, 1921–1923.

———. *Sbornik deistvuiushchikh dogovorov, soglashenii i konventsii zakliuchennykh s inostrannymi gosudarstvami.* 8 vols. Moscow, 1925–1935.

———. *Sborniki dokumentov po mezhdunarodnoi politike i mezhdunarodnomu pravu.* Ed. K. V. Antonov. 9 vols. Moscow, 1932–1934.

———. *Sovetskaia Rossiia i Pol'sha.* Moscow, 1921.

Protokoly S'ezdov i Konferentsii Vsesoiuznoi Kommunisticheskoi Partii (b). Moscow: Partiinoe izdatel'stvo, 1924.

Report of Court Proceedings in the Case of the Anti-Soviet "Bloc of Rights and Trotskyites." Moscow, March 2–13, 1938. Moscow: People's Commissariat of Justice of the U.S.S.R., 1938.

Résolutions adoptées à la IXe session plénière du C.E. de l' I.C. (Février 1928). Paris: Bureau d'Éditions [n.d.].

Rykov, A. I. *Ocherednye voprosy mezhdunarodnoi i vnutrennei politiki.* Moscow: Gosudarstvennoe izdatel'stvo, 1929.

———. *Sotsialisticheskoe stroitel'stvo i mezhdunarodnaia politika SSSR.* Moscow: Gosudarstvennoe izdatel'stvo, 1927.

———. *Stat'i i rechi.* 4 vols. Moscow: Gosudarstvennoe izdatel'stvo, 1927–1929.

R.S.F.S.R. *Vos'moi Vserossiiskii S'ezd Sovetov Rabochikh. . . .* Stenograficheskii otchet. Moscow: Gosudarstvennoe izdatel'stvo, 1921.

Savinkov, B. V., Collection. Stanford: Hoover Institution. Wislowski Collection.

"Savinkov's letter to Wrangel," October 15, 1920. Stanford: Hoover Institution. Wislowski Collection.

Savinkov, B. V., Trial of. (Translation of official report in *Pravda*, August 30, 1924.)

S'ezd Sovetov. *Vserosiiskii s'ezd sovetov.* Moscow: [n.p.] 1918–1935.

Shapiro, Leonard (ed.). *Soviet Treaty Series.* 2 vols. Washington: Georgetown University Press, 1950.

Soiuz Sovetskikh Sotsialisticheskikh Respublik. *S'ezd Sovetov Soiuza SSR.* Stenograficheskii otchet s prilozheniiami. Moscow, 1922.

———. *Vtoroi S'ezd Sovetov SSSR.* Stenograficheskii otchet. Moscow, 1924.

———. *Tretii S'ezd Sovetov SSSR.* Stenograficheskii otchet. Moscow, 1925.

———. *4 S'ezd Sovetov SSSR.* Stenograficheskii otchet. Moscow, 1927.

———. *5 S'ezd Sovetov SSSR.* Stenograficheskii otchet. Moscow, 1929.

———. *Tsentral'nyi Ispolnitel'nyi Komitet.* Stenograficheskii otchet. Moscow, 1925.

The Soviet Union and Peace. The most important of the documents issued by the government of the USSR concerning peace and disarmament from 1917 to 1929. New York: International Publishers [n.d.].

Stalin, Joseph. *Foundations of Leninism.* New York: International Publishers, 1932.

———. *Leninism. Selected Writings.* New York: International Publishers, 1942.

———. *Marxism and the National and Colonial Question.* New York: International Publishers [n.d.].

———. *Sochineniia.* 13 vols. Moscow: Ogiz, 1946.

———. *Voprosy Leninisma.* 7th edition. Moscow: Gosudarstvennoe sots.-ekon. izdatel'stvo, 1931.

Third International. *Pervyi Kongress Kommunisticheskogo Internatsionala.* Protokoly zasedanii v Moskve so 2 po 19 marta 1919 goda. Petrograd: Izdatel'stvo Kom. Internatsionala, 1921.

———. *L'Internationale Communiste.* Manifestes, thèses, résolutions du 1ᵉʳ Congrès de l' I.C. (Mars 1919) [n.p., n.d.].

———. *Vtoroi Kongress Kommunisticheskogo Internatsionala.* Stenograficheskii otchet. Petrograd: Izdatel'stvo Kom. Internatsionala, 1921

———. *III Vsemirnyi Kongress Kommunisticheskogo Internatsionala.* Stenograficheskii otchet. Petrograd: Gosudarstvennoe izdatel'stvo, 1922.

———. *Theses and Resolutions adopted at the Third World Congress of the Communist International* (June 22—July 12, 1921). New York: The Contemporary Publishing Association, 1921.

———. *IVᵉ Congrès communiste mondial.* Résolutions. Paris: Librairie de l'Humanité, 1923.

———. *Protokoll des Vierten Kongresses der Kommunistischen Internationale.* Hamburg: Verlag der Kommunistischen Internationale, 1923.

———. *Fourth Congress of the Communist International.* Abridged report of meetings held at Petrograd and Moscow, Nov. 7—Dec. 3, 1922. London: Communist Party of Great Britain [n.d.].

———. *From the Fourth to the Fifth World Congress.* Report of the Executive Committee of the Communist International. London: Communist Party of Great Britain, 1924.

———. *Piatyi Vsemirnyi Kongress Kommunisticheskogo Internatsionala.* Stenograficheskii otchet. Moscow: Gosudarstvennoe izdatel'stvo, 1925.

———. *Vᵉ Congrès de l'Internationale Communiste.* Compte rendu analytique. Paris: Librairie de l'Humanité, 1924.

———. *VIᵉ Congrès de l'Internationale Communiste.* Compte

rendu sténographique. Numéro spécial. Paris: La Correspondance Internationale, 1928.

———. *Thèses et Résolutions du VI⁰ Congrès de l'Internationale Communiste.* Paris: Bureau d'éditions [n.d.].

———. *Theses and Resolutions. XII Plenum of the Executive Committee of the Communist International* (September 1932). Moscow: Cooperative Publishing Society of Foreign Workers in the USSR, 1933.

Tivel', A., and Kheimo, M. (eds.). *10 let Kominterna v resheniiakh i tsifrakh.* Moscow: Gosudarstvennoe izdatel'stvo, 1929.

Trotsky Archives. Cambridge: Harvard University, Houghton Library.

Vneshniaia Politika SSSR. Sbornik dokumentov. 1917–1944. 4 vols. [n.p., n.d.].

DOCUMENTS ON GERMAN FOREIGN POLICY

Auswärtiges Amt. *Nachlass des Reichsministers Dr. Gustav Stresemann.* Washington, D.C.: National Archives.

———. Geheim Akten. *Das Verhältnis Deutschlands zu Russland.* Reel 33, *St. Antony's Collection.* Washington: National Archives

———. *Akten betreffend das Verhältnis Deutschlands zu Russland.* January 1, 1919—August 21, 1919. Reel 103, *St. Antony's Collection.* Washington: National Archives.

———. Deutsche Gesandtschaft Moskau. *Politische Beziehungen Russlands mit Deutschland.* Reels 785, 911. Washington: National Archives.

———. *Brockdorff-Rantzau, Nachlass* (Brandenburg Manuscript). Reel 1013. Washington: National Archives.

———. Büro des Reichsministers. *Akten betreffend Russland.* Reels 1404–1417. Washington: National Archives.

———. Büro des Reichsministers. *Akten betreffend Polen.* Reels 1424–1430. Washington: National Archives.

————. Büro des Reichsministers. *Akten betreffend Spa—Allgemeine.* Reel 1642. Washington: National Archives.

————. *Alte Reichskanzlei* (protocols of sessions of the cabinet). Reels 1664, 1669, 1670. Washington: National Archives.

————. *Akten betreffend Auswärtige Politik—Allgemeine.* Reel 1680. Washington: National Archives.

————. Büro des Staatssecretärs. *Russland.* Reels 2313–2323. Washington: National Archives.

————. Büro des Staatssecretärs. *Polnische Angelegenheiten.* Reel 2339. Washington: National Archives.

————. *Geheimakten, 1920–1936. Russland: Handakten Band 1–96.* Reel 3027. Washington: National Archives.

————. *Geheimakten, 1920–1936. Russland-Polen.* Reel 3036. Washington: National Archives.

————. *Geheimakten, 1920–1936. Russland-Polen, Kellogg Pakt, Litvinow Protokoll.* Reel 3042. Washington: National Archives.

————. *Allgemeine 1. Verhandlungen zur Ausführung des Friedensvertrags in Spa.* Reels 3462, 3463. Washington: National Archives.

————. *Briefwechsel mit Herrn Botschafter v. Dirksen,* March 1931—July 1932. Reel 3486. Washington: National Archives.

————. *Aufstand im Ruhrgebiet.* Reel 3623. Washington: National Archives.

————. Alte Reichskanzlei. *Spa Konferenz.* Reel 3674. Washington: National Archives.

Documents on German Foreign Policy 1918–1945. Series C (1933–1937). Washington: U.S. Government Printing Office, 1957.

General von Seeckt's Papers. Cambridge: Harvard University, Houghton Library.

General Wilhelm Groener's Papers. Cambridge: Harvard University, Houghton Library.

Stresemann, Gustav. *Vermächtnis.* Herausgegeben von Henry

BIBLIOGRAPHY

Bernhard unter Mitarbeit von Wolfgang Goetz und Paul Wiegler. 3 vols. Berlin: Ullstein Verlag, 1932.

DOCUMENTS ON POLISH FOREIGN POLICY

Akty i Dokumenty, dotyczace Sprawy granic Polski na Konferencji pokojowej w Paryżu, 1918–19. Paris: [n.p.], 1920.

Beck, Józef. *Beiträge zur Europäischen Politik.* Reden, Erklärungen, Interviews, 1932–1939. Essen: Essener Verlagsanstalt, 1939.

Ciechanowski Deposit. Stanford: Hoover Institution.

Delegacje polskie w Komisjach Reewakuacyjnej i Specjalnej w Moskwie. Warsaw: [n.p.], 1922, 1923.

Filasiewicz, Stanislas. *La question polonaise pendant la guerre mondiale:* Receuil des acts diplomatiques, traités et documents concernant la Pologne. 2 vols. Paris: Comité Nationale Polonais, 1920.

Komunistyczna Partia Polski. W walce o ziemie, wolność i chleb: [n.p.], 1920.

KPP w obronie niepodleglości Polski. Materialy i dokumenty. Warsaw: Ksiażka i Wiedza, 1954.

KPP. Uchwały i rezolucje. 2 vols. Warsaw: Ksiażka i Wiedza, 1953, 1955.

Kumaniecki, Dr. Kazimierz Wladyslaw. *Odbudowa Panstwowości Polskiej.* Najważniejsze Dokumenty. Warsaw: J. Czerniecki, 1924.

Pilsudski, Joseph. *L'Année 1920.* Paris: La rennaissance du Livre, 1929.

Pilsudski, Józef. *Erinnerungen und Dokumente.* Essen: Essener Verlagsanstalt, 1936.

Polish-Soviet Relations 1918–1943. Washington: Polish Embassy [n.d.].

Les problèmes polono-allemands devant les Chambres polonaises. Warsaw: [n.p.], 1931.

République de Pologne. *Les relations polono-allemandes et polono-soviétiques au course de la periode 1933–1939.*

Réceuil de documents officiels. Paris: Flammarion, 1940.
Sikorski. Władysław. *O Polska Polityke Państwowa.* Mowy i Deklaracje. Cracow: Nakładem Krakowskiej społki wydawniczej, 1923.
Les Socialistes Polonais et la défense du pays. Paris: Imprimérie Tancrède, 1921.
Współczesna Europa polityczna. Zbiór umów miedzynarodowych 1919–1939. Eds. Władysław Kulski, Michał Potulicki. Warsaw: Ksiegarnia Powszechna, 1939.
Zaleski, August. *Przemowy i deklaracje.* 2 vols. Warsaw: [n.p.], 1929, 1931.

OTHER DOCUMENTS

Documents on British Foreign Policy, 1919–1939. Eds. E. L. Woodward and R. Butler. London: H.M. Stationery Office, 1946–.
Documents on International Affairs. Eds. John Wheeler-Bennett and Stephen Heald. New York: Oxford University Press, 1929.
Papers Relating to the Foreign Relations of the United States. Washington: Government Printing Office, in progress.

SELECTED GENERAL WORKS

Bakh, M. G. *Politiko-Ekonomicheskie Vzaimootnosheniia mezhdu SSSR i Pribaltikoi za Desiat' Let* (1917–1927). Moscow: Kommunisticheskaia Akademiia, 1928.
Beck, Joseph. *Dernier rapport.* Politique polonaise 1926–1939. Neuchâtel: Éditions de la Bacounière, 1951.
Beloff, M. *The Foreign Policy of Soviet Russia, 1929–1941.* 2 vols. London: Oxford University Press, 1947, 1949.
Berndorff, H. R. *General zwischen Ost und West.* Hamburg: Hoffmann und Camp [n.d.].
Bernhard, Henry. *Finis Germaniae.* Stuttgart: Verlag Kurt Halsteinen, 1947.

Bernstorff, Graf Johann H. *Erinnerungen und Briefe.* Zurich: Polygraphischer Verlag, 1936.

Bessedovsky, Grigory. *Revelations of a Soviet Diplomat.* London: Williams & Norgate, 1931.

Blücher, Wipert V. *Deutschlands Weg nach Rapallo.* Wiesbaden: Limes Verlag, 1951.

Bonnet, George. *De Washington au Quai d'Orsay.* Geneva: Les éditions du cheval ailé, 1946.

Brand, E., and Waletsky, H. *Le communisme en Pologne.* Trois ans de combats à l'avantgarde. Paris: Librairie de l'Humanité, 1922.

Bretton, Henry L. *Stresemann and the Revision of Versailles.* Stanford: Stanford University Press, 1953.

Breyer, Richard. *Das Deutsche Reich und Polen, 1932–1937.* Würzburg: Holzner Verlag, 1955.

Buell, R. L. *Poland: Key to Europe.* New York: A. A. Knopf, 1939.

Cambridge History of Poland from Augustus II to Pilsudski (1697–1935). Cambridge: Cambridge University Press, 1941.

Carr, Edward H. *The Bolshevik Revolution, 1917–1923.* 3 vols. New York: The Macmillan Co., 1953.

———. *German-Soviet Relations between Two World Wars, 1919–1939.* Baltimore: The Johns Hopkins Press, 1951.

Castellan, George. *Le réarmament clandestin du Reich, 1930–1935.* Paris: Librairie Plon, 1954.

Chicherin, G. *Vneshniaia politika Sovetskoi Rossii za dva goda.* Moscow: Gosizdat, 1920.

Curtius, Julius. *Sechs Jahre Minister der deutschen Republik.* Heidelberg: Carl Winter Verlag, 1948.

D'Abernon, Viscount. *The Diary of an Ambassador.* 3 vols. New York: Doubleday, Doran, 1929–1931.

———. *The Eighteenth Decisive Battle of the World. Warsaw, 1920.* London: Hodder & Stoughton, 1931.

Dąbski, Jan. *Pokój Ryski*. Wspomnienia, petraktacje, tajne układy z Joffem, listy. Warsaw: [n.p.], 1931.

Debicki, Roman. *Foreign Policy of Poland, 1919–1939*. New York: F. A. Praeger, 1962.

Denikin, General A. I. *Kto spas' sovetskuiu vlast' ot gibeli.* Paris: Izdanie Soiuza Dobrovol'tsev', 1937.

———. *Ocherki Russkoi Smuty.* Berlin: Mednyi Vsadnik, [n.d.].

The Diplomats, 1919–1939. Eds. Gordon A. Craig and Felix Gilbert. Princeton, N.J.: Princeton University Press, 1953.

Dirksen, Herbert von. *Moscow, Tokyo, London; Twenty Years of German Foreign Policy.* Norman: University of Oklahoma Press, 1952.

Dmowski, Roman. *Świat powojenny i Polska.* Warsaw: M. Niklewicz, 1931.

Dziewanowski, M. K. *The Communist Party of Poland.* Cambridge: Harvard University Press, 1959.

Erusalimskii, A. S. *Germaniia, Antanta i SSSR.* Moscow: Izdatel'stvo Kommunisticheskoi Akademii, 1928.

Filippov, N. *Ukrainskaia kontr-revoliutsiia na sluzhbe u Anglii, Frantsii i Pol'shi.* Moscow: Moskovskii rabochii, 1927.

Fischer, Louis. *Men and Politics.* New York: Duell, Sloan and Pearce, 1941.

———. *The Soviets in World Affairs.* 2 vols. Revised edition. Princeton: Princeton University Press, 1951.

Fischer, Ruth. *Stalin and German Communism.* Cambridge: Harvard University Press, 1948.

Fisher, H. H. *America and the New Poland.* New York: The Macmillan Company, 1928.

François-Poncet, André. *Souvenirs d'une Ambassade à Berlin.* Paris: Flammarion, 1946.

Freund, Gerald. *Unholy Alliance.* Russian-German Relations from the Treaty of Brest-Litovsk to the Treaty of Berlin. New York: Harcourt, Brace, 1957.

Gafencu, Grigore. *Last Days of Europe*. New Haven: Yale University Press, 1948.

Gatzke, Hans W. *Stresemann and the Rearmament of Germany*. Baltimore: The Johns Hopkins Press, 1954.

Giertych, Jedrzej. *Polityka Polska w dziejach Europy*. London: Nakładem autora, 1947.

Goltz, R. von der. *Als politischer General im Osten*. Leipzig: [n.p.], 1936.

———. *Meine Sendung in Finland und im Baltikum*. Leipzig: [n.p.], 1920.

Grabowiecki, J. Grzymała. *Polityka zagraniczna Polski w roku 1924, 1925, 1926*. Warsaw: F. Hoesick, 1925–1928.

Grazhdanskaia Voina 1918–1921. Eds. A. S. Bubnov, S. S. Kamenev, R. P. Eideman. 3 vols. Moscow: Gosudarstvennoe izdatel'stvo, 1928, 1930.

Groener-Geyer, Dorothea. *General Groener, Soldat und Staatsmann*. Frankfurt am Main: Societäts-Verlag, 1955.

Halperin, S. William. *Germany Tried Democracy*. New York: Thomas Y. Crowell Company, 1946.

Heike, Otto. *Das Deutschtum in Polen, 1918–1939*. Bonn: Selbsverlag des Verfassers, 1955.

Helbig, H. *Die Moskauer Mission des Grafen Brockdorff-Rantzau*. Forschungen zur Osteuropäischen Geschichte, Vol. II. Berlin, 1955.

———. *Die Träger der Rapallo-Politik*. Göttingen: Vandenhoeck & Ruprecht, 1958.

Herbette, Jean. *Un diplomate français parle du péril bolcheviste*. Berlin: Commission des Archives du Ministère des Affaires Etrangères du Reich, 1943.

Hilger, G., and Meyer, A. G. *Incompatible Allies*. New York: The Macmillan Company, 1953.

Höltje, Christian. *Die Weimarer Republik und das Ost-Locarno-Problem, 1919–1934*. Würzburg: Holzner-Verlag, 1958.

Iul'skii, V. *Pol'sha—Avanpost interventsii*. Moscow: Ogiz, 1931.

Kaeckenbeeck, G. *The International Experiment of Upper Silesia; A Study of the Working of the Upper Silesian Settlement, 1922–1937.* London: Oxford University Press, 1942.

Kakurin, H. *Russko-Pol'skaia kampaniia 1918–1920.* Moscow: Vysshii voennyi redaktsionnyi sovet, 1922.

Kakurin, H. E., and Melikov, V. A. *Voina s Belopoliakami 1920 g.* Moscow: Gosudarstvennoe voennoe izdatel'stvo, 1925.

Kennan, George F. *The Decision to Intervene.* Princeton: Princeton University Press, 1958.

———. *Russia Leaves the War.* Princeton: Princeton University Press, 1956.

Kirkien, L. *Russia, Poland and the Curzon Line.* London: Caldra House [n.d.].

Klein, Fritz. *Die diplomatischen Beziehungen Deutschlands zur Sowjetunion, 1917–1932.* Berlin: Rütten & Loening, 1953.

Kobliakov, I. *Ot Bresta do Rapallo.* Moscow: Gosudarstvennoe izdatel'stvo politicheskoi literatury, 1954.

Kochan, Lionel. *Russia and the Weimar Republic.* Cambridge: Bowes & Bowes, 1954.

Komarnicki, Titus. *Rebirth of the Polish Republic.* London: W. Heinemann, 1957.

Kommunisticheskaia Akademiia. *Desiat' let kapitalisticheskogo okruzheniia SSSR.* Seriia v semi knigakh pod red. E. Pashukanisa i M. Spektatora. Moscow: Izdatel'stvo Kom. Akademii, 1928.

Kon, Feliks I. *Pol'sha na sluzhbe imperializma.* Moscow: Gosudarstvennoe izdatel'stvo, 1927.

Kutrzeba, Gen. Tadeusz. *Wyprawa Kijowska 1920 roku.* Warsaw: Nakład Gebethnera i Wolffa, 1937.

Laroche, Jules. *La Pologne de Pilsudski.* Souvenirs d'une ambassade, 1926–1935. Paris: Flammarion, 1953.

Litvinov, M. M. *Vneshniaia Politika SSSR. Rechi i Zaiavleniia,*

1927–1935. Moscow: Gosudarstvennoe Sotsial'no-economicheskoe izdatel'stvo, 1935.

Łukasiewicz, Juljucz. *Polska w Europie w polityce Józefa Pilsudskiego*. London: Nakładem Listów z Londynu, 1944.

Machray, Robert. *Poland, 1914–1931*. London: Allen & Unwin, 1932.

————. *The Poland of Pilsudski*. New York: Dutton, 1937.

Maiskii, I. *Vneshniaia politika RSFSR, 1917–1922*. Moscow: Izdatel'stvo "Krasnaia Nov'," 1923.

Makowski, Juljan. *Zobowiazania miedzynarodowe Polski 1919–1929*. Warsaw: Nakład Wł. Łazarskiego, 1929.

Markhlevskii, I. *Voina i mir mezhdu burzhuaznoi Pol'shei i proletarskoi Rossiei*. Moscow: Gosudarstvennoe izdatel'stvo, 1921.

Mazepa, I. *Ukraina v ogni i buri revoliutsii, 1917–1921*. Paris: Prometej, 1950.

Morrow, Ian F. D. *The Peace Settlement in the German-Polish Borderlands, A Study of Conditions Today in the Pre-War Prussian Provinces of East and West Prussia*. London: Oxford University Press, 1936.

Movchin, N. *Posledovatel'nye operatsii po opytu Marny i Visly*. Moscow: Gosudarstvennoe izdatel'stvo, 1928.

Niessel, General A. *L'évacuation des Pays Baltiques par les Allemands*. Paris: Charles-Lavauzelle, 1936.

Norden, Albert. *Zwischen Berlin und Moskau*. Zur Geschichte der deutsch-sowjetischen Beziehungen. Berlin: Dietz Verlag, 1954.

Papen, Franz von. *Memoirs*. Tr. Brian Connell. New York: Dutton, 1952.

Pashukanis, E., and Spektator, M., eds. *Desiat' let kapitalisticheskogo okruzheniia SSSR*. Moscow: Izdatel'stvo Kom. Akademii, 1928.

Petrie, Sir Charles A. *The Life and Letters of the Right Hon. Sir Austen Chamberlain*. 2 vols. London: Cassell and Company, 1940.

Pilskudska, Alexandra. *Pilsudski*. A Biography by His Wife. New York: Dodd, Mead, 1941.

Potemkin, V. P. (ed.). *Istoriia diplomatii*. 3 vols. Moscow: Ogiz, 1941.

Przybylski, Adam. *Wojna Polska, 1918–1921*. Warsaw: Wojskowy instytut naukowowydawniczy, 1930.

Rabenau, F. *Seeckt. Aus seinem Leben, 1918–1936*. Leipzig: V. Hase & Koehker Verlag, 1941.

Radek, K. *Die Auswärtige Politik Sowjet-Russlands*. Hamburg: Verlag der Kommunistischen Internationale, 1921.

————. *Germanskaia revoliutsia*. 2 vols. Moscow: Gosudarstvennoe izdatel'stvo, 1925.

————. *Der Kampf der Kommunistischen Internationale gegen Versailles und gegen die Offensive des Kapitals*. Hamburg: [n.p.], 1923.

————. *Likvidatsiia versal'skogo mira*. Petrograd: Izdanie Kommunisticheskogo Internatsionala, 1922.

————. *Na sluzhbe germanskoi revoliutsii*. Moscow: Gosudarstvennoe izdatel'stvo, 1921.

————. *Piat' let Kominterna*. Moscow: Krasnaia Nov', 1924.

————. *Vneshniaia politika Sovetskoi Rossii*. Moscow: Gosudarstvennoe izdatel'stvo, 1923.

Radek, K., and Stefanovich, R. *Perevorot v Pol'she i Pilsudskii*. Moscow: Gosudarstvennoe izdatel'stvo, 1926.

Reddaway, W. F. *Marshal Pilsudski*. London: George Routledge & Sons, 1939.

Regula, Jan Alford. *Historja Komunistycznej Partji Polski*. Warsaw: Drukprasa, 1934.

Reshetar, John S., Jr. *The Ukrainian Revolution, 1917–1920*. Princeton: Princeton University Press, 1952.

Roos, Hans. *Polen und Europa*. Tübingen: Mohr, 1957.

Rose, William J. *Poland, Old and New*. London: G. Bell, 1948.

Rosé, Adam Charles. *La Politique polonaise entre les deux guerres*. Neuchâtel: Éditions de la Bacounière, 1945.

Rosenberg, Arthur. *A History of the German Republic*. London: Methuen & Co., 1936.

Rubinshtein, N. L. *Sovetskaia diplomatiia v borb'e protiv izolatsii SSSR i ustanovlenie diplomaticheskikh otnoshenii s kapitalisticheskimi stranami*. Moscow: Izdatel'stvo Pravda, 1947.

———. *Sovetskaia Rossiia i kapitalisticheskie gosudarstva v gody perekhoda ot voiny k miru (1921–1922 g.)*. Moscow: Ogiz, 1948.

———. *Vneshniaia politika sovetskogo gosudarstva v 1921–1925 godakh*. Moscow: Gosudarstvennoe izdatel'stvo politicheskoi literatury, 1953.

Schieder, Theodor. *Die Probleme des Rapallo-Vertrags*. Köln: Westdeutscher Verlag, 1956.

Seeckt, Hans von. *Deutschland zwischen West und Ost*. Hamburg: Hanseatische Verlagsanstalt, 1933.

———. *Wege deutscher Aussenpolitik*. Leipzig: Verlag von Quelle & Meyer, 1931.

Seton-Watson, H. *Eastern Europe between the Wars, 1918–1941*. Revised edition. Cambridge: Cambridge University Press, 1946.

Shtein, B. E. *Burzhuaznye fal'sifikatory istorii (1919–1939)*. Moscow: Izdatel'stvo Akademii nauk SSSR, 1951.

Skrzyński, Count Alexander. *Poland and Peace*. London: George Allen & Unwin, 1923.

Starzewski, Jan. *Polska politika zagraniczna w latach 1914–1939*. London: Szkoła nauk politycznych i społecznych, 1950.

Stone, Julius. *Regional Guarantees of Minority Rights: A Study of Minorities Procedure in Upper Silesia*. New York: The Macmillan Company, 1933.

Strassburger, H., et al. *Danzig et quelques aspects du problème germano-polonais*. Paris: Publications de la conciliation internationale, 1932.

Stroński, Stanislaw. . . . *Pierwsze lat dziesieć (1918–1928)*. Lwów: Gubrynowicz i syn, 1928.

Suslov, P. V. *Politicheskoe obespechenie sovetsko-pol'skoi kampani 1920 goda*. Moscow: Gosudarstvennoe izdatel'stvo, 1920.

Teslar, Tadeusz. *Propaganda bolszewicka podczas wojny polskorosyjskiej 1920 roku*. Warsaw: Wojskowy instytut naukowo-oświatowy, 1938.

Thimme, Annelise. *Gustav Stresemann*. Hannover: Norddeutsche Verlagsanstalt O. Goedel, 1957.

Trotsky, L. *Kak vooruzhalas' revoliutsiia*. 3 vols. Moscow: Vysshii voennyi redaktsionnyi sovet, 1924.

———. *Die neue Etappe. Die Weltlage und unsere Aufgaben*. Hamburg: Verlag der Kom. Internationale, 1921.

———. *Sovetskaia Rossiia i burzhuaznaia Pol'sha*. Praga: Izdatel'stvo gazety "Pravda," 1920.

———. *Voina s Pol'shei*. Moscow: Literaturno-Izdatel'skii Otdel Polit. Upravleniia Revol. Voen. Soveta Respubliki, 1920.

Trotsky, L., *et al. Sowjetrussland und Polen*. Berlin: Russische Korrespondenz, 1920.

Trotsky, Leon. *The First Five Years of the Communist International*. 2 vols. New York: Pioneer Publishers, 1945.

Tukhachevsky, M. *Voina klassov*. Stat'i 1919–1920 gg. Moscow: Gosudarstvennoe izdatel'stvo, 1921.

Umiastowski, R. *Russia and the Polish Republic, 1918–1941*. London: "Aquafondata," 1946.

Vaker, Nicholas P. *Bielorussia. The Making of a Nation*. Cambridge: Harvard University Press, 1956.

Val', E. G. *Kak' Pilsudskii pogubil Denikina*. Tallinn': Izdanie avtora, 1938.

Wambaugh, Sarah. *Plebescites since the World War*. With a collection of Official Documents. Washington: Carnegie Endowment for International Peace, 1933.

Wandycz, Piotor S. *France and Her Eastern Allies 1919–1925*.

Minneapolis: The University of Minnesota Press, 1962.
Wheeler-Bennett, John W. *The Forgotten Peace, Brest-Litovsk, March 1918.* New York: William Morrow & Co., 1939.
Witos, Wincenty. *Wybor Pism i Mów.* Lwów: Spóldzielnia Wydawnicza "Wieš," 1939.
Wrangel, P. *The Memoirs of General Wrangel.* London: Williams & Norgate, 1929.
Zimmerman, Ludwig. *Deutsche Aussenpolitik in der Ära der Weimarer Republik.* Göttingen: Musterschmidt Verlag, 1958.
Żółtowski, Adam. *Border of Europe.* A Study of the Polish Eastern Provinces. London: Hollis & Carter, 1950.
Zuev, F. *Mezhdunarodnyi imperializm-Organizator napadeniia panskoi Pol'shi na Sovetskuiu Rossiiu (1919–1920).* Moscow: Gosudarstvennoe izdatel'stvo politicheskoi literatury, 1954.

PERIODICALS
Brüning, H. "Brief an R. Pechel," *Deutsche Rundschau,* Vol. 70, 1947, No. 7.
———. "Brief an St. Sopicki," *Niepodległość* (London), Vol. 4, 1952.
Dziewanowski, M. K. "Pilsudski's Federal Policy, 1919–1921," *Journal of Central European Affairs,* x, Nos. 2, 3.
Epstein, Julius. "Der Seeckt-Plan," *Der Monat,* I, No. 2.
Gąsiorowski, Z. J. "Stresemann and Poland before Locarno," *Journal of Central European Affairs,* xviii, No. 1.
———. "Stresemann and Poland after Locarno," *Journal of Central European Affairs,* xviii, No. 3.
———. "The Russian Overture to Germany of December 1924," *The Journal of Modern History,* xxx, No. 2.
Gatzke, Hans W. "Russo-German Military Collaboration during the Weimar Republic," *American Historical Review,* lxiii, No. 3.

————. "Von Rapallo nach Berlin: Stresemann und die deutsche Russlands Politik," *Vierteljahrshefte für Zeitgeschichte*, IV, No. 1.

Helbig, Wolfgang J. "Between Stresemann and Hitler. The Foreign Policy of the Bruening Government," *World Politics*, Vol. 12, No. 1.

Honigwill, Ludwik. "Dla czego Stalin rozwiazat KPP," *Wiadomości* (London), XI, No. 21.

Inprecorr (International Press Correspondence). Weekly periodical, 1922–1940.

Izvestiia, 1920–1933.

Jaworznicki, Boleslaw. "Polskoradziecki pakt o nieagresji z r. 1932," *Sprawy Miedzinarodowe* (Warsaw), V, No. 5.

————. "Rapallo i politika rapallska," *Sprawy Miedzynarodowe* (Warsaw), VIII, No. 11.

————. "Wyprawa Kijowska Pilsudskiego," *Sprawy Miedzynarodowe* (Warsaw), VIII, No. 5.

Jedrzejewicz, Waclaw. "Rokowania borysowskie w 1920 roku," *Niepodległość* (London), III, 1951.

Jeleński, K. A. "Wywiad z gen. Weygand," *Kultura* (Paris), Vol. 63, No. 6, 1953.

Kommunisticheskii International. Organ Ispolnitel'nogo Komiteta Kommunisticheskogo Internationala.

Lipski, J. "Przyczynki do polskoniemieckiej deklaracji o nieagresji," *Bellona* (London), Nos. I, II, 1951.

Mackiewicz, Józef. "Nasza Strona Medalu," *Wiadomości* (London), XI, No. 19.

Miedziński, Boguslav. "Polska politika zagraniczna w okresie przedwojennym," *Wiadomości* (London), October 26, 1952.

Nauticus, "New Germany's New Navy," *The Review of Reviews*, LXXVIII, No. 468.

Ochota, Jan. "Uniewaznienie aktów rozbiorowych przez Rosje," *Sprawy Obce* (Warsaw), No. 2, 1930.

Phelps, Reginald H. "Aus den Groener Dokumenten," *Deutsche Rundschau*, Vol. 76, No. 8.

————. "Das Baltikum," *Deutsche Rundschau,* Vol. 76, No. 10.

Pravda, 1920–1933.

Rhode, Gotthold. "Die Entstehung der Curzon-Linie," *Osteuropa,* Vol. 5, No. 2, 1955.

Ryszka, F. "Kulisy decyzji w sprawie Śląska w r. 1921," *Kwartalnik historyczny* (Warsaw), LX, No. 1, 1953.

Speidel, Helm. "Reichswehr und Rote Armee," *Vierteljahrshefte für Zeitgeschichte,* I, No. 1, 1953.

"Vrangelevshchina," *Krasnyi Arkhiv,* Vol. 2(39), 1930.

Wraga, R. "Pilsudski a Rosja," *Kultura* (Paris), Vol. 2–3, 1947.

Zorkii, A. "Pol'sko-Germanskie otnosheniia," *Mirovoe Khoziaistvo i Mirovaia Politika,* No. 2–3, February–March 1931.

INDEX

Allenstein, 68, 110
Allied Control Commission, 111, 147, 244
All-Russian Central Executive Committee (VTsIK), appeal to Poland for peace, 31; on Ruhr crisis, 130; on Soviet-Polish war, 44

Balfour, Lord Arthur J., 57
Baltic States, 40, 104, 189; Polish leadership of, 248; recognition by Entente, 108; relations with Russia, 191
Baranowicze, 51
Bavaria, Soviet Republic of, 14
Beck, Joseph, 272–73, 286n, 288; conversation with Neurath, 283; on German-Polish tensions, 281; on Hitler's speech, 282; on Polish policy, 273–74
Belgium, and occupation of Ruhr, 99, 129
Belorussia, 35; in Pilsudski's plans, 23; Polish advance into, 22; in Polish plans, 40, 248; and Riga armistice, 58; and Soviet peace offer, 51; and ties to Poland, 219
Beneš, Edvard, 169
Berlin Treaty, 186, 254, 255, 271; and proposed Soviet-Polish treaty of nonaggression, 207. *See also* Soviet Union, relations with Germany, and Germany, relations with Soviet Union
Berliner Tageblatt, 171
Berliner Volkszeitung, 276
Bernstorff, Count Johann A., 246
Berthelot, Phillippe, 242
Bessarabia, 150, 191
Bialystok, 37

Blücher, Wipert von, 76
Boerner, Captain I., 24, 25, 26
Boetticher, Major Friedrich von, 74
Borah, William E., 264–65
Borisov, 36, 37
Borodin, Michael, 186
Brest-Litovsk Peace Treaty, 17, 18
Briand, Aristide, 168–69, 179, 227; attitude toward German-Polish boundary, 216; exchange of views with Litvinov, 220–21; on French-German *rapprochement*, 212–13; on Pilsudski's return in politics, 205; on Pilsudski-Stresemann meeting, 241–42; Stresemann's friendship with, 184
Brockdorff-Rantzau, Count Ulrich, 169, 176, 177, 178, 256; attitude toward England, 125; France, 119, 120, 124, 125; Poland, 117–20, 124, 125, 153–59, 163, 192–94, 210, 210n; Russia, 117–21, 125–26, 128, 134, 152, 155–59, 170–71, 221–22, 246–47 biographical sketch of, 121–23; and Chicherin's visit in Warsaw, 172–73; conversation with Radek, 132; on Lithuanian-Polish crisis, 224, 225, 231; and Moscow disarmament conference, 128; on Pilsudski's return in politics, 205; relations with Chicherin, 124, 247; and Ruhr crisis, 129–30, 131, 134, 137–38; Stresemann's policy opposed by, 146–47
Brodovski (Bratman), 172, 207
Brüning, Heinrich, 184–85, 256, 263, 263n, 270n, 275
Budding, Carl, 264n

311

Bukharin, N. I., 62n, 126, 142; on Ruhr crisis, 130; on war danger, 237–38
Bukovina, 150
Bülow, Bernhard von, 262n–63n, 279, 280

Center Party, 68
Chamberlain, Austen, 158, 201; on Germany's entry in the League of Nations, 169; on German-Polish boundary, 167–68; on Pilsudski, 240–41; proposal of German intervention in Moscow, 219–20; on Stresemann's conversation with Pilsudski, 243
Chicherin, G. V., 37, 53, 91, 114, 141, 147, 150; accusations of Polish violations of Riga Treaty, 107; attitude toward Poland, 124; biographical sketch of, 123–24; conversation with Stresemann in September 1925, 175–78; denial of understanding with France and Poland, 134; on "East Locarno," 214; on East Prussia, 219; illness of, 251, 256–57; Kopp disavowed by, 178n; personal relations with Rantzau, 124; on Pilsudski, 219; on Pilsudski's return in politics, 205; on Polish-Lithuanian crisis, 233, 234; on Polish-Soviet boundary, 196; on Rapallo Treaty, 116; reaction to Voikov's murder, 218–19; reply to Curzon note, 50–51; and Ruhr crisis, 137–38; and Soviet relations with Germany, 220
   exchange of views on close cooperation with, 152, 155–59, 170–71, 175–78; and Germany's entry in the League of Nations, 157; negotiations during Soviet-Polish war with, 87–88
and Soviet relations with Poland, 106, 162, 164
   during Soviet-Polish war, 24, 30, 36, 56n; negotiations on nonaggression pact with, 164, 193–94, 213, 221

visit in Berlin
   September 1925, 175–78; December 1924, 188; December 1926, 228–29
visit in Paris, 178–79; visit in Warsaw, 171–75; on war danger, 219. *See also* Stresemann, Brockdorff-Rantzau
Churchill, Winston, on German cooperation with Entente during Soviet-Polish war, 83
Communist International (Comintern), *see* Third International
Communist Party of Germany, 72, 141–42; accomplice of Nazis, 187; consideration of Soviet financial support of, 269–70; Ruhr crisis, 134–35
Communist Party of Poland, 12, 192; attitude toward Versailles, 112n; and Central Army Revolutionary Committee, 43; on danger of Lithuanian-Polish war, 227–28; on danger of Polish invasion of Danzig, 275; and Pilsudski's *putsch*, 203–04; and Polish-German boundary, 65–66; and the Polish-Soviet war, 43, 47, 61–62; and revolutionary activities after World War I, 27; and role in case of war, 238–39; and Ruhr crisis, 135, 136; Second Congress of, 60, 136
Communist Party of the Soviet Union, 10; on revolutionary conditions in Germany, 269–71; and Ruhr crisis, 135
Corridor, 68, 146, 153, 161, 168, 198, 199, 214, 224, 229, 236; Hitler on, 281, 282; minority complaints from, 202; Radek on, 65; Stimson on, 264; Stresemann on, 243
Curtius, Julius, 256, 267; on Polish-German boundary, 261
Curzon, Lord George N., 48, 49, 50
Czechoslovakia, dismemberment of, 288; Pilsudski's attitude toward, 284; and Polish-Soviet war, 46
Czernin, Count Ottakar, 17–18

D'Abernon, Lord Edgar V., 54n, 111, 195n–96n, 201; on Soviet-Polish war, 83

Dąbski, Jan, at Minsk negotiations, 56–57; on Riga armistice negotiations, 58

Daniszewski, Karol, 53, 55

Danzig, 90, 110, 126, 214, 224, 253, 275, 281; allegations of Polish preparation of seizure of, 132; alleged Soviet understanding with Poland on, 141; free city of, 15, 68; free port for Poland in, 242; Nazi agitation in, 262; and Polish-Soviet war, 46; Radek on, 65

Dawes Plan, 100, 147

Denikin, General A. I., 9, 22–23, 24, 25, 26, 33n, 47

Deutscher Herrenklub, 276

Diamand, Dr. H., 211, 243

Dirksen, Herbert von, 74n, 75, 195, 260, 268, 269, 280; as Ambassador to Russia, 251; on Chicherin's illness, 257; on deterioration of Soviet-German relations, 254–55, 260; on Rapallo Treaty, 116; on Soviet-Polish treaty of nonaggression, 207, 271

Disarmament Conference, 264, 277

Dmowski, Roman, 20, 140

Dresel, Ellis L., 87n

Duchemin Protocol, 279–80

East Galicia, 41, 126, 153; Soviet attitude toward, 133, 149–50

"East Locarno," 190, 216, 232, 251

East Prussia, 68, 70, 253; alleged danger of Polish invasion of, 129; alleged Soviet understanding with Poland on, 141; approach of Red Army to, 84–85; German fear of Polish invasion of, 263, 275; internment of Soviet units in, 92; Pilsudski about, 241

Ebert, Friedrich, 70, 80

Eckhardtstein, Freiherr von, 83

Enver Pasha, correspondence with Seeckt, 90–91

Erzberger, Mathias, 69

Estonia, 36, 232; and Genoa Conference, 104–05; and Litvinov Protocol, 252; and Moscow disarmament conference, 126, 127; in Polish plans, 40; relations with Russia, 186

Evening News, 83

Fehrenbach, K., 80n

Filipowicz, Tytus, 106, 263

Finland, 189–90, 232; and Moscow disarmament conference, 126, 127; in Polish plans, 40

Fischer, Ruth, 62n, 113

Foch, Marshal Ferdinand, 67, 70; and German assistance in Soviet-Polish war, 84; visit in Poland, 132

France, alleged abandonment of Poland, 115; attitude of Pilsudski toward, 284; and Lithuanian-Polish crisis, 230; and Locarno, 183; and occupation of Ruhr, 99, 129; and Polish boundary, 264; and reaction to Soviet-German treaty of nonaggression, 196; and relations with Germany, 166
pre-Locarno negotiations with, 147, 159, 167–68, 169. *See also* Germany, relations with
and relations with Poland, 12
Polish-Soviet war, 46, 47–48, 56, 65, 93. *See also* Poland, relations with
and relations with Russia, 179
rumors on mutual understanding, 134. *See also* Russia, relations with
Stresemann's attitude toward, 144, 145, 146, 147; and Upper Silesia, 112

François-Poncet, André, 286n

Free Corps (*Freikorps*), 14; in the Baltics, 71; and Soviet-Polish war, 90

Fromageot, Henri, 242

Geneva Protocol, 159

Genoa Conference, 98, 104, 115–16, 126

German Army, Versailles limitations upon, 81

German People's Party, 144, 258

Germany, attitude toward Soviet-Polish nonaggression pact, 260–69, 271; and Brest-Litovsk negotiations, 17–18; cession of Danzig to, 224; contacts with Ukrainian terrorists, 262; and disarmament, 111; and Disarmament Conference, 264; and evaluation of Pilsudski's return in politics, 204–05, 206; fear of Polish invasion of, 263, 275; and Genoa Conference, 115–16; as guarantee against spread of Bolshevism, 110–12; information on planned Soviet invasion of Poland, 27–30; internal developments in, 13–15, 99–100, 184–85, 256; and the League of Nations, 152, 156

    entry in, 169, 200–02; Soviet attitude toward, 153–59, 166; and commitment toward, 154

and Locarno Conference, 179–80; and occupation of Ruhr, 99–100, 129ff; Pilsudski's idea of preventive war against, 280; and Polish-Lithuanian crisis, 230, 231–32, 233–36; prospects for communist revolution in, 97; prospects for cooperation with Allies, 81; and reaction to Chicherin's visit in Warsaw, 171–73; reaction to proposed Polish-Soviet treaty of nonaggression, 207–08; relations with Czechoslovakia, 179

    arbitration treaty offer to, 160

and relations with England, 158. *See also* Great Britain and relations with France, 158. *See also* France, relations with and relations with Poland

    after World War I, 109–12; arbitration treaty with, 160, 180; boundary with, 160, 177, 179; economic crisis in, 198–200; Polish evaluation of, 78–79; and trade agreement in 1930, 261.

See also Poland, relations with and relations with Russia

    in early 1920's, 98–99, 110–15; fear of Polish understanding with, 164–65; and Lithuanian-Polish crisis, 231, 260; military cooperation with, 114; neutrality treaty with, 157–58, 184, 188, 189, 196, 197, 289; reaction to proposal of nonaggression treaty with Poland, 192–95; trade agreement with, 175, 188. *See also* Soviet Union, relations with and role of officers in, 69ff; and Ruhr crisis

    appreciation of Soviet attitude during, 133–34; Polish neutrality during, 138

and Soviet-British tensions, 217; and Soviet-Polish war, 81, 82

    consideration of cooperation with Entente during, 81–84; and neutrality during, 46, 66–67, 87, 88–90, 91, 114; and relations with Russia during, 84–92 and support of minorities in Poland, 262; and Upper Silesia, 112

Gessler, Otto, 113

Gibson, Hugh, 35

Goebbels, Joseph, meeting with Beck, 283

Goering, Hermann, 277

Goltz, General Rudiger von der, 71, 76

Grabski, Władyslaw, 48

Great Britain, 169; attitude toward German-Polish boundary, 216, 264; and Lithuanian-Polish crisis, 229; and Locarno, 183; and Poland's economic crisis, 199; and Polish-Soviet war, 47–48, 93; reaction to German-Soviet treaty of nonaggression, 196; in Soviet writings on Polish-German boundary, 66; in Soviet writings on Soviet-Polish war, 65; suspension of relations with Russia, 217, 247; and Upper Silesia, 111–12. *See also* Germany, relations with

Grodno, 37
Groener, General Wilhelm, 75, 263n; and cooperation with Allies, 69–70; and evalution of Soviet-Polish war, 82; views on Poland, 69–71
Gwiazda, 55

Haking, General Richard, 83
Haller, General Joseph, 12
Hasse, Colonel Otto, 114
Hencke, Andor, 163
Herbette, Jean, 158
Hilger, Gustav, 138
Hindenburg, Paul von, 185, 245
Hitler, Adolf, 185, 277; appointment as Chancellor, 278; on direct negotiations with Poland, 284–85; Lipski received by, 283; on Pilsudski, 285; Polish Envoy received by, 281–82; putsch in Bavaria, 100; on relations with Poland, 280, 281–82
Hoesch, Leopold, 169, 242
Hoffmann, General Max, 22, 78, 84n; and Soviet-Polish war, 82
Hoover, Herbert, 185, 263
Hungary, communist revolution in, 70

Independent Socialists, 13
Ioffe, Adolf, 85n, 124, 257; at Riga armistice negotiations, 57, 58
Izvestiia, 190, 228, 266; on Soviet-Polish war, 42, 62

Junkers, 13, 14

Kahr, Gustav von, 80n, 111
Kamenev, Leo, 62, 86; negotiations in London, 52, 56n; and Soviet-Polish war, 42, 57
Kamenev, Sergei, on Soviet advance in Poland, 48–50
Kapp Putsch, 14
Karakhan, Leo, 105, 106, 124, 238, 257
Kellogg-Briand Pact, 184, 249, 250, 286; ratification of, 252
Kiev, Polish army in, 41

Kolchak, Admiral Vladimir V., 9, 22
Königsberger Hartungsche Zeitung, 89
Knoll, Roman, 126, 141, 208
Kopp, Victor, 87, 159; and activities during Soviet-Polish war, 84, 85, 90; and negotiations in Berlin after World War I, 76–77; Rantzau's conversation on Poland with, 153; role in German-Soviet cooperation, 155, 156, 177, 178; on role of Lithuania, 223; visit to Latvia, 138–39; visit to Lithuania, 139; visit to Poland, 138, 139–41
Kostrezewa, Vera, 237
Krasin, Leonid B., 86, 114, 115
Krasnaia Zvezda, attitude toward Soviet-Polish war, 62
Krestinski, Nikolai N., 124, 161–62, 177, 210, 213, 226; on Polish-Soviet nonaggression pact negotiations, 235
Królikowski, Stefan, 238
Kronstadt, 97
Kun, Bela, 27
Kutrzeba, General Tadeusz, 26, 37; inquiry on French-Polish alliance, 243–44; on Pilsudski's plans, 34

Latvia, 232; and Genoa Conference, 104–05; and Litvinov Protocol, 252; and Moscow disarmament conference, 126, 127; in Polish plans, 40; relations with Russia, 186; Soviet offer of pact with, 138–39
League of Nations, 288; and Germany's entry in, 154, 171, 179, 183, 200–02; and Lithuanian-Polish crisis, 132–33, 233, 234, 235, 236; and Locarno, 183; and minorities in Poland, 101, 262; Pilsudski's attitude toward, 203, 240, 284; and plebiscite in Upper Silesia, 99, 112; and Poland's nonaggression proposal, 216; Russia's entry in, 288; Stresemann's attitude toward, 144, 146
Lebedev, P., 114

Lenin, V. I., 10, 11; illness of, 142; and negotiations with Poland, 24–25; and NEP, 97; and opinion of Chicherin, 123; postwar plans of, 27–30; on prospects of revolution in Germany, 12–13; on Riga armistice negotiations, 57–58; on self-determination of Poland, 16, 18; on Versailles, 112; on war with Poland, 32–33, 42, 49, 51–52, 52–54, 56, 59–60, 105–06

Levi, Paul, 80–81

Lipski, Joseph, 283, 286n

Lithuania, 78, 111, 165; and Litvinov Protocol, 252; and Moscow disarmament conference, 127; and Polish advance into, 22; Polish conflict with, 132–33, 213, 214, 219, 226; in Polish plans, 40; and relations with Germany, 223, 225–26; and relations with Russia, 5; and Ruhr crisis, 130, 139. *See also* Germany, Pilsudski, Soviet Union

Litvinov, Maksim M., 29, 124, 147, 170, 171, 213, 251; appointment as Foreign Affairs Commissar, 257; assurance to Germany on Litvinov Protocol, 251–52; biographical sketch of, 257–58; conversation with Neurath in December 1932, 277; on French-Soviet nonaggression pact negotiations, 268; on Memel, 224; and Moscow disarmament conference, 126–27; on nonaggression pact with Poland, 235, 249–50, 267, 271; on relations with Germany, 152, 165–66, 260; on relations with Poland, 151, 166, 190–91, 218; on Polish-Lithuanian crisis, 227, 231, 234–36; on Ruhr crisis, 130–31

Litvinov Protocol, 266; and Baltic States, 250; and Germany's reaction toward, 250–51; and Lithuania, 250; and Poland, 249–50, 253; signature of, 251

Lloyd George, David, 35, 56n, 57, 86; and Polish-Soviet war, 47, 48, 52

Locarno Conference (Pact), 100, 175, 177, 179, 186, 188, 224; evaluation of, 183; and Germany's position after, 180; and Poland's attitude toward, 189

Loebe, Paul, 111

Ludendorff, General Erich F. W., 78, 84n

Ludwig, Emil, 271–72

Luxemburg, Rosa, 16, 61

Maiskii, Ivan, 105

Maltzan, Baron Ago von, 29, 111, 178; contacts with Russian *émigrés*, 76; negotiations with Kopp, 77; on Poland and Soviet-German cooperation, 154; political views of, 75–76

Manuilsky, Dmitrii Z., 192

Marchlewski, Julian, 27; on danger of German war against Russia, 80; and negotiations with Pilsudski, 23–26; and Soviet-Polish war, 42, 46, 60

Marienwerder, 68; plebiscite in, 110

Martov, J., on war with Poland, 42

Mazepa, I., 41

Memel, 224, 225, 229, 236; German claims on, 230; free port for Poland in, 242; occupation of, 288

Miedziński, Boguslaw, 273

Mikaszewicze, 24

Minsk, 28, 51, 52n, 53; peace negotiations at, 55–57

Mirbach, Count Wilhelm von, 87

Moltke, Hans von, 281, 285

Müller, Hermann, 77–78; on relations with Poland, 77–78

Munich Conference, 289

Nansen, Fridtjof, 131

National Democratic Party, 11

National Socialist Workers' Party, 256; election successes of, 185

Neurath, Baron Konstantin von, 277, 278, 280, 283

Niessel, General A., 76

Norman, Montagu, 198, 199

Noske, Gustav, 80

October Revolution, 9, 17
Ordzhonikidze, Z., 32n

Pact of Paris, *see* Kellogg-Briand
Pact
Papen, Franz von, 185, 275, 278, 280;
alleged plans for German-French-
Polish cooperation, 276
Patek, Stanislas, 30, 208, 218, 234;
Bukharin's speech protested by,
238; on nonaggression pact with
Russia, 267; Rykov's speech protested by, 253
Petlura, Simon, 38, 41
Pilsudski, Joseph, 37, 47, 64, 79, 259,
261, 272; alleged request for German assistance by, 80n; appearance at the League of Nations,
236, 240–41; attitude toward
France, 242; attitude toward Lithuania, 226; and battle for Warsaw, 54; and Belorussia, 33; biographical sketch of, 19–22; death
of, 289; declaration on invasion
of Ukraine, 38–39; and elections
in November 1930, 262; on Hitler,
285; Hitler's thoughts on agreement with, 280; and Lithuania,
33; and Locarno, 189; and negotiations with Denikin, 23; and negotiations with Lenin, 22–26, 27;
and political plans after World
War I, 23, 33–34, 37; and prospects
of German-Polish understanding,
211–12, 283–84; refusal to receive
Soviet representative, 125–26; reports on preventive war against
Germany, 280; retirement from
public life, 100, 131; return to
politics, 202–06; Soviet views of,
248; speech at Vinitsa, 41; and the
Ukraine, 33–34; and withdrawal
of Russian *émigrés* from Poland,
106
Poland, and agreement with Ukrainian National Republic, 38; and
attitude toward Germany's entry
in the League of Nations, 200–02;
and Baltic States, 189; as barrier
against Bolshevism, 111; Belorus-

sian minority in, 133; Briand on
change of boundary of, 169; as
cause of Russian-German tensions,
189–95; Chicherin's visit to, 171–
75; Conciliation Convention with
Russia, 274; and danger of Soviet-
German alliance, 39; and East
Galicia, 133, 149–50; and East
Prussia, 135; economic crisis in,
198; evaluation of international
position of, 78–79, 264; and Genoa
Conference, 104–05; and Litvinov
Protocol, 250, 252; and Moscow
disarmament conference, 126–28;
and national minorities in, 101,
202; and plans for "East Locarno,"
190; and Rapallo Treaty, 116–17;
and relations with Czechoslovakia
after World War I, 12; and relations with France, 10
alliance with, 107–09, 242, 243;
apprehension of policy of, 115,
148; and military plans against
Germany, 132n. *See also* France,
relations with
and relations with Germany, 12,
15, 101–02, 103, 118, 148, 211–13,
245, 261–63, 281
and arbitration treaty with,
147–48, 189; and communist
writings on boundary with, 66,
66n; and nonaggression pact
with, 283–86; and tariff war
with, 101, 261, 283. *See also*
Germany, Soviet Union, relations with
and relations with Latvia after
World War I, 12; and relations
with Lithuania, 12, 135, 223, 234
danger of war with, 229; cession
of territory of, 224, 261. *See also*
Germany, Lithuania, Soviet
Union, relations with
and relations with Rumania, 12,
101, 107–09
and alliance with, 191, 195
and relations with Russia, 12, 47,
101–02, 103, 104–09, 134, 148–49,
186, 188, 248
and nonaggression treaty with,

Poland (*cont.*)
174, 193–94, 206–08, 210, 266–
69, 272, 273, 274; and peace
negotiations with, 23–26, 34–38;
and war with, 38–59, 89–90, 93.
See also Germany, Lithuania,
Radek, Soviet Union, relations
with
and Riga armistice negotiations,
57–58; role in German-Soviet cooperation, 154–59, 176–77; and
Ruhr crisis, 129, 131–32, 138; and
Russian refugees in, 104, 106, 107;
Seeckt's views on, 72–74, 120, 258–
59; and situation in, 11–12, 100–
01; Stresemann's attitude toward,
144, 146, 147; and Ukrainian minority in, 133; and Upper Silesia,
112; and wartime plans on Soviet
Russia, 39–40
Polish Army, 12; and League of
Riflemen, 20; and offensive in
1919, 22; and Polish Legion, 20,
21
Polish Socialist Party, 11, 64; and
Pilsudski, 19
Poznań (Province), 68, 69, 90
Pravda, 210; on Soviet-Polish war,
62
Provisional Revolutionary Committee, 60; and Soviet-Polish war, 46

Radek, Karl, 62n, 81, 141, 142; on
Chicherin's visit in Warsaw, 173–
74; on relations with Poland, 25–
26, 36, 65, 109, 132, 163; on revo-
lutionary conditions in Germany,
135; on Riga Treaty, 105; and
Ruhr crisis, 135, 137–38; on Soviet
plans against Poland, 114; on
Soviet-Polish war, 42, 45–46, 90;
on treaty with Germany in 1922,
115; on Versailles, 65–66
Radowitz, 152, 157
Radziwill, Prince Janusz, 211, 244
Rakovsky, Khristian, 115, 124
Rantzau, Count Ernst, 247
Rantzau, Ulrich, *see* Brockdorff-
Rantzau

Rapallo Treaty, 98, 115–17, 120, 176,
254, 255
Rathenau, Walther, 99
Rauscher, Ulrich, 131, 164–65, 208
Red Army, 28; and cooperation
with German Army, 98–99; and
Soviet-Polish war
defeat in, 59–61; in offensive,
41; and political instructions
during, 46–47; before Warsaw,
54
Reibnitz, Baron Eugen von, 90
Revolutionary War Council, attitude toward Soviet advance in
Poland, 49–50
Rhineland, evacuation of, 147, 244,
264; occupation of, 288
Riga Treaty, 92, 165, 228, 238, 274;
accusations of violations of, 107;
armistice negotiations and preliminary treaty, 57–59, 103–04;
and East Galicia, 133, 149, 150;
and implementation of, 109, 164;
Soviet attitude toward, 105; and
Soviet transit through Poland,
139
Rozwadowski, General T., 55n
Ruhr, Red Army in, 14; threat of
occupation, 99. *See also* Germany,
Poland, Soviet Union and Ruhr
crisis
Rumania, 188; and Moscow disarmament conference, 127; and Litvinov Protocol, 250, 252. *See also*
Poland, relations with
Rykov, Aleksei I., 62n, 209; on Soviet-Polish relations, 252–53
Rzeczpospolita, 161

Sapieha, Prince Eustache, 58, 106,
107
Sauerwein, Jules, 214
Savinkov, Boris, 106, 107, 135
Saxony, communist upheaval in,
100
Schacht, Hjalmar, 198, 199
Scheffer, Paul, 163, 164
Schleicher, Kurt von, 114, 185, 275,
278; in favor of cooperation with
Russia, 276–77

Schubert, Karl von, 178, 195, 225, 226, 245; and Polish-Lithuanian crisis, 226–27; and Soviet-German cooperation, 158–59, 176–77

Seeckt, General Hans von, 69, 71–72, 75; attitude toward Poland, 71, 72–74, 113, 114, 120–21; attitude toward Russia, 72–74, 117–18, 120; political views of, 71–75, 258–59; Rantzau's policy criticized by, 120; and Soviet-Polish war contacts with Enver Pasha during, 90–91; evaluation of, 82, 85–86; and German neutrality during, 88
Stresemann's policy opposed by, 146

Serghieiev, J. N., 61

Seyda, Marjan, 139, 140

Shaposhnikov, General Boris, 32

Sikorski, General Władyslaw, 131–32

Simons, Walther, 111, 113; and proposal to negotiate with Russia, 87; on role of Lithuania in German policy, 223

Skirmunt, K., 107, 116

Sklianski, E., 49, 54; and conversation with Enver Pasha, 91

Skrzyński, Count Alexander, 150, 171; on Locarno, 189–90; on relations with Russia, 191–92; on Soviet peace offer, 34

Smilga, I. T., 56

Social Democratic Party of Germany, 13, 14, 68, 144

Sokolnikov, G. I., 42

Souvarine, B., 130

Soviet Union, attitude toward Versailles, 112; and Berlin Trade Mission, 148; and Brest-Litovsk negotiations, 17–18; and Genoa Conference, 104–05, 115–16; and Germany's entry into the League of Nations, 152, 156, 159; and internal developments in, 12, 247; and Moscow disarmament conference, 126–28; and Pilsudski's return in politics, 204–05, 206; Polish communists in, 104; and

Polish-German boundary, 65–66; and Polish-Lithuanian crisis, 133, 230, 232, 233–36; and reaction to "East Locarno," 190–91; and reaction to prospects of German-Polish understanding, 213; and relations with England, 10, 97–98, 158
and suspicion of war by, 217; and trade agreement with, 97
and relations with France, 10–11, 158, 187
and pact of nonaggression with, 220; and prospects of understanding with, 166
and relations with Germany, 11, 148, 150–51
and Locarno, 179–80, 185–86; and offer of cooperation with, 152ff; and proposal of common attack on Poland, 114; and reevaluation of, 175–78; and revolutionary conditions in, 270; and treaty of nonaggression with, 196, 197, 289. *See also* Germany, relations with
and relations with Lithuania, 223–24
and treaty of neutrality with, 228. *See also* Germany, Lithuania, relations with
and relations with Poland, 11, 148–51, 163–65, 187, 266–67
and border attacks against, 107; and peace offer to, 30–31, 36–38, 51; and self-determination of, 42, 45; and treaty of nonaggression with, 174, 178, 190, 191, 206–07, 247, 248, 267. *See also* Germany, Lithuania, Poland, relations with
and Riga armistice negotiations, 57–58; and Ruhr crisis, 129ff, 142
and denial of responsibility for Comintern, 137–38; and offer of understanding with Poland during, 138–41
and Soviet-Polish war, 39–59
and Germany's role in, 79ff, 84–85, 92; and peace conditions,

Soviet Union (*cont.*)
55–56; and Polish advance in Ukraine, 39–41; and preparation for war, 27–30, 32–33; and Soviet evaluation of, 59–67

Stresemann's attitude toward, 145–46, 148

Spartacists, 11, 13; and Polish-Soviet war, 89

Stalin, I. V., 289; appreciation of Litvinov by, 258; attitude toward revolutionary movements, 186–87; attitude toward Soviet advance in Poland, 49n, 50, 52, 52n; on CPP, 204; decision on postponing revolution in Germany, 269–71; and developments in Russia in late 1920's, 186–87; Emil Ludwig's interview with, 271–72; and Ruhr crisis, 142; on self-determination, 16–17; on Soviet-Polish war, 62–63; on Voikov's murder, 218

Sthamer, Friedrich, 198, 199

Stimson, Henry L., 264

Stolpce, 149

Stomoniakov, B., 248–49

Stresemann, Gustav, 135, 210, 261; biographical sketch of, 143–46; conversations with Chicherin, 175–78, 188–89, 213–14; on danger of war against Russia, 219; death of, 255; on French-Polish alliance, 179–80; and Lithuanian-Polish crisis, 230–31, 232, 233, 235; and minority complaints from Poland, 202; and opposition to treaty of nonaggression with Poland, 194–95; and Pilsudski's meeting with, 241, 243; political concept of, 147, 157, 162, 166, 255–56; on possibilities of German-Polish understanding, 211–12; and relations with France, 160–62

and pact with, 147–48, 159ff, 168

and relations with Poland

on boundary of, 224, 225, 229; on economic pressure on, 197–99; and signs of friendship toward, 244–45

and Ruhr crisis, 147; on Soviet relations with France and Poland, 221–22; and suggestion to Litvinov on a pact, 170

Subcarpathian Russia, 150

Supreme Allied Council, 50; attitude toward Soviet-Polish war, 48, 52; and disarmament of Germany, 71

Swit, 44

Szembek, Jan, 278

Teschen, 126

Third International, 10, 36, 60, 80, 97, 127, 142, 275; and accusations against CPP, 204; and agitation in Germany, 254; and appeal to Poland for peace, 31–32; and attacks on Poland, 109, 126, 150, 186, 192; attitude toward Versailles, 112; on danger of Polish war against Lithuania, 236–38; and Polish-Soviet war, 43–45; on revolutionary conditions in Germany, 269–71; and Ruhr crisis, 134–38; and Soviet government, 175

Thoiry, 212

Thuringia, communist upheaval in, 100, 135

Toruń, 28

Treviranus, Gottfried, 262

Trotsky, L., 24, 32n, 58, 91n, 142, 186; at Brest-Litovsk negotiations, 17; and conversations with Nansen, 131; Rantzau on Ruhr crisis, 129–30

and Soviet-Polish war, 33, 42–43, 49, 50, 53

and alleged recognition of old German boundary, 91; evaluation of, 62n; instructions concerning Germany during, 85; and responsibility for, 62

Truppenamt, 72

Tukhachevsky, General Mikhail, 42; at maneuvers in Germany, 276; and Soviet-Polish war, 53, 60–61

Ukraine, 35, 79, 150; and Pilsudski's plans on, 23, 40, 219, 248; Polish invasion of, 37, 79; and Riga preliminary treaty, 58, 103–04; and Soviet-Polish war, 39–41

Unshlikht, Josef, 32n

Upper Silesia, 15, 58, 81, 90, 91, 110, 111–12, 118, 126, 153, 161, 168, 198, 199, 214, 224; communist propaganda in, 149; German fear of Polish invasion of, 113, 129, 263, 275; Hindenburg on, 245; minority complaints from, 202; plebiscite in, 68, 99, 112; Radek on, 65; and Ruhr crisis, 132; Stresemann's policy on, 146; and Third International, 150

United States, 169; and Polish boundary, 264; and Polish-Soviet war, 48; in Soviet writings on Polish-German boundary, 66; on Soviet-Polish war, 65

Versailles Peace Treaty, 4, 14, 65, 110, 115, 184; German attitude toward, 68–69, 117; and German disarmament, 81, 98, 111–12; Groener on, 69–70; Hitler's pledge on, 282; and Polish-German boundary, 68; Radek on, 65–66; and Rantzau, 121–22; and reparations, 98, 99; revision of, 167; Seeckt as delegate at, 72; and Soviet-Polish war, 59; Stresemann against, 143, 144

Vilna, 126, 127, 132, 223, 224, 226, 228, 233

Vinitsa, 41

Voikov, Peter L., 217

Voldemaras, A., 229, 236, 244

Vossische Zeitung, 171

Walecki, Marx, 105

Wencikowski, 23

Westerplatte, 280, 283

Weygand, General Maxime, 259; on battle for Warsaw, 54, 54n–55n

Wiedenfeld, Kurt, 114

Wirth, Joseph, 99, 117, 118

Wrangel, General Peter, 9, 47, 48, 49, 50, 51, 52, 52n, 54, 55, 58, 106

Wysocki, Alfred, 278

Yegorov, Marshal, 276

Young Plan, 184, 185

Yudenich, General Nikolai N., 122

Zaleski, August, 202, 206, 244, 272; conversation with Stresemann, 215; on nonaggression pact with Russia, 248, 266–67; on relations with Russia, 208

Zetkin, Clara, 59

Zinoviev, Grigorii E., 62, 91, 142, 175, 192; on Ruhr crisis, 136–37; on negotiations with Poland, 208–09; on Soviet-Polish war, 44–45, 60